Fightin

ADVANCE PRAISE FOR THE BOOK

'History writing at its best. A fascinating and important story, beautifully, clearly and fairly told. An excellent read'—Oliver Everett, CVO, Librarian Emeritus, Royal Library, Windsor Castle; and first secretary, UK High Commission, New Delhi, 1969–73

'Judicious, elegantly argued and a joy to read, *Fighting Retreat* addresses the thorny questions of why Churchill took such a jaundiced view of India and whether his obduracy over Indian independence fed the rancour that led to Partition. As the author of seminal works on both India and Churchill, Walter Reid is well placed to supply the answers. He does so with elan and conviction. This is an important and immensely rewarding account of a hitherto puzzling conundrum'—John Keay, author of *India: A History of India* and *The Honourable Company: A History of the English East India Company*

'In this day and age, Churchill remains a controversial figure: he is seen as a great patriot in Britain but nothing less than an archetypal imperialist villain in India. Reid has put his hands into a wasp's nest to examine Churchill's attitude towards India. To his credit, he has come up with a fair and warts-and-all account that explains Churchill's attitude, even while it does not excuse it'—Manoj Joshi, distinguished fellow, Observer Research Foundation, New Delhi

'Walter Reid pulls no punches in this troubling book, and the attentive reader will have much to reconsider'—John Hussey, OBE, winner of the Templer Medal Prize for *Waterloo: The Campaign of 1815*

'Reid's account and assessment are critical and impartial. The real Winston Churchill emerges with blemishes and strengths but not as a friend of India'—General T.S. Shergill, PVSM

'This is a splendid book, clear-eyed and dispassionate, which perfectly captures the essence of Churchill's misguided ire towards India. The presentation of him and his approach to India, the various peoples of India and to Indian nationalism, is compelling. I have really, really enjoyed this. Not only does Reid write beautifully but the issues are arrayed clinically, and dispatched calmly and authoritatively. I don't think I have seen the whole subject dealt with so dispassionately. The chapter on the Bengal famine is exemplary. I agree that nuance is required in understanding Churchill's use

of language: there is a clear divide between his sometimes shocking verbal intemperance and his political actions. Reid draws a distinction between what he said and what he did. The final chapter is masterful. It certainly helped me to understand some things about Churchill for the first time'
—Robert Lyman, author of *A War of Empires* and *Slim, Master of War*

Fighting Retreat

Churchill and India

WALTER REID

HURST & COMPANY, LONDON

First published in the United Kingdom in 2024 by
C. Hurst & Co. (Publishers) Ltd.,
New Wing, Somerset House, Strand, London, WC2R 1LA
Copyright © Walter Reid 2024

First published by Penguin Random House India

Printed in the United Kingdom by Bell & Bain Ltd, Glasgow

The right of Walter Reid to be identified as the author
of this publication is asserted by him in accordance with
the Copyright, Designs and Patents Act, 1988.

Distributed in the United States, Canada and Latin America by
Oxford University Press, 198 Madison Avenue, New York, NY 10016,
United States of America.

A Cataloguing-in-Publication data record for this book
is available from the British Library.

This book is printed using paper from registered sustainable
and managed sources.

ISBN: 9781805260509

www.hurstpublishers.com

For Janet

Contents

Preface

In an earlier book on the role of the British in India, *Keeping the Jewel in the Crown: The British Betrayal of India,* I examined British policy towards the subcontinent from 1917, the year of the Montagu Declaration, to 1947 and Independence. I was not entirely surprised that my studies revealed a malign continuum of deceitful and hypocritical attempts to thwart India's entirely reasonable political aspirations.

I was, however, taken aback by the scale, nature and significance of Winston Churchill's role. I was aware of his determination not to preside over the liquidation of the British Empire, but I was not prepared for what I found: consistent, disingenuous and unprincipled opposition to any initiative which might edge India, however slightly, out of the clutches of Great Britain.

I have written in another book about Churchill's strategy in the Second World War and I found little to criticize in his conduct of that war. Indeed, I have found much to admire in most aspects of his remarkable life. He was capable of a grandeur of spirit and of concern for the generality of mankind. But not for India. Similarly, though he was for the most part surprisingly liberal in relation to Britain's colonial possessions, his hostility to India was uncompromising. The scope of my earlier book didn't allow me to focus unduly on Churchill and India; that's what this book is about.

Acknowledgements

In the course of writing and researching this book, I have been reminded yet again of how generous writers and historians are prepared to be with their time and assistance. I have made new friends and have received much valuable help and support. I have to thank Oliver Everett, John Hussey (yet again), Manoj Joshi, John Keay, Rob Lyman and General T.S. Shergill.

James Colvin very kindly allowed me access to the papers of his grandfather, Lieutenant Colonel James M.C. Colvin VC. Colonel Colvin was part of the Malakand Field Force, and awarded his Victoria Cross for his conduct in the Mohmand Valley action. His observations about Churchill, who served with him as part of the Field Force, are of interest.

Gwen McKerrell has been of enormous help in bringing my undisciplined draft into a coherent whole and assisting with research.

I particularly want to record my gratitude to Tarini Uppal, who was the senior commissioning editor at Penguin Random House India when the idea for this book was forming in my mind. She was wonderfully supportive of what was then a fairly inchoate notion, and it was great to work with her on this book as on an earlier one. Very real thanks too to her marvellous successor, Archana Nathan, and to Manali Das, the most sensitive of copy editors.

Finally, and as always, my heartfelt thanks to Janet and our wonderful family. I could say much more, but they know what they mean to me.

1

Goodbye to India

On 18 June 1898, Winston Churchill, a junior officer in the Fourth Hussars, set sail for Europe from Bombay. He cut an elegant figure in his cavalry uniform. He was good-looking: his eyes blue, his hair ginger and his countenance distinctly boyish. He had none of the jowly bulldog appearance of Karsh's famous photograph of 1941, the image that came to symbolize his defiant leadership of the British people as they fought for survival. In Bombay, after months in the saddle, his figure was lithe.

He was very different, too, from the statue by Ivor Roberts–Jones, which now stands in Parliament Square. This huge bronze image of Churchill wearing a military greatcoat, one hand resting on a stick, his legs apart and his shoulders thrust forward, is based on a press photograph taken when the Prime Minister inspected the chamber of the House of Commons after it had been destroyed by bombing in 1941. This statue rests on a plinth standing twenty feet tall (over six metres), and the effect is to convey a sense of solidity and permanence.

In 2012, this iconic statue of the man whom Alan Taylor, an historian of the left, described in a celebrated footnote simply as 'the saviour of his country'[1] was vandalized. It was sprayed with red paint to look as if red blood were emerging from Churchill's mouth, and a strip of grass, like a Mohican haircut, was placed on its head. Ten years later, in the course of Black Lives Matter protests, when Churchill was repeatedly accused of being responsible for the famine in Bengal of 1942–1943, in which millions had died, the statue was attacked again. Underneath the name, WINSTON CHURCHILL, the words 'is a racist' were daubed. The statue of the saviour of his country had to be crated up for its protection.

*

In 1945, Winston Churchill was the most famous man in the world. His fellow countrymen revered him. He had brought them to victory. He was seen as single-handedly having saved his nation from annihilation. By his force of character in 1940, he had overborne a cabinet that would have made an ignoble peace with Hitler; by his oratory and steadfastness, he had inspired the nation to hold on when Britain stood alone against all the power of Nazism, defending and preserving the flame of resistance until it could be handed on and lit in the hearts of the Russian and American peoples; by his powers of persuasion and dynamism, he was, more than anyone else, until the very last year of the war, the energizing and directing force in the Anglo–American Alliance.

And in 1945, he was applauded not only by his own countrymen. The free world recognized that it remained free, and the values that it shared continued to exist, only because of his leadership in the early years of the war. He was far from being a little Englander. He was a patriotic Briton; but his true commitment was to the world, as Lord Attlee, his lifelong colleague, opponent and friend, his deputy in the heroic years 1940–1945, averred in his tribute in the Lords after Churchill's death. He had an incredibly wide sympathy for ordinary people, wherever they might be. He was committed to causes that overrode national boundaries—to a sense of unity amongst the English-speaking peoples, for instance. He favoured European integration and the Council of Europe. The scale of his humanity was demonstrated by the way he stretched out to succour his former enemies. He did so after the South African War; he did so after the First World War; and he would have done so again after the Second World War if he had been in office. No one would disagree with the first part of the peroration to Attlee's tribute, and few would disagree with the second: 'My Lords, we have lost the greatest Englishman of our time—I think the greatest citizen of the world of our time.' In 2002, Churchill was voted the greatest Briton ever in a national poll. No one was greatly surprised. In September 2014, it was announced that Churchill's portrait would be featured on the five-pound note.

*

When the announcement about the new five-pound note was made, Benjamin Whittingham, the Labour candidate for Wyre and Preston North, tweeted that Churchill was a 'racist and white supremacist'. There had been straws in the wind. The 'racist' graffito had been scrawled on the statue's plinth just ten years after the Greatest Briton vote and eight years before the Black Lives Matter scrawls, and the subsequent crating to protect the statue of the greatest Briton ever from the hands of crowds that had toppled statues of others regarded as racist exploiters. Empire, racism, the nature of Britain's imperial history, the issue of whether a degree of involvement in slavery or imperial development meant that figures in history should not be commemorated in statues: all of those issues were suddenly very much in the air. Oxford University held a debate at the Union where the motion 'That This House Believes the British Empire was a National Disgrace' was passed easily. (It was a pretty one-sided sort of debate, with three formal speakers in favour of the motion and only one against). Meanwhile, in 2021, at the Cambridge College named after Churchill that constitutes the national and commonwealth memorial to him, there was a year-long series of discussions entitled 'Churchill, Empire and Race'. The theme was not whether or not Churchill had been a racist. That was pretty much taken for granted. It was rather an examination of different facets of a type of racism that did not need to be proved. A college spokesperson said it was 'not a debate [but] . . . specifically designed to be a more critical assessment of Churchill's imperial policy'.

The second event in the Cambridge series was a discussion entitled 'The Racial Consequences of Mr Churchill'. It was to consider 'Churchill's life and legacy in the light of his views on empire and race'. The discussion was not an open debate between two sides; on the contrary, four academics joined in a sustained attack on supposed ideas of white supremacy and eugenics.

The panellists were Dr Onyeka Nubia from Nottingham University, Professor Kehinde Andrews of Birmingham City University and Dr Madhusree Mukerjee. The chair was Professor Priyamvada Gopal from Churchill College itself. The purpose of this book is not to bolster Churchill's reputation or to argue that he was benevolent to India, but it has to be said that the contributions at the event did little damage to him. The panellists were remarkably uninformed about some of the points on which their arguments pivoted. One of them did not appear to know the difference between Ernest Bevin, a member of Churchill's cabinet and someone whom Churchill greatly admired, and Aneurin Bevan, an outspoken opponent, not to say enemy. Their contentions were that Hitler's importance in the war had been greatly overstated, that the war would have ended in the same way without Churchill, and that the war was won by the Soviet Union. There is a large measure of truth in that last point, but it does ignore the fact that the war wouldn't have begun if the Soviet Union had not allied itself with the Nazis in 1939; it also ignores the role of the United States in the defeat of Germany. It was narrated that the British Empire was the blueprint for Nazism; that the Holocaust was 'not an outlier at all'; that 'Churchill's views on race were much the same as the Nazis'; 'and that Churchill facilitated the Bengal Famine of 1943'. The 'scholarship' behind the conference has been fairly devastatingly destroyed by Andrew Roberts and Zewditu Gebreyohanes.[2]

Churchill's grandson, Sir Nicholas Soames, told the *Daily Mail* that it seemed to him 'extremely unlikely that young ladies and gentlemen will get a balanced view of Churchill's life' from the deliberations of the Cambridge programme, and he is probably right. Unless or until the revisionist wheel turns full circle, Churchill will be remembered not as the saviour of his country and of the free world but as a bigoted racist, as evil as if he had trafficked in slaves or run a plantation in the West Indies.

*

Why has his image changed so much? The 'evidence' against him in the Churchill College not-a-debate consisted mostly of criticism of racial stereotyping and of language used by Churchill and others of his time that is certainly to be deprecated but was all too common amongst men of his generation. But there is more substantive evidence to look at in relation to India; it is Churchill and India with which this book is concerned. Was the hero of 1940–1945, the saviour of his country, a racist enemy of India?

2

A Passage to India

In Bombay in 1898, standing at the stern of the ship, Churchill looked back at Wellington Pier with its tight network of wharves and narrow streets. As the troop ship moved out, its propeller disturbed the silt that was carried into the estuary by the Ulhas River and had settled around the mangrove swamps that lay on the shores of the harbour.

Just a few years later, the ramshackle buildings would be cleared to prepare for the visit of the Prince of Wales, soon to be King George V and Emperor of India. A monumental arch would be erected and called the Gateway of India. But Wellington Pier was already effectively that, and at the age of twenty-four, Churchill was departing through it, turning his back on India for the last time.

Several years later, when he was Prime Minister of Great Britain and in the middle of the struggle for his country's survival, he seriously contemplated coming back to the subcontinent. He never did so; he never even came within 1000 miles. But from across the sea, he had more influence over a prolonged period, as backbencher, Cabinet Minister and Prime Minister, on the political development of India and its struggle for independence than any other British statesman.

*

The ship moved away from the Customs House building and Cotton Green into the harbour, down the estuary and finally into the Arabian Sea. Churchill bade farewell to India, the Jewel in the Crown, the most populous, and by far the most romantic part of the British Empire. It was the acquisition of this enormous peninsula and its potential treasures that prompted Victoria's Prime Minister, Benjamin Disraeli, to promote his queen from a European throne to Empress of India.* Without India, Britain was an important power—possibly the most important power in the world—with huge possessions: Australia, Canada and New Zealand, as well as innumerable other territories scattered over the face of the globe. But with India, with its exoticism and riches, and its physical position, linking Victoria's assets in the east and the west, Britain's Empire became the greatest the world had known.

Churchill, already possessed of a great sense of history and anxious to find an element of destiny in Britain's role as in his own life, was conscious of all this. He was leaving India after spending almost two years there. In the course of that time, he had come to know parts of India—particularly the North–West Frontier Province—well. He had seen some aspects of India then. But they were limited aspects. He had been unable to see others. It is questionable whether he had any huge desire to do so. He had been immersed in military life. He had seen action for the first time and displayed personal bravery. In a small way, he had matured; in a larger sense, he never did. He had supplemented

---

* Shortly afterwards, she made him Earl of Beaconsfield. *Punch's* drawing was captioned, 'One good turn deserves another.'

the piecemeal education he had received at Harrow. He thought he had increased his confidence and benefited from self-discipline and responsibility. Others may have doubted that his confidence ever needed bolstering. He had begun the literary career on which he would depend for money for the rest of his life.

He left India with no regrets. He had been keen to escape, as he saw it, almost from the moment he arrived. Yet his destiny and that of India were inextricably linked. He would lead the opposition to the Government of India Bill in 1935, which was intended to pave the way for dominion status and ultimately independence. He would congratulate himself that the results of his efforts were that internal forces—the princes, Muslims and Hindus—were divided amongst themselves so that progress towards independence would be checked, perhaps forever. As Prime Minister, he continued to thwart moves towards self-rule, frustrating, for example, Sir Stafford Cripps's mission. In 1943, he was Prime Minister at the time of the famine in Bengal. He delayed independence as long as he had the power to do so, and it only arrived when he was out of office.

*

The mystery of Churchill and India is that the truth contains strange contradictions. Unlike most of the British men who forged the history of the Indian subcontinent in the twentieth century, Churchill had indeed spent time there. The British sovereigns rarely visited their Indian possessions as king emperors.[*] The

---

[*] Edward VII, as Prince of Wales, spent eight months in India in 1875–1876. He deprecated the way Indians were treated by the British: 'Because a man has a black face and a different religion from our own, there is no reason why he should be treated as a brute.' George V spent four months there from November 1905 to March 1906, first at the

viceroys, who reigned in their emperors' stead, generally did not remain in India for long. Lord Linlithgow, unusually, spent eight years there in that position because Churchill wanted to keep him there for reasons that will be discussed later. His was the longest viceregal reign. The other men who shaped India in the years leading up to independence in 1947 did so from afar. No prime ministers visited India when they were in office. Few secretaries of state for India spent any great time there, and the innumerable missions and commissions of inquiry enjoyed only brief stays. Churchill, by contrast, was there for twenty-two months, from November 1895 to June 1898. It would, however, be quite wrong to imagine that he was there as a matter of choice rather than regrettable necessity.

*

On 2 February 1895, Churchill was commissioned into the Fourth Hussars, aged just over twenty. His choice of career was that of his father, Lord Randolph Churchill. Randolph died at the age of forty-five, just ten days before Churchill was commissioned. He had been an aloof and unkind parent, and Churchill's sense of filial piety towards him is all the more surprising. It can be convincingly argued that much of the son's subsequent career was determined by a desire for achievements of which his father would have approved.

Great Imperial Durbar and then touring the country while he was still Prince of Wales. To his great credit, he was horrified by the way the Indians were treated. He returned as king in 1911. Edward VIII also visited India as Prince of Wales in 1921–1922 (his visit was boycotted by the Congress Party in the aftermath of the Jallianwala Bagh Massacre). His views of his subject races were much less advanced and sympathetic than those of his father.

Randolph's choice of career for his eldest son was dictated largely by what he saw as his academic failures at Harrow. It was a negative decision, and Winston was, in truth, far from positive about the army. He saw it not as an end in itself but as a vehicle for achieving distinction in public and political life, the goal that he had set himself at an early age and from which he never wavered. His father was right only in a sense: Winston had been inconsistent in his scholastic achievements. He was hopeless at what he didn't like—Mathematics and Latin—but very able at the subjects that interested him: English, History and Chemistry.* But Lord Randolph wrote off a school performance that was certainly not uniformly poor with a typically cruel letter in which he threatened to disown his son: 'If you cannot prevent yourself from leading the idle, useless, unprofitable life you have had during your school days & later months you will become a mere social wastrel, one of the hundreds of the public school failures.'[1]

Sandhurst, where he prepared for a military career, was different from school. By now, Churchill was not simply filling the school day but doing what he wanted to do, qualifying himself for success. He passed out high—twentieth out of 130. Thus, he came to the Fourth Hussars. The army had no great appeal in itself, but it was the route to eminence. What he really wanted was to play 'the game of politics'. It was 'a fine game to play', but he knew he had to prepare for it: soldiering would be fun and good for him and would inculcate responsibility and discipline.

He entered the army then, out of necessity and without much enthusiasm. Just six months after being commissioned, he admitted that the military life was not his métier. He confided this

---

* The last of these may be surprising, but in the Second World War, with the assistance of Lord Cherwell, he was keenly involved in the application of science to warfare. His interest in these matters is reflected by the space he accords them in his *History of the Second World War*.

to his mother. In truth, she had been as absent from his childhood as selfishly as Lord Randolph had been, but she was not unkind. Churchill loved her, and he poured out his intimate thoughts to her. They were, in a way, kindred souls, more or less penniless, spendthrifts when they had money and ultimately adventurers.

And if the army was only a means to an end, so, certainly, was India. It simply happened to be where his regiment was bound. It was to go to the subcontinent for nine years' service, although individual officers would come and go during that period. Their preparations began in the summer of 1895, when they marched from Aldershot to Hounslow. Life for a cavalryman could be briefly dangerous, but there were compensations. Officers were allowed five months' leave a year, including an uninterrupted spell of ten weeks. Churchill spent most of the winter not in the hunting field, where young officers were expected to be; he managed to find a more exciting way of extending his experience of life. He wangled a visit to the West Indies and the United States. He was very good at wangling. The attraction of the West Indies was that in Cuba, still occupied by Spain, government troops were active, attempting to suppress independence insurrections upcountry. As usual, his mother, Jennie, shamelessly used her extraordinarily wide list of social connections to promote her son's interests.

His commanding officer, Colonel Brabazon, had given Churchill and his friend Reggie Barnes permission to proceed 'to the seat of war', a delightfully Churchillian expression, and observe how the Spanish authorities were attempting to suppress the insurrection. Churchill did his own bit to supplement his mother's string-pulling. He always favoured 'doing business with the people at the top'. He contacted his father's old friend, Sir Henry Drummond–Wolff, the then British Ambassador in Madrid.

All this networking carried Churchill to Cuba with a favouring wind. There, he was able to observe warfare at close quarters. He was critical of the lack of discipline in the ranks of the upcountry natives, but it's to be noted that it was with them in their oppression that his sympathies lay. At this stage in his life, his instinct was to support the underdog. And not only at this stage. Why was he against the oppressed as long as they weren't Indian?

On his return, he still had months to fill. He went back to his list of contacts. In the course of three dinners, he met Henry Asquith, the former home secretary and future prime minister; Arthur Balfour, the Leader of the House, First Lord of the Treasury and also a future prime minister; Joe Chamberlain, the Colonial Secretary; Wolseley, the Commander in Chief of the British army; the President of the Local Government Board; the Chancellor of the Duchy of Lancaster; the President of the Probate Division; the Judge Advocate General; the Lord President of the Council; and the Duke of Devonshire.[2] Pretty remarkable: an agreeable young aristocrat, even an impoverished one, could do a lot if he had confidence, contacts and a beautiful, widowed mother. It was heady stuff. He found it seductive, and he regretted that he would be excluded from such events and contacts by isolation, as he saw it, in India.

In the meantime, there were interesting diversions. They were important to him, not only for the excitement they brought but crucially as elements in what wasn't then called a curriculum vitae. He tried to fill the remaining time before India as a special correspondent for the *Daily Chronicle* in Crete, where there was a rising against the Turks. Then he offered himself as a galloper, an informal aide-de-camp, to Kitchener, who was organizing an expedition up the Nile. His next attempt was to get himself attached to an expedition against a rising in Matabeleland.

All of this activity on the part of Churchill and his family came to the attention of Lord Lansdowne, the Secretary of State for War, and one of Jennie's innumerable friends. He discreetly warned her that, as there had been a minor scandal about a possibly rigged horse race affecting some of the officers of the

Fourth Hussars, it would be wise for Winston to lower his profile and be out of the country for a bit.

Winston took little notice of the advice, but he finally had to bow to the inevitable. He sailed from Southampton for India on 11 September 1896 on the *SS Britannia*. He went without enthusiasm. He had written to his mother just five weeks earlier. He had seen an opportunity to transfer to the Ninth Lancers and go to Rhodesia

> [W]here I could gain experience and derive advantage—rather than to the tedious land of India—where I shall be equally out of the pleasures of peace and the chances of war. The future is to me utterly unattractive. I look upon going to India with this unfortunate regiment . . . as useless and unprofitable exile . . . [in comparison with] a few months in South Africa with the SA medal . . . and in all probability the company's Star.[3]

*

On their arrival in Bombay, Churchill and some of his friends called over one of the many tiny boats to take them ashore. When they reached the quays and the Sassoon Dock, he tried to scramble ashore from the plunging dinghy and dislocated his shoulder. He suffered from the results of that dislocation for the rest of his life. For the thirty years in which he played polo, he had to do so with the upper part of his arm strapped to his body. Two years after his accident, he took part in the charge of the 21st Lancers at the Battle of Omdurman. Because of his injury, he couldn't use a sword, and he maintained that he had survived because he had been able to defend himself instead with a pistol.

From Bombay, Churchill and his regiment travelled by train to Bangalore via Poona. In Bangalore, despite his lack of funds, he lived well. He, Reggie Barnes and one other shared a substantial bungalow: 'a magnificent pink and white stucco palace in the

middle of a large and beautiful garden'. Each subaltern had a
butler, two 'dressing boys', or valets, and a syce, or groom, for
every horse or pony. They shared the services of two gardeners,
three *bhistis* (water carriers) four *dhobis* (washermen) and a
watchman. Churchill resumed his schoolboy hobby of collecting
butterflies and began an interest in gardening, which, at the level
of landscaping rather than weeding, was to remain with him for
most of his life. Within a month or two, he had planted 250 rose
trees of seventy different varieties, and every morning, he filled
three great basins with fresh flowers.

He also met Pamela Plowden, 'the most beautiful girl I've ever
seen'. She was the first great love of his life. They never became
engaged. But they remained very close friends throughout his life.
Although seven months older than he, she was still alive at the
time of his death. They explored Hyderabad on elephants: 'You
dare not walk or the natives spit at Europeans—which provokes
retaliations leading to riots.'

Pamela impressed him, but most of the English women he
met in India did not. In his first letter from the subcontinent to his
mother, he related that he 'saw a lot of horrid Anglo–Indian* women
at the races—nasty vulgar creatures all looking as though they
thought themselves great beauties. I fear me they are a sorry lot'.[4] He
had little contact with Indian people, but the British he met did not
impress him: 'Nice people in India are few and far between. They are
like oases in the desert. This is an abominable country to live long in.
Comfort you get—company you miss.'[5] He didn't make much of an
effort. 'The vulgar Anglo–Indians' commented on his failure to call
on them, 'as is the absurd custom of the country'.

Churchill found regimental life devoid of any stimulating
company, a 'land of snobs and bores'.[6] Life was 'stupid, dull &

---

* 'Anglo–Indian' was later often used to denote someone of mixed race.
Here he meant an English resident in India.

uninteresting' and Churchill despaired of meeting 'more of the influential people who rule the country and unless I get *good letters of introduction* to the *very best* (not socially best) people out here my stay is likely to be utterly valueless'.[7] He was frustrated by the uninspired people that he met and by the fact that he did not have the contacts in India that would allow him access to the people who mattered. When he talked about 'the people who mattered', he meant the British, who framed and implemented policy. There is no hint that he wanted to meet Indian politicians, let alone advocates of independence. The limitations of military life frustrated him too. His colleagues' interests were confined to polo and racing, and although he sought to improve himself by reading extensively and did indeed do so, the climate made this an effort.

To be fair to him, he was indeed confined in a claustrophobic bubble, which meant that he was never able to make a proper assessment of India. In Cuba, he had sided with the insurgents. If he had been able to meet Indian politicians or even senior British administrators, he would have assembled a scaffolding of knowledge on which to build later when he addressed his mind to the Government of India. He was conscious of his limited contact with the great country in which he found himself, '[p]oked away in a garrison town which resembles a third-rate watering place, out of season & without the sea . . . The only valuable knowledge I take away from India (soldiering apart) could have been gathered equally well in [his London house] Cumberland Place'.[8]

*

The greatest legacy of Churchill's time in India was the opportunity it afforded him for self-education. If he could learn little about the Indian world, he could at least educate himself in the politics, history and public life of Britain. He was conscious of the piecemeal nature of his own education and, in later life, regretted the fact that he had not gone to Oxford or Cambridge and become familiar with the discipline of studying both sides of a problem and arriving at a balanced judgement. And so, resisting the torpor that enveloped his friends, he settled down to a structured and demanding course of reading.

Before he went out, he had already tried to do some preparatory research about India. He prepared by reading a book called *Twenty-One Days in India* by George Robert Aberigh–Mackay, who had been principal of Rajkumar College, Indore. The book's subtitle was *The Tour of Sir Ali Baba, K.C.B.* It consisted of a satirical depiction of different Indian and Anglo–Indian characters, from the 'Great Ornamental' viceroy to the 'Bengali Baboo'. Now in India, he read *Indian Polity* by Sir George Chesney. The book argued that 'the state of anarchy and universal strife throughout the land, which was replaced by the peace everywhere established under British rule, must have been attended with a degree of suffering that far outweighs the defects inseparable from a rule by foreigners'. This was about the extent of his research on the subcontinent, and Chesney's conclusion is a fair summation of Churchill's settled and continuing judgement: that overall British rule had conferred vast benefits on the Indian population that far outweighed any trifling drawbacks.

His reading of wider works was infinitely more rigorous. He pestered Jennie with incessant demands for reading material. Between September 1896 and April 1897, she sent him twelve volumes of Macaulay (eight of the *History* and four of essays); twenty-seven volumes of the *Annual Register* and two volumes of Adam Smith's *Wealth of Nations*. The volumes of the *Annual Register*, first published in 1758 by Edmund Burke, narrate the major events of succeeding years. Initially, when it concentrated on the Seven Years' War, 1756–1763, its format was to set out the events of the year followed by what were called 'state papers', which included the parliamentary speeches relating to the events. Churchill's demanding approach was not to look at the papers until he had analysed the events and set out his own opinions. He then read the debates. 'After reading I reconsider and finally write. I hope by a persevering continuance of this practice to build up a scaffolding of logical and consistent views which will perhaps tend to the creation of a logical and consistent mind.'[9]

He analysed what he read and did so in the letters that he wrote to his mother and his brother Jack. How interested they were in his thoughts on literature must be questionable. His mother was preoccupied with her rackety social life and her financial problems, and Jack, five years younger than Winston, was still at Harrow. Winston reported to her on the different literary styles of Macaulay and Gibbon, on his thoughts about a translation of Plato, and about a book that particularly interested him and which will be discussed later: *The Martyrdom of Man* by William Winwood Reade. He found himself reluctantly concurring in Reade's criticism of Christianity.

His mother was also expected to read lengthy and detailed comments on British politics, which the young soldier followed avidly. His comments were, of course, wildly out of date; he made them on the basis of English newspapers that had taken weeks to arrive, and by the time his own thoughts had reached Jennie, she must have felt that she was reading history. She was also expected to admire his pen sketches of men who were among her intimate friends but whom Churchill only knew from the parliamentary reports.

In his political views, he was far from the caricature of reactionary young cavalry blood. He told his mother, 'I am a Liberal in all but name. My views excite the pious horror of the Mess.' Again,

Among the leaders of the Tory party are two whom I despise
and detest as politicians above all others—Mr Balfour and
George Curzon. The one—a languid lazy lackadaisical cynic—
the unmonumental figurehead of the Conservative Party; the
other the spoiled darling of politics—blown with conceit—
insolent from undeserved success—the typification of the
superior Oxford prig.[10]

He was conscious that his reading of Gibbon and Macaulay and
the golden period of the Annual Register tended to affect his
literary style. 'I suppressed with difficulty an impulse to become
sententious. Gibbon and Macaulay, however much they may
improve one's composition of essays or reports, do not lend
themselves to letter writing.' The style of these masters may not
have permanently affected his letter writing, but it impressed itself
on his speeches and his formal composition for the rest of his
life, and his contribution to literature and oratory would have
been infinitely less remarkable if it had not been for the sticky
afternoons in the bungalow.

He exchanged letters with the Reverend J.E.C. Weldon, his
former headmaster at Harrow. Weldon responded to Churchill's
desire for self-improvement, telling him to consider taking up Latin
or even Greek. He was unaware of Churchill's lack of opportunity
to study the administration of India. He told him that he would
be a witness to 'the most interesting administrative work that
has ever been done among men' and at a particularly interesting
time in Indian history. He asked his former pupil to tell him,
as Churchill could not, what he thought of the intellectual and
moral capacities of the natives. Interestingly, he ended his advice
by telling Churchill to 'think more of others than of yourself [and
to] be ready to learn from those that are below you'.

3

Soldiering on the Frontier

The young Winston took his military duties seriously and was appointed adjutant and then Brigade Major at a far earlier stage than would have been the case if he had remained with the regiment in England. He took his polo no less seriously. He was a distinguished player, and his regiment did well at the Hyderabad polo tournament. At Secunderabad, the Fourth Hussars won a first-class tournament, the first British regiment to do so after such a short time in India. Churchill found polo useful in allowing social contact between the army and the Indian princes, against whose teams they often played. That provided some contact with the people of India, if only at a rarefied and unrepresentative level.

He struggled to survive on what he ironically described as 'the generous rewards of the Queen–Empress'—his pay was just £120 a year—and his very limited private allowance.

[A]ll the rest had to be borrowed at usurious rates of interest from the all-too accommodating native bankers. Every officer was warned against these gentlemen. I always found them most agreeable; very fat, very urbane, quite honest and merciless

rapacious. All you had to do was to sign little bits of paper, and produce a polo pony as if by magic. The smiling financier rose to his feet, covered his face with his hands, replaced his slippers, and trotted off contentedly till that day three months. They only charged 2% a month [Churchill's emphasis] and made quite a good living out of it, considering they hardly ever had a bad debt.[1]

This was how he made his first contact with the mercantile, chiefly Hindu, classes, as opposed to the 'manly, martial races' whom he commanded. His perceptions of the supposed differences would inform his political position almost half a century later. We will return to this topic.

Money was then a frequent subject of correspondence with his mother. The cavalry was not the place for a poor man, and Churchill was a poor man. An officer could not subsist on his pay. It was reckoned that at least £600 a year of private income was necessary for existence in a cavalry regiment. Churchill's parents were as financially irresponsible as he was, and his father's assets when he died amounted to about the same figure as his debts. Jennie had an income of about £2700 a year from her own father's settlement from which to meet her considerable requirements in addition to those of her two sons. Winston thought that in his regiment he would need £500 a year on top of his pay of £120; he also had initial expenses of about £650 for items like his polo ponies and a charger. His aunt, Duchess Lily, the second wife of the eighth Duke of Marlborough, helped out by giving him £200 to buy the charger.

The correspondence between mother and son on the subject of finance is full of delicious irony. Each urged on the other self-restraint and prudence, of which neither was capable. It was said of Jennie that 'in money matters' (the same could be said of sexual matters) 'she was without sense of proportion. The value of money meant nothing to her: what counted with her were the things she

got for money, not the amount she had to pay for them'.[2] It only took her three years after Lord Randolph's death to build up debts of her own of about £14,000. She was told she would have to raise a loan to be paid off at the rate of £700 a year, and in the event of her death, her sons would have to take it over. Winston was very unhappy about the implied reduction in his allowance:

> I sympathise with all your extravagances—even more than you do with mine—it just seems suicidal to me when you spent £200 on a ball dress* as it does to you when I purchased a new polo pony for £100. And yet I feel that you ought to have the dress and & I a polo pony. The pinch of the whole matter is we are damned poor.[3]

Soon, Jennie could no longer afford to pay Winston his allowance at all. He raised a loan of £3500 to pay her an income for him and Jack for three years and to pay off £400 of debt that he had accumulated with tailors and other tradesmen. The settlement that her father had made for her allowed Jennie an income but no access to capital. The capital would pass to Winston on her death, but it was less than the £3500 that she was borrowing.[4]

Wealth and poverty are relative matters, but Winston's life in India was not without embarrassing reminders about money matters. Cheques were dishonoured. When Jennie went to the bank to pay his allowance, she would find that the whole of the quarter's allowance had been anticipated. For an even greater spendthrift, she could be quite tiring:

> I would only repeat that I cannot help you anymore & if you have any grit in you and & are worth yr salt you will try & live within yr income & cut down yr expenses in order to do

---

* About £25,000 today. Some dress; some price.

it. You cannot but feel ashamed of yrself under the present circumstances—I haven't the heart to write any more . . . [5]

*

Winston's letters are heavily burdened with references to his desire to get out of India and indeed the army as soon as possible, but in the meantime, at least to get as many medals and as much public attention as possible. Jennie allowed herself to be mildly irritated by his desire to quit India prematurely. Despite that, he kept on pressing her to use her contacts: 'This my dearest Mamma must depend on you.'[6] Turkey had declared war on Greece. He wanted to go to Greece as a special correspondent, and 'You know the King of Greece'. Not many young men had this kind of connection. He sailed from Bombay on leave on board the *HMS Ganges* on 8 May 1897, but alas, the Greeks sued for peace three days later. He used the three months' leave to explore Italy as well as attend the famous fancy dress ball held by the Duchess of Devonshire in Devonshire House in Piccadilly. Lady Randolph went as the Empress Theodora.* When he was staying with Duchess Lily

---

* Of whom Gibbon had written,

> The beauty of Theodora was the subject of . . . flattering praise, and the source of . . . exquisite delight. Her features were delicate and regular; her complexion, though somewhat pale, was tinged with a natural colour; every sensation was instantly expressed by the vivacity of her eyes; her easy motions displayed the graces of a small but elegant figure . . . But this form was degraded by the facility with which it was exposed to the public eye, and prostituted to licentious desire. Her venal charms were abandoned to a promiscuous crowd of citizens and strangers of every rank, and of every profession: the fortunate lover who had been promised a night of enjoyment, was often driven from her bed by a stronger or more wealthy favourite; and when she passed through the streets, her presence was avoided by all who wished to escape either the scandal or the temptation.

Churchill had read Gibbon. His mother may not have done so.

and her husband, Lord William Beresford, for the Goodwood Races, he read in the newspapers that there had been a revolt of Pathan tribesmen on the North–West Frontier and that a Field Force of three brigades had been formed by Sir Bindon Blood. Churchill had made friends with this magnificently named general the year before and had obtained a promise that if he ever commanded another expedition on the frontier, he would allow Churchill to accompany him. Now Winston telegraphed the general, reminding him of his promise, and took the train from Brindisi to catch the Indian Mail. He was attached to the Field Force as a war correspondent for the *Daily Telegraph*. To his considerable annoyance, his reports did not appear under his name but were simply signed by 'a young officer'. But 'the great thing is to get to the front'.

On his way to the Field Force's base of operations at Nowshera, Churchill broke his journey at Rawalpindi and visited the sergeant's mess while a sing-song was in progress. He said that the best song he heard was:

> Great White Mother, far across the sea,
> Ruler of the Empire may she ever be.
> Long May She Reign, glorious and free,
> In the Great White Motherland.[7]

Lieutenant (later Lieutenant Colonel) James Colvin was a relation of Bindon Blood, and had been summoned from leave to be part of the Field Force. On his arrival on 13 September 1897 he dined with Blood and then met Lieutenant Churchill, 'who was acting as war correspondent for some London daily paper'. Colvin noted Churchill's enthusiasm for action (for which read medals). He found him bumptious. Many did, and it is not a surprise to learn from Colvin that when they returned home by ship Churchill was sent to Coventry by his fellow-officers (though not by Colvin).

In the aftermath of a raid on the Mamund Valley, Bindon Blood ordered that the valley be laid waste. Churchill recalled the operation: the systematic destruction of village after village; the wells filled up; the cutting down of trees that provided shade; the burning of the crops; and the destruction of the reservoirs. He was shocked by this, but not more than he was by the brutality of the tribesmen and by the British policy of taking no prisoners, even when their opponents were wounded. He saw Sikh troops set fire to a wounded man. James Colvin, who was awarded the Victoria Cross for his part in the action, supplied a cameo of Churchill. 'At the time we were in a small nullah* and suddenly Winston Churchill appeared, flourishing his drawn revolver: I was in a beastly funk . . . and there seemed no real reason for drawing it . . . so I was jolly glad when he put it back in his holster.'[8.]

Churchill's appraisal of the situation may have been realistic. Colvin reports that their men were falling back in disarray. The Sikh non-commissioned officers couldn't stem the retreat and appealed to the two officers. 'Winston said, "Colvin, this won't do. Let's hold our hands across the nullah". So we stood in the nullah with our hands stretched across it and [the men] gradually began to stand still and stop going back.'[9] We shall see later that Churchill developed a low opinion of Indian troops in general.

At last Churchill was seeing action. On 19 September 1897, under fire and fearing for the safety of his pony, he dismounted and went forward on foot. He was one of the last to retire. The danger was real enough. Two officers with him were killed, and he and another subaltern carried a wounded sepoy for some distance 'and might perhaps, had there been any gallery, have received some notice'. The two of them remained where they were until the enemy was within forty yards. Churchill and his companion,

---

* A dry river bed

Bethune, fired their revolvers at the enemy. 'They actually threw stones at us. It was a horrible business.'

Later, he picked up a rifle that a wounded man had dropped and fired forty rounds 'with some effect' at close quarters. He thought he hit four men. 'At any rate they fell.' His reports and reflections are self-regarding and insensitive, but he had been brave enough; he had nearly been caught by the tribesmen, and the fate of a British officer in the hands of the Pathans was not an enviable one. His courage was as obvious as his motives. He was quite frank about them. He told his mother that he 'rode on my grey pony all along the skirmish line where everyone else was lying down in cover. Foolish perhaps but I play for high stakes and given an audience there is no act too daring or too noble. Without the Gallery things are different'.[10] Whatever the motives, he was effective. Bindon Blood appointed him to an Indian regiment that had run short of officers, the 31st Punjaub (*sic*) Infantry. Blood wrote to Winston's Hussar commander, Colonel Brabazon, that the young officer was 'working away equal to two ordinary subalterns'. Blood went on to say that if Churchill got a chance, he would get the VC or a DSO; he was aware of what Churchill was after. But army command didn't like the unofficial way in which Churchill had spirited himself from Bangalore to the frontier and wasted little time in recalling him to the Fourth Hussars.

The reports he sent back to the press were vivid but sanitized. He did not reveal that British and Indian troops had been thrown back, and he was silent on the atrocities that the insurgents inflicted on the wounded whom they captured. Equally, he did not mention that British and Indian troops were ready to 'finish off' wounded insurgents who came into their hands, even if *they* didn't mutilate them first. He could not mention that the British troops were supplied with dum-dum expanding bullets,* later

---

* So called because they were originally developed at Dumdum, near Calcutta, by the British.

banned by the Hague Convention of 1899. As a serving British officer, he could not do so, but what is interesting is that privately, he was horrified by the effect of the bullets and told his family and friends about them in disapproving terms.[11]

His candour about his desire for medals is remarkable. He told his mother in a letter dated 19 September 1897, that Blood had made him his orderly officer and that this meant that he would get a medal and perhaps a couple of clasps—but he was conscious that what was going on in Egypt was more publicized and therefore tended to attract more clasps and medals. As it was, he had to make do with the Campaign Medal and a Mention in Despatches. The Mention referred to his courage and resolution and the way in which he made himself useful at a critical moment.

Lloyd George once said that Churchill would use his grandmother's hide to make a drum on which to signal his success. Back in Bangalore by the end of October 1897, he started work on *The Story of the Malakand Field Force*. Simultaneously, he was working on his first and only novel, *Savrola*.*

In one part of the *Malakand* manuscript, there is an amendment that reflects Churchill's views on race. A passage that said 'the prestige of the dominant race enables them to keep up appearances before the native troops' was amended to read: 'the prestige of the dominant race enables them to maintain their superiority over the native troops'.[12] Churchill was horrified to

---

* *Savrola* was serialized in 1898 and published as a book in 1900. It was dedicated to the Officers of the 4th Hussars, and is similar in genre to Anthony Hope's *The Prisoner of Zenda*. The heroine seems to have been modelled on Jennie, the hero on Churchill himself, and a nurse on Churchill's own nurse, Mrs Everest. The book was, of course, written for money, and it was a modest financial success. It was, on the whole, well received by critics. Churchill claimed that he consistently urged his friends to abstain from reading it.

discover 'weapons of the 19th century . . . in the hands of the savages, of the stone age'.[13]

It is too easy to be simplistic about his views. They were fairly subtle, and nuances could result in apparent contradictions. This ambivalence was always going to be there, although less so as the years passed. He could support a 'forward' imperial policy on the grounds that civilization had to prevail over savagery, but regret the practical consequences of the policy, 'an awful business'.[14] He was aware not only of the need to suppress 'savagery', but also of the danger of leaving unannexed territories between British possessions and the Russian frontier. *The Story of the Malakand Field Force* was widely criticized for advocating the forward policy. The *United Service Gazette*, the *Pall Mall Gazette*, the *Review of Reviews* and the *Daily News* all accused him of that. The *Scotsman*, alone in Britain, noted his ambivalence.[15] The *Times of India* also recognized his reservations about forward policy, which Churchill emphasized in a follow-up article on 'The Ethics of Frontier Policy', which justified forwardness only on the grounds that having started, it was impossible not to continue. More generally, even the Prince of Wales wrote to him favourably. Churchill's literary ambition was whetted. He began to talk of a life of Garibaldi (a disruptive revolutionary and an instructive choice) and a history of the American Civil War.

*

He was wildly inconsistent in his expressed opinions about the qualities of Indian troops. He referred to them later on the basis of his experience in these early days, of his acquaintance with them on the Western Front in the First World War, in Mesopotamia afterwards and in the Second World War, particularly Burma. He *sometimes* treated them with respect and admiration; but at other times and much more often, he was witheringly disparaging. In his history of the Second World War, he talked of what he had seen of 'the steadfast Indian corps in the cruel winter of 1914',[16] but made no mention of their essential services in other theatres—most notably Mesopotamia, where Indian troops had played the largest part in defeating the Ottomans. In his account of the First World War, *The World Crisis*, he gave a more balanced account of the Indian contribution but focused to an extent on the logistical problems of transport.

*

During his period on the North–West Frontier, he was impressed by the bravery and dash of Muslims and Sikhs. It is as well to examine his partiality for Muslims a little more, because it was to inform his views on the Indian communities. In his partiality, he was following his father. Lord Randolph Churchill combined a knowledge of India (he had been Secretary of State for India) with a preference for Muslims. In this, he had been influenced by Wilfred S. Blunt, who encouraged him 'to make himself, in Parliament, the champion of Islam'. Blunt later became an equal friend of Winston. Randolph Churchill's political influence on his son was strong, and Winston was quoting from him when he said, as he often did, that British rule in India was 'a sheet of oil spread over and keeping free from storms, a vast and profound ocean of humanity'.

For the rest of his life, Churchill continued to make a great distinction between Muslims and Hindus when he talked about India, an issue that will be discussed at length later. He was always conscious not only of this division in Indian society but also of the separate interests of the princes and the lower castes. To an extent, he played up his concern for the more vulnerable peoples as an extension of divide-and-rule tactics, but his emotional sympathies for the weak and vulnerable were always an undeniable and generous aspect of his character.

His favourable view of the bravery of Muslims, which he had observed on the North–West Frontier, was reinforced by his experience of the First World War. In a note on 'The importance of fair dealings with Moslems of India' he said that: 'During the Great War the Moslems of India confounded the hopes of their disloyalty entertained by the Germans and their Turkish ally and readily went to the colours. The Punjab alone furnished 180,000 Moslem recruits.'*

In his romantic imagination, he contrasted the clean-living, hard-fighting Muslims and their adventurous lives on the rocky hillsides of the North–West Frontier with the easy existence of the money-grabbing boxwallahs in the cities, like those who had lent him money to supplement the paltry rewards of the Queen–Emperor. Many British people found it easier to get along with the Muslims because they could dine and eat beef with them, whereas the Hindus thought the feringhee, the white foreigner, a *mleccha*, unclean; this inability to share a meal deepened their dislike of Hindus generally. And, like many Victorians, Churchill felt more affinity for monotheistic religions like Islam as opposed to the multiplicity of Hindu gods. In 1943, Churchill said, 'I'm pro-Moslem—the only quality of the Hindus is that there is a lot of them and that is a vice.'[17]

---

* Unusually for his generation, the young Churchill was in favour of the Turkish ally, the Ottoman Empire, saw it as a mechanism of maintaining peace in India and even talked of fighting for the Turks in the Greco-Turkish War of 1897. See on the subject generally, Warren Dockter, A., 'Men of Martial Nature: Reconsidering Churchill and Indian Muslims', published on June 23, 2014 by Centre for Imperial and Global History Exeter.

But his preference for Muslims was qualified by a concern about conflicting loyalties. During the Malakand campaign in 1897, Churchill had been dismayed by what he called Muslim 'superstition and credulity' when the Mullahs' preaching threatened to dissolve oaths of loyalty.[18] This worry became a very real one at the start of the First World War, when, despite immense but clumsy efforts, Britain failed to detach the Ottoman Empire from Germany's embrace. The result was that throughout the war, it was feared that the Grand Mufti's call would unite the Empire's very numerous Muslim subjects, mostly in India, in rebellion against the Raj. This nightmare was at the root of much of Britain's convoluted and frequently contradictory policies in the Middle East between 1914 and 1918.

Immediately after the end of the First World War, there were widespread risings in the Arab parts of the Ottoman Empire that had been entrusted to Britain as mandates. There was a fear that this would develop into a larger Muslim uprising. Indian Muslims had indeed been concerned by what they thought was an anti-Islamic bias in the peace negotiations at Versailles, reflected in the British intention to abolish the Caliphate. In an extension of the 'Great Game', which Imperialist Russia had played with Victorian Britain, it was thought that Soviet Russia was now fomenting Indian Muslim distress. Churchill and Edwin Montagu, the Secretary of State for India, took these concerns very seriously and were exasperated by Lloyd George's hostility to the Turks.[19]

Churchill had, by this stage, developed an almost paranoid fear of Soviet Russia and overestimated the threat, as did Curzon, the Foreign Secretary. The Russian bear was now a communist bear, but the dynamics were the same as in Kipling's days: destabilization from the north, through Afghanistan. Edwin

Montagu even believed that Gandhi was manipulated by international communism.

*

I have parted company with Churchill in India in order to deal with his views on the relative qualities of the Muslims and the Hindus. These views were important when he had responsibility and influence as a mature politician. Returning to his time as a young officer, it has to be said that overall, Churchill's interaction with the ordinary Indian soldier when he was with the Fourth Hussars was superficial. He thought it 'quite unnecessary' to learn Hindi: 'All natives here speak English perfectly and I cannot see any good in wasting my time acquiring a dialect which I shall never use.'[20]* He was condescending: 'There was no doubt that [the Indian troops] liked having a white officer among them when fighting . . . They watched him carefully to see how things were going. If you grinned, they grinned. So I grinned industriously.'

His general view of the Indian Army was finally more influenced by a mutiny in Singapore in February 1915 than by what 8,00,000 brave and loyal Indian soldiers did for the Empire in the First World War.

*

At the end of 1897, he took a four-day train journey from Bangalore to Calcutta, then India's capital. He had only sixty

---

* In fact, stationed in Bangalore as he was, the local language was not Hindi but Kannada; and the inclusive language of the Indian Army was not Hindi but Urdu.

hours in the city, and he spent them lobbying for a transfer to Egypt.

By now he was beginning to look around for a parliamentary seat, but popular acclaim was always on his mind, and when he was staying at Meerut for a polo tournament as a guest of Sir Bindon Blood, he got wind of an expedition going to Tirah on the North–West Frontier to suppress another rising. He took the risk of heading not for his depot but for Peshawar, the railhead for the expedition, despite the risk that if he were not accepted at Headquarters, he would return to Bangalore having overstayed his leave. He reached the Khyber Pass on 7 March 1898, and made contact with Sir William Lockhart, commanding officer, and Colonel (later) General Ian Hamilton. Hamilton was already a friend: the networks were everywhere. Churchill was hopeful that he could find conspicuous employment in this theatre until he could get to Egypt. Unfortunately, 'the outlook is I fear pacific. The Tribes will probably submit'.[21] On the other hand, he told his mother, he had now made himself familiar with pretty much all of the North–West Frontier.

*

Of all the strings that were pulled and plucked, most were still connected to Egypt, where Kitchener, the Sirdar, continued up the Nile, constructing a railway and supported by an ever-increasing army, Egyptian and British. By February 1898, because he had been attached to a Field Force, Winston was entitled to a full three months' leave on full pay. He decided to use this by proceeding to Egypt. As usual, his plans pivoted around his mother. She was indeed spending part of the winter of 1898 in Egypt: 'Your wits and tact and beauty should overcome all obstacles.' It was pretty shameless for a son to pimp his mother like this, but Jennie Churchill needed no encouragement to deploy her charms.* And thus it was that Churchill sailed away from Bombay and from India forever on 18 June 1898.

---

* She is said to have had 200 lovers. Roy Jenkins described this as a suspiciously round number.

4

Colonial Adventures

Egypt was good for Churchill. He had always expected it to be.
He had told his mother that, having won a medal or two in India,
he could, '[t]hence hot-foot to Egypt—to return with two more
decorations in a year or two—and beat my sword into an iron
despatch box'.[1]

Kitchener went to enormous trouble to avoid having
Churchill around, but even that silent hero could not resist the
efforts of the Churchills, mother and son, and their dragooned
supporters. Initially, Winston was in Egypt as a correspondent
for the *Morning Post,* but inevitably, he wore down the Sirdar
and obtained a temporary posting with the 21st Lancers. As
is well known, he took part in the British Army's last major
cavalry charge at the Battle of Omdurman on 2 September 1898.
The regiment found itself by mistake in a ravine, effectively
ambushed.* Thanks to his dislocated shoulder and his Mauser,

---

* He was to be the last survivor of the charge. When he was told that
the only other man who had taken part had died, so that he could now
claim his title, he said, 'That was remarkably decent of him.'

Churchill managed to shoot dead at least three of the enemy and survived hand-to-hand fighting in which twenty-two of his fellows were killed. He was exhilarated by the experience and regretted that he hadn't been able to renew the charge and kill another fifty or sixty of the enemy. The battle ended in an overwhelming victory. More than 30,000 Dervishes were killed at the cost of twenty-eight British officers and men. It was hardly a conflict between equals. At Omdurman, Kitchener had fifty-two Maxim machine guns.

Churchill's immediate reaction was that of a thoughtless young soldier whose blood was up. 'Talk of fun!' said Churchill. 'Where will you beat this? All Dervishes who did not immediately surrender were shot or bayonetted.' That included the wounded.*

Churchill's reaction to this bloody episode is instructive. His grandmother's skin was turned into another drum: this time, *The River War,* a two-volume account of the campaign, contained a sympathetic study of the Sudanese revolt against British rule. The puzzle again: he was always liberal to subject races provided they weren't Indian.

By the time the book was published in 1899, the heat of battle had been displaced by more considered reflections. He was entirely sympathetic to the rebellious Sudanese and critical of British jingoism. He deplored Kitchener's desecration of the tomb of the Sudanese leader, the Mahdi, and of his skull, and he deprecated the slaughter of the wounded Dervish soldiers.

*

---

* It was in the same year as Omdurman that Hilaire Belloc wrote, 'Whatever happens we have got/The Maxim gun and they have not.'

In 1899, he resigned his commission and obtained a contract with the *Morning Post* as a correspondent reporting on the South African War. A salary of £250 per month made him the highest-paid war correspondent of the day. He acquitted himself with great distinction when an armoured train on a reconnaissance mission was ambushed. Displaying cool resolution, he, a civilian, took command and organized a successful attempt to free the engine. Subsequently captured by the Boers, he escaped and, in an exciting series of adventures, made his way back through Portuguese East Africa to Durban. His exploits were just what were needed during the demoralizing events of 'Black Week', and on the strength of his new fame, he was able to combine his role as a war correspondent with a commission in the South African Light Horse. He was under the command of his friend Sir Ian Hamilton, fighting the kind of war he wanted, galloping over the veldt, frequently in the thick of the fray, sending off eagerly read despatches to London, sustained by supplies from Fortnum and Mason and attended by his own valet. Two books were produced this time: *London to Ladysmith via Pretoria* and *Ian Hamilton's March*.

*

He returned to London, where his experiences in South Africa had made him a personality of some consequence. By a combination of determination, accident and his mother's charms, he had fought in three wars, acquired a chestful of medals, written several books and established his capacity to pay his way as a journalist. He had learned to be dismissive about the abilities of senior officers. He had seen enough of war on a small scale to think that he could direct it on a large scale. These perceptions would have important consequences, both for good and for bad, in both world wars.

He had by no means lost his belief in the beneficial influence of the British Empire, but there remained a chasm between his sympathy for rebellious Boers and insurgent Dervishes, on the one hand, and his later attitude towards the inhabitants of India, on the other.

5

Politics—'A Fine Game to Play'

The first part of his preparation for greatness was complete. He now turned to what really mattered to him: politics. Despite the covert liberalism he had revealed to his mother, he had been flirting with Conservative Party managers since 1897. Now, on his return from India, a by-election was to take place in the Lancashire seat of Oldham.

He stood as a Conservative Party candidate. In one sense, it wasn't surprising that he stood as a Tory. Randolph Churchill had been one, after all. And yet, in another sense, it was a little peculiar. While Randolph *had* been a Conservative like his own parents, he was far from a representative of what Macaulay had called 'those stern unbending Tories'. Indeed, from the managers' point of view, he was a hopeless party politician. Randolph and other junior Conservatives including Arthur Balfour were frequently referred to as 'the Fourth Party' because of their independent line. He founded the Primrose League, a populist Conservative organization, and, as a member of the National Union of Conservative Associations, became associated, possibly mistakenly, with 'Tory democracy'. The movement was more democratic than Tory. He regarded its policy as chiefly support for the monarchy, the House of Lords and the Church of England, but Tory so far, he was also in favour of leasehold reform, and his florid and outspoken oratory created the impression of radicalism, possibly irresponsible and meretricious. His precipitate and ill-judged resignation from Salisbury's Cabinet in December 1886 reinforced the impression of what the Prime Minister called a 'wayward and headstrong disposition'. He never held office again.

'Popular' or 'one nation' Toryism and 'the property-owning democracy' are notions that are associated with Randolph Churchill largely by those who have not inquired too closely into the matter. Winston Churchill probably cared about the lot of ordinary men and women more than Randolph did. He tried to do something about it from his early doctrinaire days alongside Lloyd George in the pre-First World War Liberal Cabinet right on to his last days, in his second administration after 1951, when he urged his Chancellor, Rab Butler, to be good to the old-age pensioners.

When Randolph had stood unsuccessfully for the Central Division of Birmingham in 1885, he had called for an Imperial Commercial Union—the rejection of Free Trade in favour of Imperial Preference. These were causes that would, in time, shake and divide the Conservative Party, and Joe Chamberlain, who later championed the policy, acknowledged that he had been influenced by Lord Randolph Churchill. But it took Joe, rather than Randolph, to change the weather, and it is difficult to see that the latter's legacy had any lasting effect on the Conservative Party. Winston's relationship with his father's legacy was a tortured one, never free from a sense that he had disappointed him, and in many ways, he tried to live out his career in accordance with his father's precepts. But on Free Trade—particularly when the Conservatives debated its final abandonment in the 1930s—Winston never followed Randolph.

Indeed, he left the Conservative Party for the Liberal Party in 1904 rather than abandon Free Trade. His attachment to Free Trade, which had formerly been supported by both main parties but now became preponderantly a Liberal enthusiasm, had implications, as will be shown, for his policy on India.

So, although it was as a Conservative that Winston stood for Parliament in the Oldham by-election of 1899, his commitment to party politics was pretty weak. In the light of all the facts, it is not remotely cynical to say that he was much more interested in his own future than in the future of any political party. That is not to say that he was entirely selfish. There were causes about which he felt strongly and on which he was prepared to imperil his career, but certainly at this stage he was much more like an old-fashioned Whig than a Tory—a generous, paternalistic Whig rather than a radical liberal. Whiggism was what he learned from the Gibbon and Macaulay that he had read in India. He had been disappointed by Salisbury's failure in 1897 to support the Cretans in their revolt against Turkey. When he had told his mother that he was a Liberal in all but name, he added, 'Were it not for Irish Home Rule—to which I will never consent—I would enter Parliament as a Liberal. As it is—Tory democracy will have to be the standard under which I shall range myself.'[1]

Just as this Tory democracy wasn't quite what his father had stood for, so Winston's liberalism would be 'Liberal Imperialism', a position that only part of the Liberal Party adopted. He was not 'imperialist' in the expansionist sense. He said that 'patriotism shades into cant; imperialism sinks to jingoism'. He was for the maintenance and consolidation of the Empire, possibly involving some form of Federation.

At the 1899 by-election, Churchill didn't do badly, losing by just 1300 votes. He made a good impression on the electorate, and he kept the constituency warm. He visited with his cousin, the Duke of Marlborough, when the prospect of renewed war in South Africa coupled with his dramatic exploits in that country made Churchill a popular candidate—some Liberals in the constituency even wrote to say that they would vote for him regardless of politics. Churchill and Marlborough capitalized on these sentiments by visiting South Africa before returning to the constituency in August 1900 in advance of a General Election the following month. The duke threw some money around, promising £400 towards his cousin's election expenses and £100 a year in support of the local party. Despite local enthusiasm for the war, Churchill was cautiously guarded, saying that he was not there representing any policy of jingo annexation but simply as a young man who wanted to see his country powerful abroad and its people happy at home. In that General Election campaign, Churchill was supported by his spirited mother, and he was able to persuade Joe Chamberlain, Colonial Secretary and a huge draw, to speak on his behalf.

The strengths of the parties were quite closely balanced. This was a two-member seat. At the last by-election, the two Liberal candidates had been elected, and the two Conservative candidates were the losers. This time, one Liberal and one Conservative were elected. There had been a slight move away from the Conservatives in Lancashire. Two factors had strengthened the Liberal vote slightly since the by-election, and particularly since the last General Election in 1895. The Liberal Government of 1892–1895 had allowed the Indian Government to place an import duty on textiles, which was unpopular in a cotton county, but the measure had been reversed by the Conservatives and was now slipping from memory. And the Liberal position on the clerical tithes issue was welcomed in a non-conformist and low-church county. But although the tide was thus against the Conservatives, Churchill had now been around the constituency for some time and was liked. He had a personal vote said to have been about 400.[2] And overall, he enjoyed a majority of just over

230 against the less popular Liberal candidate, Walter Runciman.* And thus he returned from his colonial perambulations to a seat in the imperial parliament, as it was often called at this time, in the capital of the mother country.

*

Churchill made his maiden speech on 18 February 1901. Although he supported the war in South Africa, he upset some of his own party with a declaration in favour of the rebels in their fight for their independence: 'if I were a Boer I hope I should be fighting in the field'. This was a pretty remarkable statement from a very junior member of the party that embodied support for the empire and imperial values. His sympathies in these years for those who wanted their independence were consistent, which has to be acknowledged and later examined against his dogged opposition to Indian independence.

Although he came from a privileged, landed background, Churchill was widely regarded as not quite a gentleman, bumptious and vulgar. He received no office from Salisbury or his nephew, Arthur Balfour, who took over as Prime Minister in May 1902.† In addition to his unconventional views on the Boers, his position

---

* Walter Runciman's political career wasn't greatly held back by his defeat. He was returned for Dewsbury, though the Liberal Leader, Henry Campbell-Bannerman, described him as 'a pugnacious, sectional partisan who will be . . . a mutineer whenever mutiny is possible'. When Churchill jumped ship to the Liberals, he and Runciman were colleagues. Later, when Churchill had returned to the Conservative fold and Runciman had become increasingly disillusioned with the Liberals, they were colleagues again in the National Government in 1931.
† 'Robert' was the Christian name of Balfour's uncle, the Marquess of Salisbury. Hence the quip at the time when the premiership passed to his nephew, 'Bob's your uncle'.

on social issues was not that of a typical Tory. As MP for Oldham, he took social issues into account. He was much influenced by Seebohm Rowntree's study of poverty in York in 1899.* 'I see little glory in an Empire which can rule the waves and is unable to flush its sewers.'[3] He had already become attracted to the idea of a coalition central party, a concept that always appealed to him and that was finally achieved in a way in the 1940 coalition and which he would have liked to have seen perpetuated. Even after 1950, he was still talking of a return to coalition.

*

It was not long before he realized he could no longer sit on the Tory benches. In 1903, Joe Chamberlain broke ranks with the Conservative leadership and began his great campaign for Tariff Reform: binding the Empire together and imposing tariffs on third parties. Churchill knew more about what Joe Chamberlain was doing than most people. In April 1902, Joe Chamberlain was invited to have dinner in the House of Commons with the young Churchill and the group of parliamentarians known as 'The Hughligans', a play on the name of Lord Hugh Cecil. The Hughligans were a bunch of young politicians who chose to make their names by being difficult, obstreperous critics of the Tory Party and, in particular, of the urbane Arthur Balfour. As Chamberlain arrived, he looked closely at his hosts and said, 'I am dining in very bad company.' The Hughligans had reason to be grateful to Chamberlain for condescending to join the precocious band of troublemakers for dinner. In 1902, at the age of 65, he was at the height of his powers, moving from the position

---

* In 1901, Churchill wrote a very detailed review of Rowntree's book. It does not appear to have been published until printed in Churchill, W.S., and Gilbert, M., *Winston S Churchill Companion Volume II Part 1.*

of a committed radical, even a republican, to promulgating the concept of the British Empire as a world-dominating influence on the world.

The Hughligans had, as usual, been critical of government policy, in this case an issue about a journalist who was being denied entry to Britain because of an article he had written in the course of the South African War. Churchill and his friends weighed in, telling Chamberlain how wrong the government had been. 'What's the use,' Chamberlain replied, 'of supporting your own government only when it is right?' But Churchill recorded that 'as he mellowed, he became most gay and captivating. I never remember having heard him talk better'. As he rose to leave, he paused at the door and, turning, said with much deliberation, 'You young gentlemen have entertained me royally, and in return I will give you a priceless secret. Tariffs! There are the politics of the future and of the near future. Study them closely and make yourselves masters of them, and you will not regret your hospitality to me.'[4]

Tariffs! By advocating the end of Free Trade and its replacement with preferential imperial trade, Joe Chamberlain was about to split the Tory Party and consign it to the opposition benches for twenty years, just as he had earlier done with the Liberal Party over the union with Ireland. The task to which he set himself was an immense one, and he would not see it completed in his lifetime. It was his younger son, Neville Chamberlain, who would end in 1932 what his father had begun in 1903. Between these two years, the debate over Free Trade divided political Britain to a greater extent than any other issue since the abolition of the Corn Laws in 1846. The passion it aroused was at least as great as that caused by the constitutional crisis of 1910–1911 or the conflict over the implementation of the Brexit referendum.

*

Nowadays, few people will remember what Free Trade was all about, let alone the peculiar veneration the doctrine was accorded. Since it is relevant to Churchill's career in the first decade of the twentieth century and again in the 1930s, especially as it bears on his attitude towards India, a brief discussion is needed.

At the most elementary level, Free Trade meant allowing goods, initially foodstuffs, to enter Britain free of import taxes. Until the abolition of the Corn Laws, which has just been mentioned, imported grain and other items were taxed on their arrival in British ports. There were a number of reasons for this, but the principal one was to protect the interests of the mainly Tory landed interests. The effect was, of course, to inflate the price of food at the cost of starvation, as in the famine years of 1845 and 1846.

So, at one level, the abolition of the Corn Laws was simply a practical measure to alleviate starvation by opening up the ports to the produce of the world. But Free Trade came to be seen as much more than that. It allowed the untaxed importation of more than just foodstuffs. All sorts of products were brought in to be worked on in the factories that the Industrial Revolution had built. Britain became very prosperous, and Free Trade seemed to be the root of that prosperity. There was virtually no challenge to the belief that Free Trade was the cause of and inexorably linked to Britain's commercial success.

For almost all of the second half of the nineteenth century, then, Free Trade was regarded as the basis of Britain's economic success and international pre-eminence. It was more than that. It was a revelation of enlightenment that stood in contrast to the blind simplicity of the past. It was a *good* phenomenon. It was inherently implicated in British liberalism, both with an upper- and lower-case initial letter.

World peace was also involved. Even before 1846, Richard Cobden had asked in a speech at Covent Garden,

Free Trade! What is it? Why, breaking down the barriers that separate nations; those barriers, behind which nestle the feelings of pride, revenge, hatred, and jealousy, which every now and then burst their bounds, and deluge whole countries with blood; those feelings which nourish the poison of war and conquest . . .[5]

Cobden and others saw Free Trade as 'a great pacificator'. Lloyd George said (six years before the outbreak of the First World War) that in the last fifty years there had not been a single war with any first-class power. 'Free Trade is slowly but surely clearing a path through the dense and dark thicket of armaments to the sunny land of brotherhood amongst nations.'[6] So Free Trade had a moral dimension as well as an economic one. The alternative to Free Trade was in no one's interests and certainly not in the interests of the advancement of a fair and just society. It thus became, truly, something close to an item of religious faith.

To challenge Free Trade was to advocate rejecting all that had been done by way of moral advancement and commitment to the amelioration of the human condition in the nineteenth century. Questioning it was like saying that there were two views on whether cruelty to children was necessarily a bad thing.

Why did Chamberlain challenge the doctrine? By the end of the nineteenth century, although Britain was far and away the richest country in the world, her lead was diminishing, and Germany and the United States threatened to catch up with her. One way of dealing with that—but a desirable aim in its own right in the eyes of some—was to transfer the fairly loose and variegated elements of the British Empire into a cohesive whole. There was no formal constitution of that empire. Some bits—trading stations and so forth—were held for utilitarian reasons; some were regarded as temporary possessions; some, chiefly in the English-speaking communities, were for keeping and perhaps ultimately some sort of independence. India may sometimes have been thought of as being in this last category—a famous speech by Lord Macaulay, which will be referred to later, appeared, perhaps, to countenance that—but only after centuries. The relationship between Britain and her possessions was different in each case and was very often vague and nebulous.

Joseph Chamberlain and the other 'new imperialists' such as Lord Milner, Leo Amery, of whom much more later, and Lord Curzon, wanted to formalize the relationship and to bind together the heterogeneous bits and pieces that appeared, in a famous phrase, to have been assembled in a fit of absence of mind,* into a strong, permanent polity that would be prosperous, powerful and a force for good in the world. To this end, it would seek to avoid penal taxes within itself; internal trade would be favoured, and discriminatory tariffs would be applied against the outside world.

If the fiscal climate within the Empire were to be benign under this new regime of Imperial Preference, why did Churchill oppose it, as he did now and was to do again when the consummation of the policy was achieved in 1932, and why did he see India in particular as a threat to the interests of his constituents? The answer to the more general question is partly that he was wedded to the Victorian orthodoxy in this, as in so many other ways, remaining all his life part of the Whiggish ascendancy. 'Free food' had been the battle cry of his heroes, and he clung to their credo. But there was also an Indian dimension. The abolition of Free Trade meant that tariffs could be adjusted to tax cotton imports from Britain, thereby stimulating the indigenous Indian cotton industry. This worried Churchill in 1904, as the representative of

---

* 'We seem, as it were, to have conquered and peopled half the world in a fit of absence of mind.' J.R. Seeley, Professor of Modern History, Cambridge, in his lectures, 'The Expansion of England', published in 1883.

a cotton constituency. It worried him again in the 1930s during the discussion of the 1935 Government of India Bill. Just as fiscal change in 1904 threatened the cotton industry, so did political change in 1935.

*

On 25 May 1903, Churchill wrote to Balfour pointing out that Joe Chamberlain had recently advocated preferential tariffs with the colonies and had revealed 'plain Protectionist intentions'. Churchill was concerned that Balfour and Bonar Law were said to have agreed with him in all this. He hoped that no irrevocable decision had been taken to alter 'the Free Trade character' of the country. If the party had made an irrevocable decision, he would, he said, have to 'reconsider my position in politics'.[7] Balfour's reply was evasive: 'The matter is one of difficulty, and requires the most wary walking.'*

Chamberlain was aware of Churchill's reservations. As early as August 1903, he wrote saying that he had never thought that Churchill was what was called a 'loyal supporter'. He expected he would drift to 'the other side' before long.[8]

On 19 February 1904, at the inaugural meeting of the Free Trade League, Churchill spoke about the effects of protectionism on shipping. 'Why,' he asked, 'should so many ships come to British Ports? . . . Other harbours are just as wide and deep as ours; other climates are quite as genial—other skies are just as blue. Why should the world's shipping labour in the chops of the Bristol Channel, or crowd up the dreary reaches of the Mersey?

---

* Balfour sought to preserve party unity by going to great lengths to avoid committing himself to Tariff Reform. Several years later, he asked his niece, Baffy Dugdale, if he had been for or against it. 'That, Uncle Arthur,' she replied, 'is what we all wanted to know.'

It is because our harbours are more nearly as nature made them; because the perverted ingenuity of man has not been occupied in obstructing them with fiscal stake nets and tariff mudbars. That is why they come.'[9]

The Conservative Party was now split between Chamberlain's supporters and a group of about sixty 'Free Fooders'. While Arthur Balfour and the party leadership looked on in helpless inaction, Churchill, more decisive than the other Free Fooders, took a momentous step. On 31 May 1904, he crossed the floor and took his seat beside David Lloyd George on the Liberal benches.

6

The Young Radical

Churchill rationalized what the Tories regarded as treachery by claiming that they had changed their position—as indeed they had—and arguing that his position was consistent with the views of his father, whose life he was then engaged in writing. His move was not an impulsive one. He had already been in touch with the North West Manchester Liberal Association and agreed to stand as their candidate at the upcoming General Election on a Free Trade ticket.

In his new campaign, he emerged increasingly as perhaps the most prominent spokesman for Free Trade. He attacked the idea that Colonial Preferences could distinguish between food and other products. He attacked Chamberlain, too, because Chamberlain had been at the Colonial Office and not the India Office when he drew up his scheme, and he had thereby ignored India, 'that most truly bright and precious gem of the Crown'. These were his father's words, and it was significant that he used them.

The argument against protectionism was based on what Churchill regarded as a great principle: 'the principle that this country should be free to purchase its supplies of food wherever it chooses and whenever it chooses in the open markets of the world'.[1] But even more than food, cotton was what mattered in Manchester and Lancashire, and the Lancashire connection weighed heavily and was critical for Churchill now. Indeed, right through the 1930s, India was at the heart of the Lancashire programme. This is an important element in Churchill's attitude towards the subcontinent. Churchill claimed that within thirty miles of the Free Trade Hall in Manchester, more human beings were concentrated than on any other part of the globe, that they were dependent on the condition of a crop at one end of the world, cotton, and the state of a market at the other, and that on this artificial basis, 'through the inestimable advantages of enterprise they had been able to create industrial success which, it is no exaggeration to say, is the economic marvel of the world'.

This was the case for opposing Joe Chamberlain, but long after the Free Trade debate had been forgotten, it remained the case for cotton—and the case for the control of India.

When he changed parties and stood for North–West Manchester as a Liberal at the 1906 General Election, the political boundaries were pretty porous. He was standing as a Liberal in a traditionally Tory constituency, but as his son, the junior Randolph Churchill, put it,

[A]lthough Manchester had for nearly fifty years been a Tory stronghold, it was, after all, the city of Cobden and Bright [John Bright was for ten years its MP. Cobden and Bright were the great advocates of Free Trade] and the Free Trade Hall stood—still stands for that matter—as a witness and reminder in the North–West division of Manchester to the enthusiasm that their Anti-Corn Law League, anti-tariff policies aroused there.[2]

Churchill received a great deal of traditional Tory support. It should particularly be noted that the Manchester Guardian Society for the Protection of Trade and the British Cotton Growing Association endorsed his candidacy: the cotton industry of Lancashire had no wish to see India stretching its muscles and challenging England's textile monopoly. The link between Churchill and the Lancashire cotton bosses did not break when he moved to another constituency. In 1908, when Churchill was a member for Dundee and President of the Board of Trade, the cotton industry was in economic difficulties, and there was a trade dispute between the master cotton spinners and the unions. The employers ordered a lockout, and 1,20,000 men were affected in the Bolton and Oldham parts of Lancashire. Thousands of weavers were also out of work as a result of the lack of yarn. In November, the employers agreed to postpone the reduction of wages, which had been the root of the problem until March, and Churchill took it upon himself to try to resolve the problem. Even though he was on his honeymoon, he ordered his officials at the Board of Trade to send him reports on the negotiations, and he made proposals to both sides, proposing the use of a sliding scale.

*

But it would be wrong—and unfair to a man who defies simple categorization—to imagine that because he supported Manchester's interests at India's expense, he was without a liberal conscience.

There had been a series of pogroms in Czarist Russia over the last twenty-five years, which resulted in large numbers of Jewish emigrants arriving in Britain, many of them without skills. There had been an extreme reaction to this. In March 1902, a Royal Commission on alien immigration was set up as a result of panic about non-existent invading swarms. In 1904, the Government introduced an Aliens Bill.

Churchill was sceptical. Lord Randolph Churchill had been friendly with many Jews. There was a substantial Jewish element in North–East Manchester, and many of Winston's prominent supporters were Jews. He always had a disproportionately high number of Jews amongst his friends in the constituency—and elsewhere—to the extent that his son Randolph later said that 'during this period he was sometimes invited into Gentile society'.

He was an early supporter of Zionism. Now, studying the Aliens Bill, he wrote to one of his friends, Nathan Laski, pointing out that the reality was that all aliens in Great Britain amounted only to a one-hundred-and-fortieth part of the population and that they were increasing at a rate of only 7000 a year. According to the Aliens Commission itself, Germany had proportionately twice as many and France four times as many foreigners as Britain.[3] He went on to conclude that it was 'the simple immigrant, the political refugee, the helpless and the poor' who would be 'harassed and hustled at the pleasure of petty officials without the smallest right of appeal to the broad justice of the English courts'. The Bill was simply an attempt to gratify a small but noisy section among the Government's own supporters. The letter was published in the *Manchester Guardian*. The Bill was sent to the Grand Committee.* Churchill was on the Standing Committee on Law and took a significant part in opposing the Bill. On one occasion, he caused considerable irritation by speaking seven times on one amendment alone. In the face of all this, the Conservative Government abandoned the Bill. Again, Churchill was on the side of progress.

---

* Churchill pointed out that in the year before the Deceased Wife's Sister Bill had not been sent to Committee because it was regarded as too controversial.

He gained a great deal of kudos from the Jewish community for his opposition to the Aliens Bill. His liberal credentials, it is true, suffered a little in 1906 when he acquiesced in the passage by the Liberal administration, of which he would become a member, of a new, albeit less extreme, Aliens Bill. But largely as a result of his influence, that act proved to be ineffective—so much so that by 1911, he had to address the issue again, for which he now had personal responsibility as Home Secretary.* The King had intervened, complaining that London was infested with men and women whose presence would not be tolerated in any other country. The 1906 Act was not, in fact, revised until 1915. The delay was more a matter of pressure on the parliamentary timetable than anything to do with Churchill, but the revisions he had in mind had been very limited.

*

---

* The revival of interest in aliens was partly the result of the Sidney Street Siege or 'Battle of Stepney', the culmination of a strange conspiracy that might have been imagined by Joseph Conrad, involving 'Peter the Painter', and Latvian revolutionaries who frequented the Anarchists Club. The siege was unusual in that the police required military assistance, was filmed by the newfangled Pathé News and was attended by Churchill in his role as Home Secretary. It would have been highly irregular if he had been intervening in operational police matters, but he probably wasn't. The footage suggests he was just enjoying the excitement. His presence was bizarre, all the same. Arthur Balfour said in the House that it appeared that Churchill and a photographer were risking valuable lives. 'I understand what the photographer was doing, but what was the right hon. Gentleman doing? That I neither understood at the time, nor do I understand now.' The siege cost the lives of a policeman, a fireman and one of the revolutionaries.

These responsibilities were still in the future. In December 1905, Sir Henry Campbell–Bannerman became Prime Minister. Churchill now took his first step up the ministerial ladder, being appointed Under-Secretary at the Colonial Office. Shortly afterwards, at the General Election, he was elected as the MP for North West Manchester, part of the great Liberal landslide. As the Colonial Secretary, Lord Elgin, was in the House of Lords, Churchill had a prominent role in handling colonial matters in the Commons. India was the responsibility not of the Colonial Office but of the India Office, but for those colonies for which Churchill was responsible, he adopted a sensitive and sympathetic approach. He was, of course, paternalistic. He did not challenge the idea that British rule was a good thing for the subject peoples, but he was concerned for the material well-being of these peoples and took a close interest in their condition.

In 1908, Asquith succeeded Campbell–Bannerman as Prime Minister. He brought Churchill into the Cabinet as President of the Board of Trade. He was thirty-three and the youngest cabinet minister since 1866. At that time, a Member of Parliament accepting 'an office of profit under the Crown' was obliged to resign his seat and stand again. He lost the consequent by-election at North West Manchester but was asked to stand for the safe seat of Dundee.

The main issue at both the Manchester and Dundee by-elections was, again, Free Trade. Though Churchill lost in Manchester, not everyone was happy to see him go. The *Manchester Guardian* reported that Lancashire businessmen ignored party lines and sent compliments to the new President of the Board of Trade. The British Cotton Growing Association applauded what Churchill had done at the Colonial Office by improving access to cotton growing parts of Nigeria. He received a telegram from the Manchester Stock Exchange: 'What's the use of a WC without a seat?'

When he went from Manchester to Dundee, which he represented from 1908 until 1922, he moved geographically but remained very much within the Free Trade community, a trading community that depended for its existence on Indian textiles. The prosperity of Dundee was based on jute.* The Indian connection persisted. Jute is primarily produced in Bengal, and its versatility was recognized from the seventeenth century onwards when the British started to trade in the commodity. Dundee, in particular, grew rich on it. The jute barons processed jute and sold it over the world. As in the case of cotton, there was always a risk of tension between the large manufacturers in Britain and the much smaller producers in India itself. From the early days of the East India Company, measures—sometimes involving the destruction of the mills—were taken to inhibit the Indian operations. All the same, towards the end of the nineteenth century, the Indian competition increasingly threatened the British end of the trade.

At the beginning of the twentieth century, about 60 per cent of India's imports came from Britain, with a concentration on textiles, machinery and iron and steel products. This tame export market was a critical element in the British economy. If it had not been for the surplus in the UK–India trade, there would have been a damaging deficit in trade with the rest of the world.

In Dundee, as well, Churchill continued to be made aware of the problems of the cotton industry. Dundee, only to a slightly lesser extent than Kirkcaldy, thirty miles to the south, had an important linoleum industry, and linoleum is made by spreading an oily skin onto a backing of cotton sheeting. On the shores of the Tay and Forth estuaries, enormous quantities

---

* Along with two other 'J's. The others are jam and journalism.

of linoleum were created, to cover domestic and public flooring and even the decking of ships—all of it resting on the basis of Indian cotton.

So for twenty-one years, Churchill was dependent on political support for the cotton interest, and the British cotton interest was uncomfortably aware that its prosperity rested on resisting Indian economic autonomy. Independence was even more unthinkable. His connection with the cotton mafia did not end when he stopped representing a cotton seat; as will be seen, he was briefed by the cotton trade when he was attempting to wreck the Government of India Bill in the 1930s.

7

'Prizes of the Game'

For the moment, we depart from a close consideration of Churchill's career, leaving him on his honeymoon (a few days at Blenheim, followed by visits to Lake Maggiore and Venice), enjoying the company of Clementine, and weighing the respective appeal of the cotton masters and their employees with the help of his sliding scale.

In the years between 1908 and the late 1920s, India did not greatly occupy his mind. That's not to say that his mind wasn't occupied. At the Board of Trade, he worked closely with the Chancellor of the Exchequer, Lloyd George. It was a fruitful partnership in which he espoused truly radical policies. He and Lloyd George effectively created and then imposed on the government a social policy of their own, a policy that took Britain down a route of social reform that would lead to the creation of the Welfare State after the Second World War. Indeed, Churchill recruited the young William Beveridge, who would later be the architect of that Welfare State, to facilitate a programme of unemployment insurance and welfare reforms. The King complained to Asquith about the virulence of Churchill's attacks on the aristocracy as he toured the country, arguing for Lloyd George's 'People's Budget' and against the House of Lords, which opposed it. Again, note that Churchill remained progressive, liberal and radical.

The policy that Lloyd George and Churchill promoted was so coherent and pervasive that it impinged even on the evolution of foreign policy. They wanted money spent on domestic issues rather than armaments, and thus argued against the inevitability of war with Germany and the emphasis on expensive naval preparations that this inevitability implied.

In 1910, Churchill was promoted to the Home Office and had the opportunity to help the police stake out the anarchists in Sidney Street.* In his new role, he was less seized by the need for naval economy, and at the time of the Agadir Crisis with Germany in the summer of 1911, he composed an important paper for the Cabinet arguing for a policy of imperial defence: His move to First Lord of the Admiralty in October 1911 was a logical development.

The War supervened, and Churchill took a prominent part in the direction of the War from his position at the Admiralty. His duties there led to his involvement in the Gallipoli campaign, a naval attempt to force the strait of the Dardanelles, which failed, followed by military landings on Turkey's Gallipoli peninsula, which also failed. The campaign was a disaster, but not primarily because of Churchill. He knew that the Gallipoli campaign could not be won by a naval force alone, but the Secretary of State for War, Kitchener, was not prepared to supply the necessary troops, telling Churchill to press on with the naval exercise. The brilliant but erratic First Sea Lord, Fisher, cracked, resigned and disappeared. The military force that was landed at the Gallipoli Peninsula, under Churchill's old friend, Sir Ian Hamilton, was

---

* See footnote, p. 54.

unable to advance from a vulnerable stretch of coastline and ultimately withdrew.

After much delay, the Commission of Inquiry, which reported on the debacle substantially exonerated Churchill. His was not the largest responsibility. Kitchener and Fisher were much more to blame. All the same, he had been carried away and overexcited, and in the popular mind, he was very much identified with the disastrous enterprise. He was already vulnerable when Asquith was obliged to go into coalition with the Conservatives. Churchill was hated by the Tories. Their contempt for his treacherous desertion was compounded by his disloyalty towards his class when he had toured the country, wrapped in the Red Flag, supporting Lloyd George's attack on the dukes. Now they demanded his scalp.

To his enormous dismay, he was thrown out of the Admiralty, the Cabinet and the War Council. He was allowed the honorific post of Chancellor of the Duchy of Lancaster, which offered him no consolation. He descended into a gloom from which Clemmie thought he would die and through which he lived thanks to the support of his family and his discovery of a love for painting. He sought active service and commanded the sixth battalion of the Royal Scots Fusiliers on the Western Front.

When Lloyd George replaced Asquith in December 1916, he worked hard to persuade the Conservative leader, Bonar Law, to agree that Churchill should return to government—outside the war cabinet—as Minister for Munitions in July 1917. He was still hated by the Conservatives, and they insisted that he would not be allowed any role in the conduct of the war. The fact that he was not within the Cabinet seems to have satisfied Bonar Law; nonetheless, his appointment was formally deplored by 100 Conservative Members of Parliament (MPs) and the Conservative press.

*

After the December 1918 General Election, Churchill's rehabilitation continued. He returned to the Cabinet as Secretary of State for War and Air, where, surprisingly, in view of his later criticism of Baldwin for failing to spend money on the armed forces, he enthusiastically sought to reduce defence expenditure. In February 1921, he was appointed Colonial Secretary.

Lloyd George had proposed Winston's transfer from the War Office to the Colonial Office on New Year's Day. The move was accepted—and possibly offered—because of tensions that had arisen between Churchill and the Prime Minister, particularly over Russia. Churchill had been obsessed with destroying Bolshevism before it could become properly established. In addition, in his desire to reduce defence spending, Churchill had already taken some interest in the Middle East, which was part of the Colonial Secretary's area of responsibility.

His role at the Colonial Office will be dealt with shortly. First, we must examine his reaction at the War Office to a pivotal event in the history of British India.

8

Jallianwala Bagh

Of all the atrocities that occurred in India during Churchill's political lifetime, there is at least one for which he bears no responsibility, though as Secretary of State for War he had to react to it: the Jallianwala Bagh Massacre.

At 6.30 p.m. on 13 April 1919, General Reginald Dyer*, together with ninety soldiers, fifty of them armed, and two armoured cars equipped with machine-guns, arrived at Jallianwala Bagh, an open area near the centre of Amritsar. The Bagh, or field, is about seven acres in area and surrounded by high walls. There were five narrow entrances, some locked, and one larger one, all effectively sealed by the troops and the armoured vehicles. The Bagh was filled with 10,000 to 20,000 people.

Without directing these people to disperse and without firing any shots over their heads, Dyer ordered his troops to fire into the densest part of the crowd. Firing continued for six minutes, by which time about 1650 rounds had been discharged. The crowd was so dense that several people could be hit by a single

---

* Technically a temporary brigadier general.

bullet. Apart from the shooting, many were killed in the stampede to escape or by throwing themselves into a narrow well. Three hundred and seventy-nine people were killed, and another 1500 wounded. Three and a half hours later, the curfew came into force. No one was allowed access to Jallianwala Bagh, and the dead and wounded were left, the latter watching the stray dogs gnaw at the remains of the former.

*

Few people in India will need to be told what the Jallianwala Bagh Massacre was, but few people in Britain will have heard of it. If they have, they will know it as the Amritsar Massacre. Amritsar is the city in Punjab that contains the specially sacred Sikh shrine, the Golden Temple. On 13 April 1919, there were many pilgrims in Jallianwala Bagh—nowadays misguidedly populated with heritage items that threaten to destroy its desolate sadness. There may also have been some protesters complaining about the two arrests, others who had been worshipping at the Golden Temple, others still who had come to Amritsar for the annual horse and cattle sale. On one account, a poem in praise of peace was being recited when Dyer and his men arrived.

The background to the massacre lies in British fears that an onslaught on India was likely from the Afghan border, an irruption in the tradition of the Great Game, and the interaction between Russia and the British Empire, which had lain behind so much of the disorder on the North–West Frontier in the nineteenth century. It was a given for Britain in Tsarist times that Russia sought to foment dissent in the area and thus destabilise and ultimately displace British rule in India. There was some basis for these fears, although they risked becoming crystallized in folklore. Similarly, now, after the Russian Revolution, there was a fear, maybe exaggerated, of Russia's desire to export Bolshevism. That was, of course, the theory and idea of Marxism; how far it was physically feasible in 1920, when the continued survival of the revolution even in Russia itself was in question, must be in doubt.

Dyer's superior officer was a man with a confusingly similar name. The Lieutenant Governor of the Punjab was Sir Michael O'Dwyer. He was able, by his lights, but tough. He was ready to use aircraft against rioters. When he had been appointed, he had been told by the viceroy that the Punjab was the most combustible part of India. It was not only vulnerable to attack from the North–West Frontier; it also contained a mix of communities. Amritsar was home to Hindus, Muslims and Sikhs.

The two men, Dyer and O'Dwyer, acted on each other. General Reginald Dyer was a substantive Colonel and a man of action. Twenty years earlier, at staff college, he had been described as 'happiest when crawling over a Burmese stockade with a revolver in his mouth'. His excitable personality was exacerbated in April 1919. Physically, he was suffering from the effects of a painful illness. He was also reacting badly to separation from his wife. Dyer thought that the *hartal* announced by Gandhi on 6 April 1919 was no more than a cover for a mass rising. Hartal was in reality a non-violent traditional expression of mourning or regret, but it was an elusive concept that could be interpreted in different ways. Gandhi's announcement led to demonstrations and processions, as well as the closing of shops and public transport.

O'Dwyer, too, was in a highly nervous state. He thought that only extreme action could avert a second Mutiny, as the first War of Independence was inevitably referred to by the British at that time. The British still thought a lot about the Mutiny. It was only a little over half a century ago and it was relayed to young officers as a horror story that informed their thinking as they tried to control a vastly superior number of native troops. O'Dwyer was convinced that the admittedly serious disorders in the Punjab needed to be checked urgently if a second mutiny were not to break out. His telegrams to the viceroy (some sent *en clair* and intercepted by Soviet Intelligence) 'made the flesh creep and strongly suggested that he was in the grip of hysteria'.[1] His response involved martial law, aerial attacks and mass floggings.

Tension was indeed high throughout India, and not only in the Punjab. India had strongly supported Britain in the First World War. It was believed that the result of this was, as Madan Mohan Malaviya said, that the war had 'put the clock . . . fifty years forward'. It was assumed that there would be extensive reforms after the war to allow Indians to take their legitimate part in the administration of their own country. Instead, in March 1919, the Defence of India Regulations Act, passed during the war as an emergency measure, was extended indefinitely under the Anarchical and Revolutionary Crimes Act. This legislation is known as the Rowlatt Act because it was based on the recommendations of a judge, Sir Sidney Rowlatt, who advised that activists should be deported or imprisoned without trial for up to two years. The Black Act, as Gandhi called it, contained wide-ranging powers: imprisonment without trial, control of the press and freedom for the authorities to regard anything they didn't like as terrorism or revolution. Possession of seditious newspapers would be sufficient evidence of guilt. Even moderate Indian politicians felt bitterly let down by this reaction to their wartime loyalty. The most violent protests against the act took place in the Punjab.

There was particular tension in the streets of Amritsar. Five Englishmen had already been killed, and there had been an assault on an English woman missionary on her bicycle. In the aftermath, Indians were forced to crawl on their stomachs down the road on which she had been attacked, saluting if they saw a white face.

This was the background as people gathered in Jallianwala Bagh on the morning of 13 April. Emotions were strong, but there was no definite threat to public order. Then the men and the armoured cars arrived. Soldiers deployed—Gurkhas, Sikhs and men of Sind—knelt, took aim and, on Dyer's command, shot into the crowd at point-blank range.

*

These facts are pretty well agreed upon, although there is dispute over the precise number of the victims. But beyond these facts, there was a wide divergence over exactly what had happened and why. Speculation and research continue. There was much of it in 2019, the centenary of the massacre. Some believe that Dyer was deliberately injected into Amritsar in order to do exactly what he did. Others, and I am one of them, tend to the cock-up rather than conspiracy school. That debate will continue. What I want to do here is look at the reaction to the terrible events at Jallianwala Bagh and assess Churchill's personal reaction.

*

For what he did at Amritsar, Dyer has rightly been execrated by history. But at the time, he wasn't universally condemned. The split of opinion between India and Britain was remarkable—much more marked than might have been expected. Nehru thought that what had happened was 'absolutely immoral, indecent [and] to use public school language, it was the height of bad form'.[2] Until Amritsar, there had been a lingering hope that, at the end of the day, Britain would do the decent thing. Now the Raj seemed incapable of decency. India felt misled and betrayed, and from now on, the movement for independence was seen as a necessarily adversarial clash rather than a process characterized by good faith and collaboration.

In the debate in the Commons that would review the massacre, the Labour politician, J.C. Wedgwood, said that the massacre had 'destroyed our reputation throughout the world . . . and damns

us for all time'. That sentence sums up the effect of Jallianwala
Bagh. In the minds of the Indians, or at least of the politically
interested classes of Indians, it drew a line under the idea that
Britain's rule was essentially reasonable. Having ordered his men
to fire, and after watching the shooting, which included targeting
anyone who tried to climb the walls or run to the exit, Dyer asked
one of his officers, 'Do you think they've had enough?' Without
waiting for a response, he said, 'No, we'll give them four rounds
more.' He was dealing a fatal blow not just to the helpless victims,
but to Britain's moral authority.

In Britain, the reaction to Jallianwala Bagh was not clear-cut.
So far as the formal process is concerned, a Scottish judge, Lord
Hunter, was sent out to India to investigate the massacre. After
extremely lengthy proceedings, Dyer was recalled to England and
censured because he had not given a warning to the demonstrators
and told them that they must disperse, nor had he offered medical
aid. He was dismissed from the service and remained on half pay
and his army pension. He suffered a stroke. He told his family he
didn't want to get better. 'I only want to die and to know from my
Maker whether I did right or wrong.'

Dyer died in 1927. O'Dwyer lived until March 1940.
Horrified by what had happened at Jallianwala Bagh, a young
Sikh, Udham Singh, determined to avenge the massacre. After
a long and circuitous odyssey that lasted more than twenty years
and took him to twenty countries and four continents, he came
face to face with O'Dwyer when the latter concluded speaking at
a meeting of the East India Association at Caxton Hall in March
1940. He shot O'Dwyer in the heart, killing him instantly, and
injured three others, including the Marquess of Zetland, the
Secretary of State for India. He was hanged at Pentonville Prison.
In so far as Brits remember him at all, which is remarkably little, he
is regarded as an assassin who may well have chosen his victim in
mistake for Dyer (there are spelling inconsistencies in his diaries).

In India, where his remains now lie, Udham Singh is regarded as a hero. His death is marked annually in Punjab, and there is a ten-foot-high statue of him just outside the Bagh.

*

Dyer's sacking was the formal outcome. It was accompanied by the response of parliament and the country at large. The first thing to say is that the general public in Britain was much less interested in the episode than Indian opinion had been. That was bound to be the case: India was a long way off, and crass though it may seem to say so, 397 deaths were a small number compared to British casualties a year earlier in just the last four months of the Great War: 3,14,000 casualties, or 1,00,000 deaths, on the Western Front alone. The Jallianwalla Bagh Massacre coincided with the Spanish flu, which killed 2,28,000 in Britain and around one million in the Punjab. None of that makes what Dyer did the least bit more acceptable, and his was a man-made phenomenon, but human perception is partial and fallible.

So in Britain, Dyer had supporters among the readers of the *Morning Post* and the right-wing members of the Conservative Party. There were those who claimed that he had 'saved the empire'. The *Morning Post* raised the sum of £26,000—perhaps a million pounds today—for Dyer and presented him with a Sword of Honour. Dyer said that he did what he did to achieve moral superiority over a disaffected populace, and many British thought he had done the right thing. Not only the British in England: Maud Diver, for instance, an Englishwoman who lived in India, now almost forgotten but in the first half of the twentieth century a bestselling author and a favourite of the royal family:

> At Amritsar strong action had already been taken . . . The
> sobering effect of it spread in widening circles . . . No more

trouble here or at Amritsar . . . [I]n no time the poor deluded
beggars in the city were shouting—'Martial law *ki jai*!' [Long
live Martial law!] as fervently as they ever shouted for Gandhi
& Co.[3]

O'Dwyer, too, all these years until he was shot at Caxton Hall,
continued to support Dyer and argued against any more fooling
around with self-government. 'The fact is, as everyone, British or
Indian, who understands the East will, if honest, admit, that 99
per cent of the people do not care a brass farthing for the "forms of
government" about which Congress lawyers are always arguing.'[4]

As in the backwoods, so, tautologically, in the House of
Lords. A majority of peers approved Dyer's actions and passed a
motion supporting him. In the Commons the tone of the debate
was slightly more measured. Here, Churchill was at the centre of
events, and in this Indian matter, he performed well. It will be
remembered that the Indian Army was the responsibility of the
Indian Government and not the Government in London, but Dyer
was a serving British officer, and it fell to Churchill, as Secretary
of State for War, to review the report on his behaviour. He had
already declared that the massacre had been a monstrous event
and rejected the suggestion by Dyer's supporters that he had saved
the Empire. He readily concluded that Dyer was a dangerous man
who could not be left in charge. The Cabinet agreed, and their
decision that Dyer should be summarily dismissed was conveyed
by Churchill to the Army Council.

Churchill did not have an easy time when the matter came
to be debated. His views were not those of the whole House.
Sir William Joynson–Hicks, for instance, who would become
an outstandingly blinkered and reactionary Home Secretary,
'Jix', was warmly received when he said that Dyer had been
the country's saviour. In the course of a seven-hour debate on
8 July 1919, Dyer was also vigorously defended by Sir Edward

Carson. India was 'seething with rebellion and anarchy', there was an underground conspiracy to destroy the Raj and drive India out of Egypt.[5]

At the end of the day, the Commons supported the Government and their handling of the matter by 247 votes to thirty-seven. That was a remarkable outcome. Such a ringing endorsement of the disciplinary measures that had been imposed on Dyer, and the fact that the motion was so carried by an overwhelmingly reactionary House, was almost entirely Churchill's achievement. This was Churchill in a humane and liberal posture, and what he did in a speech that was one of his greatest peacetime discourses falls into contrast with his later hostility to India. That is the paradox to which this narrative continually returns.

*

The starting point in the debate was that the Conservative majority was bitterly resentful. Dyer, as they saw it, was being condemned for defending the Raj. There was an even more unpleasant motive behind the Conservative opposition to Hunter's inquiry: that it had been set up by a Secretary of State for India who was a Jew, Edwin Montagu. Latent anti-Semitism was in the air.[6] Montagu spoke first in the debate and had a very rough time of it. He criticized Dyer's statement to the Hunter Commission, in which he said that he had intended to 'teach a moral lesson to the Punjab'. The Conservatives thought that he was quite right to do so. Carson followed with his powerful defence of Dyer, whom he described as 'a gallant officer of thirty-four years' service'. He was interrupted by Josiah Wedgwood: 'Five hundred people were shot.' Carson was undeterred: Dyer was 'without a blemish upon his record'. The tone of the debate was becoming very violent. Members later described it as a return to the vehemence of pre-war days.

Churchill's speech was very different. It was described as a personal triumph. *The Times* said that it had been 'amazingly skilful' and had 'turned the House . . . completely round . . . It was not only a brilliant speech, but one that persuaded and made the result certain'. What Churchill did was start with a moderate, detailed consideration of correct military procedure, stressing that Dyer was entitled to a fair hearing. Having established this more temperate atmosphere, he proceeded forensically to elaborate the case against Dyer, showing that the unanimous decision of the Army Council had been sound and based on the firmest of evidence.

Churchill's views were always tempered by responsibility. When he was not in a position of authority, he could say the most outrageous, foolish and offensive things, but when he was in a position of power, a judgement that could be spectacularly wayward was held in check. Because he said many appalling things about India and Indians when he was not in a position of authority, it is worth looking carefully at his words on this occasion when he contemplated the shootings from a standpoint of legal responsibility:

> However we may dwell upon the difficulties of General Dyer
> during the Amritsar riots, upon the anxious and critical situation
> in the Punjab, upon the danger to Europeans throughout
> that province, upon the long delays which have taken place in
> reaching a decision about this officer . . . one tremendous fact
> stands out—I mean the slaughter of nearly 400 persons and
> the wounding of probably three or four times as many, at the
> Jallianwala Bagh on 13 April.
>
> That is an episode which appears to me to be without
> precedent or parallel in the modern history of the British
> Empire. It is an event of an entirely different order from any
> of those tragical occurrences which take place when troops

are brought into collision with the civil population. It is an extraordinary event, a monstrous event, an event which stands in singular and sinister isolation.[7]

He went on to speak about other cases of officers firing on Indian crowds in Punjab in April 1919. He sought to draw out the circumstances in which this could be justified. Whether the crowd was armed was important. No more force should be used than is necessary to secure compliance with the law. Officers should confine themselves 'to a limited and definite objective'. He did not suggest that it was easy to make a quick decision in difficult circumstances. But he said that in general, officers could arrive at the right decision in much more trying circumstances than Dyer had faced. Above all, he recognized, as the Conservative Party and the readers of the *Morning Post* did not, that Dyer's behaviour had intruded into a special and unspeakable dimension:

> There is surely one general prohibition which we can make. I mean a prohibition against what is called 'frightfulness'. What I mean by frightfulness is the inflicting of great slaughter or massacre upon a particular crowd of people, with the intention of terrorizing not merely the rest of the crowd, but the whole district or the whole country.[8]

This was the point, which Dyer's supporters failed to acknowledge but which Dyer himself had admitted: he was attempting to break the morale of a people. Churchill did not mince his words:

> Let me marshal the facts. The crowd was unarmed, except with bludgeons. It was not attacking anybody or anything. It was holding a seditious meeting. When fire had been opened upon it to disperse it, it tried to run away.

Pinned up in a narrow place considerably smaller than Trafalgar Square, with hardly any exits and packed together so that one bullet would drive through three or four bodies, the people ran madly this way and the other.[9]

Churchill's speech was masterly and recognized as such.* He had managed to say nothing to support the extremists on the right, but without saying anything to which they could strenuously object. Like the best examples of advocacy, his speech was the result of a careful analysis of the psychology of his opponents.

Part of his tactics had been to identify what had happened at Jallianwala Bagh as outrageous but anomalous, a 'monstrous event standing out in sinister isolation'. That argument obviously worked less well in India, where the *Lahore Tribune* said that 'frightfulness was more the rule than the exception', than in London. But few would have spoken as he did. There was a great deal of feeling in British India and at home that O'Dwyer and Dyer had been absolutely right to take the action they did and that by doing so they had averted a mass rising, which would have struck at the whole basis of British control of India. Ahead of the events at Amritsar, Churchill had been affected by concern about the vulnerable state of the Raj. As Secretary of State for War, he approved bringing in reinforcements from East and Central Africa to support the Indian Army. He did not allow these concerns to influence the stand he took over Dyer. In the course of Churchill's speech, he established his own credentials as liberal and very different from Dyer's.

---

* Though one of those present, Colin Coote, said that Churchill had saved the day by 'boring the House into tranquillity with an endless discourse on military law'. But it was a sardonic comment, intended to amuse. [Colin Coote, *A Companion of Honour: The Story of Walter Elliot in Scotland and in Westminster*. London, Collins, 1965.]

We shall read of Churchill saying some terrible things. We shall see him opposing the India Bill in 1935 and thwarting its attempt to provide a route to self-government. We shall see his frustrating moves towards independence during the second war. But in all fairness, we must take aboard and give him credit for his liberal views and his leadership in the Amritsar debate.

9

Creating Kingdoms at the Stroke of a Pen

In February 1921, Churchill was appointed Colonial Secretary. Lloyd George had proposed the transfer from the War Office to the Colonial Office on New Year's Day. The move was accepted—and possibly offered—because of tensions that had arisen between Churchill and the Prime Minister.

*

Coming to the Colonial Office meant a return to a matter that had occupied him just before the First World War. In the spring of 1914, Britain had been convulsed by the Ulster Crisis. The extent of this crisis, which created a massive fissure in British politics, and the fact of just how close Britain came to civil war and the army to mutiny are overlooked today simply because of the even graver national crisis represented by the outbreak of the war itself in August 1914. Churchill's position is of interest because it bears on his views about imperial cohesion and the rights of minorities.

Churchill's attitude towards Ireland was even more inconsistent than on other matters. His father had been a strong supporter of Ulster's resistance to Home Rule: 'Ulster will fight and Ulster will be right.' But Winston's response to Ulster's intransigence veered all over the place. At times, ahead of the First World War, he said that he would resign at the first shot if Ulster were coerced in any way. At other times, he said that there were worse things than bloodshed. As always, however, responsibility nudged him to an extent towards sounder judgement, and as colonial secretary in 1921, he came to support the south, even as the Troubles unrolled and the Auxiliaries and the Black and Tans exchanged atrocities with the IRA.* He took part in secret discussions in which he tried to promote a peaceful settlement, and he declared that he would resign from the Cabinet if force were employed.

He signed the treaty that established the Free State along with Michael Collins, with whom he had become friendly. Churchill said, 'I may be signing my political death warrant.' Collins said, 'I may be signing my actual death warrant.' He was right; months later, he was ambushed in County Cork and shot in the head.

At the cost of jumping ahead for a few lines, contrast his policy on Ireland with his policy on India. Churchill told a meeting of ministers in February 1922 that there was an idea that was prevalent that the British Raj was doomed and that India would gradually be handed over to the Indians. He said that he was strongly opposed to this idea and that, on the contrary, he believed that our position on India should be strengthened. He had no sympathy with what he regarded as a temporary and aberrant view on 'the expediency of granting democratic institutions to backward nations which had no capacity for self-government'.[1] In September of the same

---

* Now, 'the Troubles' is used to refer exclusively to the problems of the 1970s and later. But the phrase was first used to describe what the IRA called the 'War of Independence' in the 1920s.

year, he wrote to his first love and lifelong dear friend whom he'd met in India, Pamela Plowden, now Lady Lytton and wife of the Governor of Bengal, making a distinction between Ireland, which he could see becoming independent, and India. 'I do not needless to say apply the reasoning [about Ireland] to the East . . . [O]ur true duty in India lies to those three hundred millions whose lives and means of existence would be squandered if entrusted to the chatterboxes who are supposed to speak for India today.'[2]

*

His other very significant responsibility at the Colonial Office was the Middle East. As a result of the distribution of spoils after the Great War, Britain found herself in control of huge tracts of the former Ottoman Empire—Palestine and Mesopotamia. Ostensibly, these undefined and ungoverned areas, 'the Mandates', were held in trust until they were ready for self-determined independence. Their value in terms of oil, at least in the case of Mesopotamia, was not yet fully recognized, and their inhabitants, who had initially welcomed liberation from Turkish rule, soon turned on the liberators. This created the risk of the Muslim–British conflict already referred to, with its consequent danger for India.

Churchill created and presided over a new Middle East Department within the Colonial Office. Here, he had enormous responsibilities. The Mandates extended the size of the British Empire by 9 per cent. In reality, Britain could do pretty much what she wanted with them. France received mandates over Syria and Lebanon and made no pretence of doing anything other than incorporating them into the French Empire as tightly and permanently as any other parts of that Empire, paying no respect to their fiduciary responsibilities or their responsibility to the League. Britain could have done likewise. For France, mandates were just colonies under another name.

Had Churchill been the expansionist imperialist that he is invariably represented as having been, he could have done the same as the French. Presiding over this, the 'third British Empire' could have appealed enormously to Churchill. But it didn't.

Clementine, who always thought she was much more liberal than her husband, amused herself by suggesting that he could play up the imperial dimension of his new role and that it would please the populace to 'resume our lofty but unconscious contempt of the Foreigner'.[3]

Churchill had, in fact, little relish for the grandiose elements of his role as Colonial Secretary, the maker of kingdoms and moulder of the Empire. It is now often assumed that Britain enthusiastically grabbed these territories because of their oil potential; as has been said, at the time, the existence of the oil was considerably understated. Far from being an imperial expansionist, Churchill did not think that Britain should take on these mandates. He recommended, for instance, that the Palestine mandate be given to the United States. Palestine was, of course, going to prove an enormously difficult political problem, but Lloyd George insisted that Britain take it on.

He would have preferred a job closer to home and more involved in domestic politics. He was annoyed not to be made Chancellor of the Exchequer when that post became vacant shortly after his appointment to the Colonial Office. There are differing views on how committed Churchill was to the work of his new department. Some said that he was interested only in Ireland and Iraq,[4] whereas Lord Curzon, the Foreign Secretary, thought that Churchill was trying to encroach on *his* responsibilities. 'He wants to grab everything into his new dept, and to be a sort of Asiatic Foreign Secretary.'[5] Churchill certainly was insistent about being allowed to create the new Middle East Department.

He devoted enormous but ultimately fruitless efforts to trying to reconcile the interests of the Arabs and the Jews in Palestine, which, by virtue of the Balfour Declaration, Britain had said would be a Jewish state. Not *the* Jewish state, and the declaration was not to affect the interests of the Arab inhabitants. Britain never did manage to resolve this problem and ultimately handed back this League of Nations mandate over Palestine to the League's successor, the United Nations Organization. Negotiations for the surrender of the mandate began in 1947, the same year that Britain, exhausted and financially bankrupted by the Second World War, gave up on India. For those who still believed in Britain's imperial destiny—and there were many who did—these were demoralizing days, whose shadow still lingers on for some three quarters of a century later.

*

It is hardly surprising that Churchill saw the Middle East, if not as a poisoned chalice, then at least as an unappealing one. His responsibilities seemed more likely to damage his career than enhance it. Between 1918 and 1921, there had been widespread risings in the area. The initial reaction of the liberated peoples quickly changed from presenting garlands to their liberators to shooting at them, much as would happen after the allied invasion eighty years later.

As Secretary of State for War and Air, Churchill had already been responsible for policing these new territories. He favoured the economical use of airpower as a means of subduing the insurgents. At the Colonial Office, he continued this policy. Protesters were machine-gunned, bombed and, if Churchill had had his way, would have been gassed. Airpower 'may ultimately lead to a form of control over semi-civilised countries which will be found very effective and infinitely cheaper [than the deployment of land forces] . . . I am strongly in favour of using poisoned gas against uncivilised tribes'. He was talking about non-lethal gas, which he thought was much less objectionable than shrapnel and high explosives. But whatever his language, he was never a monster, and indeed, he was horrified to hear that at one point the RAF had driven villagers into a lake where they bombed them.

As at the War Office, so at the Colonial Office, he deprecated the cost involved, and as the uprisings came to their climax in 1920, 'the Year of Catastrophe', he accelerated a speedy withdrawal from the area. Britain, while retaining trade and defence responsibilities, sought, however unsuccessfully, to prepare the mandates for some kind of independence, as indeed the League of Nations expected.

The whole concept of the Middle East Mandates was flawed. It predicated taking what were arbitrary local government components of the Ottoman Empire and reconstituting them as independent kingdoms with some sort of democratic or liberal system of government. There was no logical definition of boundaries, which were mere lines in the sand. There was no tradition of democracy or liberal ideas, and there were no middle classes to provide stability. Religion and tribal allegiances, which were the basis of cohesion in the area, were ignored.

The project, like similar essays in the following century, was doomed to failure. Churchill at least got Britain in and out pretty nimbly and avoided being stuck with an intractable problem. In that respect, his policy with the bits and pieces of Mesopotamia was more successful than the Palestine negotiations.

The Mesopotamia Exit was largely engineered in Cairo, where Churchill presided over a conference in 1921 at which the necessary arrangements were made with remarkable speed. He enjoyed himself hugely as the man on the spot directing events. He was never averse to luxury, and here he had it in abundance. He established himself in the Mena House Hotel, the former palace and hunting lodge of the Khedive Ismael, just twelve kilometres from Cairo, with an entourage of forty-two people that included Clemmie. He disposed of business briskly, establishing Faisal, deposed in French Syria, as king of Iraq, carving out the new Emirate of Jordan, and making Abdullah, Faisal's brother and hitherto something of a bandit, its ruler. He still had time to paint so many pictures that he was able to have a special exhibition.

*

The Indian dimension to Churchill's life in these years, compared to what was to come later, was limited and, it has to be said, was more of an irritant than a source of pleasure. It must be remembered that India had its own government, over which the viceroy in India presided, at the end of a thread that led to the India Office and the Secretary of State for India in London. The Indian Army was also independent of the British Army. In 1914, the Indian Army was 1,60,000 strong, and only a third were British.[6] The particular beauty was, as Lord Salisbury put it, that India was 'an English barrack in the Oriental seas from which we may draw any number of troops without paying for them'.[7]

Mesopotamia, the part of the Ottoman Empire from which the Mandates were carved out, was run by the Indian Government and not the British Government, and the troops that fought there during the war and that garrisoned it afterwards were largely, although not exclusively, Indian. There were therefore plenty of opportunities for tension.

Throughout 1921 and 1922, Churchill fought very hard to contain the amount of money being spent and the number of troops deployed in the Middle East. He fought hard with the War Office, which he regarded as extravagant. They wanted to maintain as many non-combatant British troops as combatant British troops. Ideally, he'd have had no British troops at all, and worked towards the arrangement that the policing would be done by the Royal Air Force, Indian Troops and Arab Levies. In this, he was supported by the British Commander, General Haldane.

The temperature in Basra had reached 128 degrees Fahrenheit. 'This is not a white man's country and it is absurd to pretend it is. The British troops hate it, and naturally so . . .'[8] Lloyd George was with Churchill, wanting no British troops in Iraq; the War Office, on the other hand, wanted over 18,000.

But while Churchill thought that policing was best done by British airmen and Indian soldiers, he was furiously indignant, as he would be again in relation to British forces in the Western Desert in the Second World War, about the proportion of what he called 'followers' or 'the tail' of non-combatant troops in relation to fighting troops. On 13 December 1921, he exploded to Sir Percy Cox, the British political officer:

> The latest War Office returns give number of Indian followers in Iraq on November 14 as 21,632. This is a shocking figure. Please inform me what is its explanation and what steps you are taking to repatriate and discharge all these people who are living on the British taxpayer. There are 4,000 more Indian followers than there are Indian soldiers.[9]

This was not Churchill's first experience of Indian troops. At the outset of the war, as First Lord of the Admiralty, he had concerns about getting troops from India to the Western Front. Working with Kitchener, by the end of September 1914, he had managed to move all 50,000 troops of the Indian Corps from Bombay and Karachi to Marseille—remarkably, without the Germans having been aware of the movement. When he was out of government in 1916, he fretted about the Indian and African troops who had volunteered for service in the Imperial Army but had not been allotted a war station. When '[n]early 1,000 men—English men, Britishers, men of our own race—are knocked into bundles of bloody rags every twenty-four hours, and carried away to hasty graves . . .'[10] A few weeks later, he returned to the same charge:

'I have heard nothing which indicates that any attempt is being made to use the manpower of India, or India's great resources, effectively in the war. The India Office attitude is one of general apathy and obstruction.'[11]*

*

The Mandates were quasi-colonies. India was a colony. What do we learn from the Middle East years? What is clear from Churchill's time at the Colonial Office is that he was anything but expansionist. In his view the cost of policing and retaining the new territories was much more important than any prestige that derived from its possession.

Churchill's remit had included Egypt, where a commission under Lord Milner published a report in February 1921 that recommended internal self-government and the abolition of the British protectorate. Churchill fought strenuously for the retention of Egypt within the Empire. He lost the battle but in the course of it emerged, according to Curzon as, with Lloyd George, 'the strongest Jingoes in the Cabinet [who] want to concede nothing and to stamp out rebellion in Egypt by fire and sword.'[12] The mandates were new. Egypt, like India, had been part of the panoply of the Empire for much longer,† and like India, Egypt had exoticism, romance and the allure of antiquity.

---

* Between 1914 and 1918, according to Martin Gilbert, India provided one soldier for every 225 of its inhabitants; New Zealand one for every five; Great Britain one for every seven; Australia one for every ten; Canada one for every eleven; and South Africa one for every forty-four. There were 14,00,000 Indians in the Indian Army, of whom 8,50,000 were moved to theatres of war.

† Egypt's position as an imperial possession only went back in law to the start of the Great War, when Britain declared it a protectorate, but *de facto* the connection was much older.

The reference to Lloyd George and Churchill as two 'Jingoes' is crude and simplistic. There was a developing tension between them. Lloyd George wanted to accelerate demobilization after the war, while Churchill felt constrained to slow it down. Part of the reason was the revival of problems in Ireland, but in a list of thirteen reasons that he gave to Lloyd George for avoiding precipitate demobilization, the fifth concentrated on the disorders in India and the thirteenth on the situation on the Afghan frontier.

This last concern didn't arise for the first time after the war. Churchill had been clear from an early stage in the war, of the dangers to Britain—and British India—of an alliance between the Muslims in the Turkish empire and the Muslims in the British Empire. Early in the war, before the Ottoman Empire had declared for Germany and Austria–Hungary, Churchill, alone in the Cabinet, favoured a pro-Turkey policy. There were about 20 million Muslims in Turkey. He was aware that there were 62 million Muslims in India and a further 10 million in Egypt* and he had a geopolitical grasp of the need not to alienate Muslims in the Empire. It was only later that other prominent politicians apprehended the dangers of a declaration of *jihad* from Istanbul. This apprehension, as it crystallized, prompted the rash of uncoordinated and conflicting promises that were made in the course of the war to different Arab leaders. These concerns emerged again in the context of the Dardanelles Campaign, when it was thought that British Muslim subjects would be placated if an independent Muslim State were set up in the Arab parts of the Ottoman Empire. Kitchener was in favour of transferring Mecca from Turkish to British control. It has to be said that Kitchener's views received fairly short shrift from his colleagues.

Churchill was thought by Lord Curzon, a former viceroy himself, to be reacting against Kitchener's wish to become viceroy.[13]

---

* Censuses of 1901 and 1907, respectively.

An even more improbably piece of gossip was reported to Margot Asquith by her husband in March 1915. Edwin Montague, then Chancellor of the Duchy of Lancaster, was terrified that *Churchill* would be viceroy.[14] As will be seen, it was not the last time that this improbable appointment was canvassed.

More generally, what do these years tell us about Churchill's attitude towards the Empire and India?

He can only be painted with a broad brush. Throughout his life, he was described, rightly, as mercurial. His charm was in his irrepressible vitality, but that vitality was subject only to a limited element of focus. There were, then, inconsistencies. He could feel genuinely for the working classes in Dundee, whose circumstances were so extraordinarily different from his own. He could agitate against the privileges of the rich with the enthusiasm of a socialist firebrand, but he was gripped in the post-war world by the dangers of Bolshevism. He exulted, to his own embarrassment, in the excitement of directing war, but his first instinct after the defeat of Germany in a conflict in which so many of his friends had died was to desire to send a 'fat grain ship' to Hamburg. There is a moving glimpse of him in the Second World War, when he watched a film of British bombers carrying the war into Germany. After all the suffering of the blitz and the bombing of British cities, he might have been expected to exult in the turn of fortunes. Instead, as the lights went up, tears were running down his cheeks. 'What beasts we have become.'

This concern for humanity is a consistent feature of the man. In it lay his greatness. It has to be weighed and taken into account alongside the racist utterances, which will be looked at later. Despite his ducal background, he always felt for the vulnerable sections of society in Britain and around the world.

*

We see that he didn't want the mandated acquisitions. To that extent, he was an accountant rather than an imperialist. He recommended that the Palestine mandate be given to the United States, which didn't want it. He was a Zionist, but he was not blindly partisan. In the Middle East and in London, he presided over long and difficult meetings with the Palestinians, Arabs and Jews, at which he urged the parties to come together in compromise. He failed, as did everyone else. But his role had been patient, informed and reasoned. That is not how I would describe his attitude towards India.

Problems in the area did not disappear immediately after the Cairo Conference. Exacerbating the problems among the Arabs was the fact that a final peace with Turkey had not yet been signed. Pamphlets were being circulated in the area in Urdu, calling on Muslim Indian troops to murder their officers and desert. The Turks were also arming some of the sheikhs.

*

But overall, the Colonial Office years were much more agreeable for Churchill than he had expected and indeed enhanced his standing. Nobody blamed him for failing to resolve Palestine, where his efforts at reconciliation had been immense. Ireland was judged a success. And he was not the only one who was gratified by the Cairo Conference, which he described as a meeting of the Forty Thieves. He enjoyed saying that he had created the Emirate of Jordan with the stroke of his pen one bright Sunday afternoon, with time left to make several paintings of Jerusalem before the light went out.

10

Out of Office

In November 1922, a General Election took place. Churchill stood again for Dundee. He was suffering from the serious after-effects of an appendicitis operation and was scarcely able to campaign. Clemmie appeared on his behalf until the very last days of the campaign. The mood had changed. When he did appear, he was heckled and shouted down. 'What about Gallipoli'? Despite the Enquiry, which exonerated him, he never shook off a taint that still lingers even today. The two Liberal candidates were defeated by a Labour candidate and a famous advocate of prohibition. Churchill, as always, was genuinely magnanimous. He declared that, given the conditions of the working class in Dundee, they were right to demand change. In public, he was buoyant. As he got on his train for London, a Dundonian reporter asked if it were true that he was being given a knighthood. He replied that he was not. He was returning south as plain Mr Churchill, 'without a prefix, a suffix or an appendix'. In reality, he was devastated by the turn of events and disappeared from active politics for fifteen months.

*

His career had indubitably suffered a setback. In the course of his political lifetime, it met many setbacks. The move from the Conservative Party to the Liberal Party in 1904 had been risky. His fall after Gallipoli had been potentially more dangerous. It could well have marked the end, and at the time, he thought it probably had. Afterwards, he was very grateful to Lloyd George for giving him a second chance, 'a remount', probably because he thought Churchill would be less of a threat in the Government than out of it.

The defeat in the 1922 election was accompanied by other blows. His youngest daughter, Marigold, had died of meningitis. Clementine suffered a nervous collapse. Lady Randolph died following the amputation of a leg. Churchill took a four-month holiday in the South of France. Holidays were not periods of inaction for him, and he spent the time beginning to write a huge (and still important) history of the First World War, *The World Crisis*.[*]

His difficulty was in accommodating himself to a changed political landscape. The coalition that Asquith formed between the Liberal Party and the Conservatives in 1915 survived his replacement by Lloyd George. At a personal level, Lloyd George, 'the man who had won the war', was almost unassailable.[†]

At the 1918 General Election, called 'the Coupon Election' because the coalition handed out a slip of paper to the candidates it endorsed, the Government won a huge majority. But it depended on its Conservative supporters. Bonar Law had 344 Conservatives. Labour came forward for the first time with a substantial vote of

---

[*] Arthur Balfour, always reliable for a good remark talked of, 'Winston's brilliant autobiography, disguised as a history of the universe.'

[†] In 1918, Bonar Law said that Lloyd George could be Prime Minister for life if he wanted. He was very wrong. Lloyd George fell from power just four years later and never held office again.

142 MPs. The Liberals were third, with 115 members, but even that overstated their strength because they were split between Lloyd George's 'National Liberals' and Asquith's official Liberal Party. Asquith had sixty-two MPs, and Lloyd George, the Prime Minister, only fifty-three.

Lloyd George's personal popularity was enormous, but his political support in Parliament was obviously fragile. His government depended on Conservative votes, and the Conservatives fairly soon tired of supporting a man they had always hated. At a famous meeting of the party at the Carlton Club in 1922, they voted for the Party to go its own way. Lloyd George was deposed. For a year, until the 1923 General Election, the Government was a Conservative Government. After the minority MacDonald Government from 1923 to 1924, the Conservatives returned and formed a government until 1929. From 1929 until 1931, MacDonald again presided over a minority Labour Government, but from 1931 until the outbreak of war, the Conservatives formed a government, the National Government, which they dominated despite Labour and Liberal elements.

So 1922 was the end of the great Liberal Party, one of the dominating influences on nineteenth-century life, not just politically but perhaps to an even greater extent morally. In the century that followed, it never again formed an administration and was only represented in coalition governments. A great political earthquake had taken place.*

---

* But the politics of the inter-war years will not be understood unless it is remembered that no one knew that Liberal England had died. There was always a real fear among the opponents of Liberalism that its fortunes would revive. At a personal level, Churchill remained wary of Lloyd George right into the Second World War.

This left Churchill with a problem. His move to the Liberal Party in 1904 had not been a difficult one. He had never had an obvious affinity with the Tories. That made coming back to them, 're-ratting', as he called it, 'in itself an awkward manoeuvre, even more difficult.'* In 1904, the issue of Free Trade genuinely mattered to Churchill, and at heart he was of a Whiggish disposition. Moreover, he never greatly liked the Conservatives, particularly the Unionist element, and the Conservatives were pretty ambivalent about him. On the other hand, he had come to dislike Bolshevism greatly and to an extent to conflate Bolshevism with Socialism, which did chime in with Conservative prejudices. That fitted in with the Unionists, as he often called the Conservative Party, but until the outbreak of the Second World War, while he had the support of the Tory press and of much of the party in the country, he was regarded by many Tory MPs with distrust and suspicion, a mercurial (that word again) opportunist. After his magnificent leadership in the Second War, his position was unassailable, but more because of support in the party than in Parliament.

So after 1922, he began to edge towards the Tories. As late as December 1923, he stood again as a Liberal, at Leicester West. He was defeated by the Labour candidate and was thus reinforced in his prevailing instinct, to oppose Socialism. The break came when, after the following General Election, the Liberals decided to support a minority Labour Government under Ramsay MacDonald. His intention was to stand as an independent, relying on support from both the Liberals and the Conservatives, and at the by-election in the Westminster Abbey Division in March 1924, he stood unsuccessfully against the Conservatives but, note, as a 'Constitutionalist, independent

---

* 'Anyone can rat,' said Churchill, 'but it takes a certain amount of ingenuity to re-rat.'

anti-Socialist'. The chorus girls of Daly's theatre sat up all night addressing envelopes and dispatching the election address. The edging to the right was completed when, shortly afterwards, he was adopted by the local Conservative Association as their candidate for Epping. Even then, he stood not as a Conservative but again as a 'Constitutionalist'. He could not bring himself to use the uncomfortable Conservative label.

*

The move away from radicalism played a role in the development of his convictions. Because Churchill lived until 1965, it is easy to assume that he was still quite a young man in 1924. He was not. Particularly as it affected his views on India, it is important to remember where his roots were planted. He was in fact forty-nine, and surprised that he had not died the early death that he had always expected. His youthful nonchalance was leaving him. He had been greatly affected by the First World War, not only for the tragedy of the deaths, which distressed this humane man, but because of the way in which it upturned the certainties of life and the geopolitical structure on which these certainties rested. When he came in 1930 to write *My Early Life*, a delightful and beautifully written account of his life from his birth to the time when he entered the House of Commons, he was recording an elegy: 'I was a child of the Victorian era, when the structure of our country seemed firmly set, when its position in trade and on the seas was unrivalled, and when the realisation of the greatness of our Empire and of our duty to preserve it was ever growing stronger.'[1]

The drift to the right can be discerned as early as the latter years of the First World War. Even before the war, while still MP for Oldham, part of the appeal for him of a Liberal–Conservative coalition was to block the development of socialism and communism. Now, as he saw the growth of the Labour Party, he became more concerned about the threat to the kind of society of which he approved and its replacement by doctrinaire ideology. When Duff Cooper had dinner with Churchill in January 1920, he reported that 'Winston said that he was all out to fight Labour. It was his one object in Politics.' He was becoming 'splendidly reactionary'.[2] There is a caesura between the young, liberal Churchill and the Churchill who hated and feared the implications of Socialist theory. This was Churchill for the rest of his life.

On this reading, after his defeat at Dundee, his return to the Tories was pretty inevitable. He had lunch with Sir Robert Horne, the former Chancellor of the Exchequer. He said, 'I am what I always have been—a Tory Democrat. Force of circumstance has compelled me to serve with another party, but my views have never changed, and I would be glad to give effect to them by re-joining the Conservatives.'[3] It would be truer to say that his views *had* changed under the influence of events. The *Glasgow Herald* said that Churchill was 'undoubtedly preparing the way of return to the party he had left many years ago'.[4]

So, far from being the radical firebrand, Lloyd George's henchman, whose treachery to his own class was so deprecated by the King, he had now become a traditionalist who deprecated the passing of the old order, the disappearance of the great European dynasties, and the threats to Britain's imperial strength. This change of attitude affected his view of the Empire and of India.

Churchill and India would collide in 1930, when he was at the forefront of opposition to steps that were designed, albeit agonizingly slowly, to lead India towards some sort of self-government. Before we concentrate on this crucial time for both Churchill and Britain's relations with the Indian subcontinent, we look at Churchill's last period in office before the Second World War.

*

The 1924 General Election saw Churchill elected for Epping. He was in Parliament but not yet in Government. The Carlton Club resolution in 1922 had separated the Tories from the Liberals, but it also caused a minor fissure in the Conservative Party. One or two prominent Tories, such as Churchill, Austen Chamberlain and F.E. Smith (Lord Birkenhead), remained apart. There were other difficulties too. The Conservative Cabinet was beginning to do the unthinkable and toy with the idea of adopting the scheme of Imperial Preferences advocated by Joe Chamberlain, which had threatened Free Trade and caused Churchill's defection in 1904.

A great deal of effort was devoted to getting the dissidents on board and thus defusing a Lloyd Georgian coup. The invitation from the new Prime Minister, Stanley Baldwin, asking Churchill to come to Downing Street was the culmination of this strategy. Churchill said that Baldwin asked him to become Chancellor, that he replied that he would indeed be glad to become Chancellor of the Duchy of Lancaster, the largely honorific government position he had held during the war, and that Baldwin replied that he meant Chancellor of the Exchequer. The story may have been true because it was extraordinary, by ordinary standards, that the double renegade, whose political career had appeared to flounder disastrously, was being invited to accept one of the highest positions at the Prime Minister's disposal—and one, moreover, for which Churchill displayed no obvious qualifications. 'I should have liked to have answered, "Will the bloody duck swim?", but as it was a formal and important conversation I replied, 'This fulfils my ambition. I still have my father's robe as Chancellor. I shall be proud to serve you in this splendid office.'[5] The story

may have been true, but I very much doubt it. Baldwin needed
Churchill back and had to pay a high price, and Churchill, who
never undervalued himself, knew that.

If this book were a review of Churchill's politics as a whole,
a lot of space would be devoted to his time as Chancellor of the
Exchequer. But it isn't, and there won't be. That doesn't mean that
he confined himself narrowly to his departmental brief. He never
did. Even in his first office, Under-Secretary for the Colonies, a
very junior member of the government, his super-abundant self-
confidence carried him brashly into areas that had nothing to do
with him. A flavour of this approach can be conveyed by what
he said when, just back in the Conservative Party, as Chancellor,
he took the Chair of a Cabinet Committee during the General
Strike. Two other principal members were the Home Secretary,
Joynson–Hicks ('Jix') and the Secretary for War, Worthington-
Evans ('Worthy'). 'I have done your job for eighteen months, Jix,
and yours for two years, Worthy, so I had better unfold my plan.'[6]
As Roy Jenkins nicely put it, 'He assumed the authority of the
Treasury within the Government as though he had the combined
Exchequer experience of Gladstone, Disraeli, Lloyd George and
Bonar Law, and he behaved towards his colleagues as though he
had the most unassailable of Conservative credentials.'[7]

A number of broad observations can be made about Churchill's
time as Chancellor for the sake of the insights they give. I said
earlier that he was not an obvious choice for Chancellor; he had
no experience at the Exchequer or in the other departments that
mesh closely with it. But he is now recognized as having been a
rather good Chancellor. At one time, there was some controversy
about his performance. That centred on the return to the Gold
Standard. Until 1914, the value of the pound was fixed in relation
to the price of gold. In that year, the linkage was removed, and
fiscal discipline—and national self-respect—suffered in the
exigencies of wartime. America had also abandoned the Gold

Standard, but the United States returned to pre-war gold parity in 1919. The effect was to leave the pound at an embarrassingly low rate of exchange relative to the dollar. Relinking the pound to pre-war parity in 1925, as Churchill did, implied a rise of about 10 per cent in its value, and the effect of that on the economy was painful. He was criticized at the time and continued to be for many years. The criticism was stimulated by the pamphlet written by the economist John Maynard Keynes, *The Economic Consequences of Mr Churchill*, a very conscious reference to his hugely popular *The Economic Consequences of the Peace*.

It was a slightly unfair personalization of the issue, doubly unfair because Churchill had worked hard with Keynes to avoid a return to parity. At the Treasury, no one was more opposed to returning to the Gold Standard than the Chancellor himself. He fought vigorously against the opposition of all his senior advisors, deploying arguments obtained, among others, from Keynes and Reginald McKenna, a former Chancellor.*

Roy Jenkins, another former Chancellor, put it well:

> As the Gold battle unfolded so there was a sense of even such a rumbustious character as Churchill being swept downstream by the force of a compelling current protesting, but nonetheless essentially impotent. The Treasury was against him, the Bank was against him, the committee presided over first by Austen Chamberlain and then by Bradbury [a former Permanent Secretary of the Treasury] was against him. Snowden, his Labour 'shadow' was against him. Baldwin . . . played no part in the decision, but would have been against Churchill had he attempted to decide otherwise. The two tufts of ground—

---

* And although McKenna strongly supported Keynes, he acknowledged that, as a matter of practical politics, Churchill had no alternative but to go back to gold.

Keynes and McKenna—on which he attempted to stand
proved, for varying reasons unsatisfactory footholds.[8]

As Chancellor, Churchill worked extraordinarily hard. He had
done so in the past, and he would do so again, but the impression
of his vitality and enthusiasm is particularly marked at this period.
He worked in the evenings and at the weekends. He exhausted his
associates, as he would do in the war, with the long and draining
sessions that he imposed on them. He immersed himself in
detail and mastered the technical aspects of his brief. Some who
admire Churchill, even claiming to model themselves on him,
are taken in by his bombast and rodomontade. It can mislead.
Even in the most famous of his wartime rhetoric, with its florid
and magnificent perorations, the bulk of the speech consisted of
painstaking analysis and a forensic recitation of detail. Churchill's
status as one of the outstanding Chancellors of the twentieth
century is underlined by the fact that he delivered no fewer than
five budgets. He should not be underrated.

The budgets that he introduced were not, apart from the
return to the Gold Standard, dramatic. And even that had been
so expected that it generated a feeling of inevitability rather than
drama. But the pantomimes with the Gladstonian despatch box
outside Number 11 Downing Street were more theatrical than ever.
Churchill loved the play-acting. The marches on Westminster,
flanked by friends, family and Treasury officials, were impressive
affairs. The budget speeches themselves were delivered with style
and humour. But the contents were pretty technical; they were
economists' budgets.

Perhaps surprisingly for someone who is forever associated
with the defence of the British Isles, they were far from a
warmonger's budget. Possibly the most noticeable feature was
his stinginess with money for the forces, particularly the Navy.
His expenditure was based on the dubious assumption that there

would be no naval wars for the foreseeable future, an assumption from which Britain would suffer at the outbreak of the Second World War. Eschewing the grand schemes and legacy gestures that Chancellors enjoy, his consistent concern was for what he referred to, with genuine compassion, if condescendingly, as 'the little people'. He was about as far from being one of the little people as could be imagined, but his concern for ordinary men and women, at home and abroad, was a heart-warming and redeeming feature of his approach throughout his political career.

The General Election of 1929 resulted in a minority Labour Government. The Tories were out of office until 1931. When they returned to Government in that year as part of the National Government, Churchill was excluded. The reason he was excluded may have had a little to do with the fact that the party continued to move towards the abolition of Free Trade while Churchill remained unenthusiastic. At the 1923 General Election, Churchill had stood on an avowedly anti-Protectionist ticket. He did signal that his views were not cast in stone when he spoke at a Conservative meeting in Liverpool on 7 May 1924. The fact remained, however, that he could draw Free Traders around him to oppose Government views that were increasingly favourable to Tariff Reform and Imperial Protection. Free Trade was finally abandoned by Neville Chamberlain when *he* became Chancellor.

*

The other respect in which Churchill differed from his colleagues was over India. The Conservative Party was moving steadily towards giving India something like dominion status (although no one knew what dominion status meant). Whatever it meant, Churchill was against it, and it was on this issue that he resigned from the shadow cabinet during the Labour minority Government. It was the Indian question, more than his other eccentricities (an obsession with the dangers of German rearmament and a romantic desire to lead a squadron of cavaliers to the rescue of King Edward VIII and Mrs Simpson), that kept Churchill in the wilderness throughout the 1930s.

Given that he devoted a large part of that decade to wrecking and thwarting British policy on India, the modern reader may be astonished that during his last year or so at the Exchequer, Churchill was repeatedly considered for appointment as Secretary of State for India with the responsibility for creating and implementing a liberal policy of reform.

Baldwin was rather fond of Churchill. Like Asquith, earlier in Churchill's career, the Prime Minister viewed him with an amused tolerance. As the 1929 election approached, Baldwin asked Thomas Jones, the Deputy Secretary to the Cabinet, whether Churchill would be a good Secretary of State for India. Jones thought it 'a splendid notion'. A week later, he recorded in his diary that he had said that Churchill would rise to the height of a great opportunity.[9] As the days passed, the matter was discussed further. Leo Amery, at this time Colonial Secretary and never Churchill's greatest admirer, wasn't keen. He favoured putting him in charge of a mission to coordinate the fighting services, where he 'would be kept happy and busy planning wars in Afghanistan and elsewhere'. He even suggested Churchill as Foreign Secretary. Neville Chamberlain told Amery that he thought the Prime Minister would not 'run such a risk [as appointing Churchill to the India Office] and would dread to find himself waking up at night in a cold sweat at the thought of Winston's indiscretions'. Amery countered that 'Winston was not really so rash as picturesque', a judgement that contains some insight. Amery was also correct in discerning the crux of the matter: Churchill was 'fundamentally opposed to all ideas of Empire development and Empire preference'.[10]

In all these discussions, his many enemies in the Conservative Party revealed nervousness about his position. He was not to be trusted because he was simply out of office. It was suspected that he was already in negotiations with Lloyd George to be second in command of a new political grouping. There was no substance to these rumours, but there was a pretty general feeling that everything should have been done to make sure that Churchill did not steal the party leadership. Scarcely any senior Conservative politician was not busily engaged in trying to trim the pinion feathers of the interloping cuckoo. Baldwin alone, secure as leader of the party, regarded Churchill benignly. One is tempted to see the man of destiny being roped down by puny Lilliputians, but that reflection is prompted by the misleading refractions of the prism of the Second World War. The demands of that conflict made Churchill as essential and suitable for office in 1940 as he would have been disastrous in 1930.

His rivals had every reason to be uneasy. Churchill's friends in the Tory press filled their papers with speculation about his future. It was taken for granted that he was due a rest from the Treasury. His successor there was thought to be likely to be Chamberlain. From Delhi, the viceroy, Irwin, wrote to Churchill on 27 March 1929, referring to this speculation. He wished Churchill 'all of the reward that virtue deserves! Good luck my dear Winston'.[11] Irwin was distinctly progressive in India. We shall return to him in a later chapter. He was being disingenuous when he wrote to his dear Winston. He had already been asked for his own views on Churchill and India and had made it clear that he did not favour Churchill's appointment as Secretary of State. He wrote to Baldwin that he could

> [s]ee a great hand for [Winston] to play over India with his capacity for seeing the big thing & presenting a broad case. But I think my doubts tend to outweigh my confidence that it would be a good appointment . . .

India today seems to be vy much at a crossways . . .
She needs the guidance of somebody with courage: and
with vision—but with both the courage and the vision of a
real desire to help India, and make themselves felt through
sympathy with all her difficulties. The 'inferiority complex'
is just now very inferior & very complex: & India is very
sore. And I am sure that more than half her problems are
psychological & of that order of difficulty. How would
W.S.C. fit into these necessities? F.E. [Smith]* did an
incredible amount of harm here . . . by the impression he
produced upon sensitive and self-important Indians visiting
England, whom either he would not see & so mortified: or
saw and produced the impression of one out of sympathy &
rather disposed to despise.

Frankly I should fear that Winston at bottom would have
rather the same point of view & would never be able—as one
never can—to conceal it. I remember his attitude of mind vis
à vis Indians in Kenya & I doubt.† And he has become—or
perhaps it's more true to say—has always been, a much more
vigorous Imperialist in the 1890 to 1900 sense of the word
than you & me. If I thought that Winston would really be
interested & would really be liberal minded to India I might
say different: but I can't bring myself to believe that this is
constitutionally likely.[12]

---

* An outstandingly illiberal Secretary of State for India during
1924–1928.
† As Colonial Secretary in 1921, Churchill supported the right of the
East African administration to deny Indians equal rights with Europeans
to land purchase. Montagu rejected the views that he regarded as
distasteful which, 'might have been written by a European settler of a
most fanatical type'.

Despite Baldwin's high regard for Irwin, he decided to mention his thoughts to Churchill. Churchill:

> Mr Baldwin seemed to feel that as I had carried the Transvaal Constitution through the House in 1906, and the Irish Free State Constitution in 1920, it would be in general harmony with my sentiments and my record to preside over a third great measure of self-government for another part of the Empire. I was not attracted by this plan.[13]

He was never actually offered the job. It's interesting that as perceptive a political observer as Baldwin still saw Churchill at this point as liberal in Imperial—and in particular Indian—matters.

He had, as Churchill surmised, been impressed by Churchill's conciliatory work in the House in regard to the Transvaal constitution in 1906, after the South African War, and the Irish Free State Constitution in 1922. Churchill set out his reasons for saying that he didn't want the job twenty years later. He was aware that a Royal Commission headed by Sir John Simon had gone out to India in 1928 to make an exhaustive tour and study. Their report was to be published shortly, and he feared that its recommendations would not accord with his views. F.E. Smith was perhaps his closest political friend. He had, from the Indian Office, kept Churchill abreast of developments in India. Churchill shared 'his deep misgivings about that vast sub-continent'.[14] In addition, the viceroy issued a declaration known by his name, the Irwin Declaration, in October 1929, which will be looked at later. It committed the British Government to encouraging India down the road towards some sort of self-rule.

These developments about which Churchill and F.E. Smith held such deep misgivings—the Simon Commission, the Irwin Declaration and the adoption by the Conservative Party of a philosophy that was deeply distasteful to 'a European Settler of a most fanatical type'—were developments that combined to propel Churchill out of the shadow cabinet after the 1929 election had been lost. He pitched himself into a policy of violent opposition to anything resembling Indian Home Rule. In doing so, he tainted his image in the eyes of all, even mildly, liberal spectators, created turmoil in the Conservative Party, and established an image of himself as an enemy to India, an image that most Indians cannot forgive, however much they admire other aspects of his life and achievements.

11

A Future for India

Churchill and India came together in four main engagements. The first is the early period, when he lived there and formed his first views of the country. His experiences and his preference for the Muslim community and the so-called martial races were established then. This was followed in the next period, spanning the First World War, by more distant reflection: observation of the colonies and the Empire generally. His views developed. As we have seen, these views were in general of a mildly liberal character, certainly patronizing, but essentially benevolent. The third period was the leadership of the die-hards in the campaign to derail the 1935 India Bill, which was intended to pave the way to India's self-government, though not independence.

When outright defeat of the government's legislation became evidently impossible, he settled for separating the different elements—the crystallization of divide and rule. In these years, his middle Indian period, from 1930 to 1935, he moved from the relative pragmatism of his early years to the settled, doctrinaire and extreme position that he would occupy for the rest of his life. His views were formed as British governments, a minority

Labour government under Ramsay MacDonald from May 1929 until October 1931 and thereafter a Conservative-dominated National Government, first under MacDonald and then under the Conservative Stanley Baldwin, sought first to work out what policy on India should be and then enacted that policy in the form of the Government of India Bill of 1935, a huge piece of legislation designed to create a federal system that would ultimately lead the way to self-government and perhaps a never-promised independence. As a decade, the 1930s were not, for the most part, good for Churchill. He was out of office until September 1939. When he was underemployed, he tended to become depressed and introverted, and he spent a lot of time in these years at Chartwell, his house in Kent, where he drank too much and could bore his friends with self-regarding monologues. These were not his best years.

His final engagement was in the period between becoming Prime Minister in 1940 and losing the General Election of 1945. During these five years, when he was heroically striving to save his country, and by extension, that part of the world that was still free, he found an astonishing amount of time and energy to devote to a sustained and bitter campaign to thwart any move towards Indian independence.

Before looking at Churchill's *response* to policy-making, let us briefly look at what the government's policy on India was.

*

A 1950 Colonial Office paper[1] disarmingly said that Britain 'as a seafaring and trading nation . . . had long been a collector of islands and peninsulas'. Immediately after the loss of the American Colonies in 1776, Britain sought what is called her 'Second Empire'. The lesson of America had been that large tracts of land that needed policing were expensive. The emphasis now was on this collection not of extents of land but of islands and peninsulas, and not just any old islands and peninsulas, but those that would favour trade and protect the sea routes. There was no question of exercising a benign influence on less-favoured parts of the globe. The motive for Empire was entirely selfish. The early territories were acquired in search of valuable raw materials. Mercantilist policy involved closing off routes and markets against competition. As there was competition with other nations such as the Netherlands and France, it became important to acquire points of strategic importance from which to defend the acquisitions, and later coaling and refitting stations also became important.

Of the dependencies with which the 1950 paper was dealing, three-quarters had been obtained in little more than the previous eighty years, when the motives for acquisition had become confused. The African territories, for instance, were largely acquired in the spirit of competition with other European nations and without regard for any certainty that they would be profitable. There was a collective view that no self-respecting European power could exist without an Empire. At the end of the First World War, as has been seen, the Ottoman territories over which Britain obtained her mandates increased the superficial area of the Empire very significantly.

*

India was acquired in the first period of the second Empire, not directly by Britain but by the East India Company, a semi-private mercantile body whose interests were purely commercial. For a variety of reasons, partly military competition with France, and partly the need to defend itself against Indian rulers, the Company deployed an increasingly powerful army, and its territories extended.

From time to time, London felt obliged to temper the greed and aggressiveness of the Company with some elements of restraint and decency, and the East India Company was by degrees brought under the control of the British Government. The attempts were never wholly successful. The final straw was the First War of Independence in 1857, which was treated by the imperial Parliament as an indictment of the Company's role. Legislation in the following year effectively put an end to the Company. From 1858, the whole of India and its armies were controlled directly by the British Government. The reaction to the War of Independence was two-fold. On the one hand, Britain had to show Indians that 'it was hopeless to endeavour to resist the power of the White Man'.[2] On the other hand, the government had already sought to promote moral aspects of British rule to ensure that the liberal, cultural benefits of education were extended to the natives of the subcontinent and that the spread of Christianity was encouraged—though it was never enforced. Now it had to formulate a wholesale and systematic policy for the huge area and vast population for which it was directly responsible.

By this time, we are in the period of imperial acquisition for acquisition's sake and not the period of commercial cherry-picking. Those parts of India that were not already under British control were acquired either directly by military annexation or indirectly by treaties with the princes. As late as 1900, a small British presence ruled two-thirds of the subcontinent directly and the remaining third, the Princely States, only indirectly. At that date, there were 674 Princely States with a population of 73 million, one-fifth of all India. The princes generally governed in the British interest; they were paid to do so, and British political officers made sure that they did. The princes were treated with deference, in the optative mood ('would that you might do such and such'). But in addition to the optative mood, there was a Gatling gun in the background and a gunship in the bay. In *British* India, Indians did not even *appear* to rule. There was no need for the optative mood. In 1909, there were no Indians at all on the viceroy's Council.

The viceroy presided over the Government of India. He was what his title suggested: the substitute for the King. His personal powers were indeed far in excess of anything that his royal master possessed, and he enjoyed surroundings of splendour and luxury far in excess of his sovereign.

India had become, without any particular planning, a distinct and peculiar part of the British Empire. Indeed, it was only because of India that Britain could claim to be an Empire. It was after the formal abolition of the East India Company in 1874 that the title 'Empress of India' was statutorily conferred on Queen Victoria.* *With* India, Britain had a true Empire, riches and exotic glamour. *With* India, Britain had the greatest Empire the world had ever known—an Empire on which the sun never set. Without it, she had a ragbag of commercial enterprises. India therefore peculiarly and enormously mattered to Britain and underpinned Britain's prestige.

At the same time, an increasingly morally serious Britain, now dominated by its middle classes, could not be entirely at ease with the fact that a handful of white men ruled over unrepresented masses, that atrocities were regularly reported, and that practices such as widows being burned on their husbands' funeral pyres were tolerated. It's easy to assume that Britain's attitude towards India was entirely cynical or selfish. That was not the case, and both increasingly serious-minded viceroys like Curzon (1898–1905) and Parliament itself, particularly after the Liberal landslide of 1906, were determined to ameliorate, as they saw it, the Government of India. The Indian Civil Service was an institution

---

* She very much wanted it, but it was with some difficulty that Disraeli got the legislation through the Commons.

of which Britain could be proud. Men (no women, of course) who joined the Service did enjoy a higher standard of living than they would at home, and some were certainly influenced by this consideration. But that does not explain wholly the intense competition to gain admission, which required hard work and the attainment of the highest standards of scholarship.

Those who finished their service in the subcontinent could retire to the shires with a comfortable sufficiency and generous pensions, but the graveyards of India are full of decaying monuments to men, their wives, and—most poignantly—their children, who did not survive climate and pestilence. Today we may think the approach condescending, but what truly is amazing is the idealism, probity and self-sacrifice with which these district commissioners, judges and collectors sought to discharge their self-imposed duties. Nothing could be more different from the knavery, corruption and peculation of the East India Company.

*

Following the 1906 election, John Morley became Secretary of State for India. He was bookish and earnest; proud, as he said, to have been made Secretary of State as a 'humble man of letters'. He had unimpeachable radical credentials and a contempt for jingoism. Improbably, in concert with the viceroy, the Earl of Minto, a Tory appointed by the previous government, and on the face of it, not a reformer, he made the first systematic attempt to reform the Government of India. They worked on what became known as the Morley–Minto Reforms, or more correctly, the Indian Councils Act of 1909. Morley believed that the British were in India 'to implant . . . those ideas of justice, law, humanity that are the foundations of our own civilisation'. Unquestionably, he hoped that limited reforms would separate moderates in India from those who were regarded as extremists. But at any rate, he *did* extend the franchise and increase the number of Indians on the provincial and central legislative councils. *Responsible* government is not self-government. There was some responsibility towards the tiny electorate, but control of only a limited number of functions was devolved to the elected representatives. Overall control was firmly retained by Britain.

The Indian National Congress was founded in 1885 by Alan Octavian Hume, a retired Indian Civil Service official. Congress was not then sectarian, although from the outset there were far more Hindus than Muslims. There was a huge chasm between the aspirations of Congress and the ideas of the government. It is important to take this chasm aboard. Almost to the very end, even when Britain acknowledged that independence was ultimately inevitable, it was still assumed that it could only arrive when, in its culture, its amenities and its organization, the subcontinent was peaceable, prosperous and indistinguishable from an English county.

Lord Kimberley, Liberal Secretary of State for India for most of the period 1882–1894, said that 'the notion of a parliamentary representation of so vast a country, almost as large as Europe, containing so large a number of different races, is one of the wildest imaginations that ever entered the minds of men'. Minto, who rode in the French Grand National and elsewhere under the name of 'Mr Rolly', felt the same way. He wrote to Morley in 1907: 'We are no advocates of representative government for India in the Western sense of the term. It could never be akin to the instincts of the many races composing the population of the Indian Empire. It would be a western importation uncongenial to eastern tastes.' Morley didn't disagree. He rejected 'the intention or desire to attempt the transportation of any European form of representative government to Indian soil'. In 1909, Minto told the House of Lords that he thought it neither desirable, possible nor even conceivable that British political institutions should be extended to India. 'If I were attempting to set up a parliamentary system in India, or if it could be said that this chapter of reforms led directly or necessarily up to the establishment of a parliamentary system in India, I, for one, would have nothing at all to do with it'. A strangely contorted sentence, but we know what he meant. What was at the heart of the Indian tragedy of the twentieth century was that these essential reservations of even liberal policymakers were not shared with Indian politicians.

*

Britain's assumption that India would possibly never—and certainly not in the next hundred years—be ready for self-government is important to understand. It was very widespread, indeed universal, until about the 1930s, and even after that and right up to independence in 1947, the assumption permeated the thinking of all but a small, advanced minority. Curzon had been an ultra-conscientious viceroy. He had approached the viceroyalty in a spirit of humility and dedication. And yet he looked at the proposed Morley–Minto Reforms with horror: 'It is often said, "Why not make some prominent native a member of the Executive Council?" The answer is that on the whole continent there is not an Indian fit for the post.' Lord Milner, who probably had more influence on twentieth-century British colonial policy than anyone else, was equally forthright: 'The idea of extending what is described as "colonial self-government" to India . . . is a hopeless absurdity.'[3]

Politicians are to be judged by the standards of their time, but what is difficult to excuse is the fact that when these architects of Indian policy expressed their views, they did not spell out the fact that their ideas of self-government and devolution were wedded to the assumption that there would probably never be self-government for India as there might be for the old dominions of Australia and Canada. The whole dialogue between Britain and India in the twentieth century was flawed by this silent assumption, never shared with Indians. It was a conversation in which words meant different things to different interlocutors. That is why Indian politicians repeatedly felt betrayed by their British counterparts.

*

The next attempt to address what was increasingly seen as the Indian *problem* came in the form of the Montagu–Chelmsford Reforms of 1917. There was no doubt that there was a problem. As India came out of the First World War, there was great confusion. The Khilafat (or Caliphate) Movement promoted the Muslim cause and demanded the restoration of the Caliph, formerly the Sultan of Turkey, which was supported strangely enough by Hindus as well as Muslims. Symbols of British rule were attacked. Punjab, in particular, was in disarray. The publication of *Mother India*, discussed further below, revealed appalling social conditions in India, particularly for women. The 1921 census showed that about 2 million girls were married before the age of ten, and about 1,00,000 of them were widowed before the same age.

In 1917, the Secretary of State for India, Edwin Montagu, set out the Government's policy for India. On a quick reading, the Montagu Declaration, as history knows it, seemed to reassure nationalists. Supporters of independence read it as a promise of independence. Supporters of the status quo could see that it was not. The critical part of the Declaration was this:

The policy of His Majesty's Government, with which the Government of India are in complete accord, is that of the

> increasing association of Indians in every branch of the
> administration, and the gradual development of self-governing
> institutions, with a view to the progressive realisation of
> responsible government in India *as an integral part of the
> British Empire.*

I stress these last words because they meant that India was not,
as the foregoing words seem to suggest, to be self-governing and
independent. Unlike the dominions, Canada and Australia, a self-
governing India was to be permanently bound in to the Empire.
The government knew exactly what it was doing: in the course
of drafting, the words 'responsible government', replaced what
had originally been 'self-government'. The revision was Curzon's,
and it was important. There might be responsible institutions, but
there would not be a self-governing country. Any village in the
Empire could have a responsible government.

Alongside the Declaration, the Montagu–Chelmsford Reforms
or 'Montford', properly the Government of India Act 1919,
represented a move forward from Morley–Minto. The electorate
was extended to five and a half million for the provincial authorities
and one and a half million for the central legislature—pathetic
figures: the population of India at the time was 263 million. Eleven
provinces were created in which 'safe' responsibilities in areas such
as public health, education and agriculture were placed in the
hands of elected Indian representatives. The responsibilities that
cut ice—police, finance, justice and the press—were 'reserved'.
The existence of two separate and parallel levels of government
was described as diarchy. Three out of the seven ministers on the
viceroy's Executive Council were now Indian.

What mattered was the Declaration, which preceded the
reforms. Everyone could read what they wanted into it, but no
one knew what it meant. So obscure was it that it had to be

clarified twelve years later in another Declaration, by the then viceroy, Lord Irwin.

No one that mattered in India was taken in. The remarkable Annie Besant, an English Theosophist who had moved to India in 1893, combined her work in theosophy with support for the National Movement and became the first woman President of Congress at the December 1917 party meeting in Calcutta. She dismissed the Montagu–Chelmsford Reforms scathingly: they were 'unworthy of England to offer and India to accept'. Gandhi saw the British 'reforms' as being ultimately aimed at the consolidation of British power. Furthermore, in March 1919, just six months after the reforms were announced, the Defence of India Regulations Act was consolidated into savage measures in the Rowlatt Act. A fiercely repressive regime had been created.

The ambiguities of the Montagu Declaration, the limited scope of the Montagu–Chelmsford Reforms, and the savagery of the Rowlatt Act created a profound sense of disillusion. India had loyally supported the war in terms of money and men and had assumed that there would be a substantial reward for their loyalty. Their disillusionment was compounded by the Jallianwala Bagh Massacre, which seemed to deprive Britain of all moral authority.

12

The Irwin Declaration

In the rapid political changes of the time, two Secretaries of State followed Montagu between March 1922 and November 1924, when the Conservative Prime Minister, Stanley Baldwin, forming his second government, appointed Churchill's friend, the Earl of Birkenhead, the former F.E. Smith.

In the 1920s, Smith soared across the political sky like a dazzling comet, finally and sadly falling to earth, burned out and broken by drink, financing his elevated lifestyle through second-rate journalism. Along with his huge abilities, he had vices in abundance. He was quite without morality. In relation to India, he was an unashamed spokesman for the Tory die-hards. But he was intellectually prodigious, capable of working very hard and effectively, and there were always surprises. He spoke out in the House of Lords to condemn those who supported General Dyer, a hero in that House. More predictably, he regarded the Congress Party with contempt. He saw its representatives as self-serving and ambitious, with no true identity with the illiterate masses. He told the viceroy, Lord Reading, that alone in the Cabinet he continued to oppose the Montagu–Chelmsford policy and did not believe that India would be capable of achieving dominion status for centuries, if ever.

*

The Montagu–Chelmsford Indian Councils Act provided that there should be a review of its effectiveness after ten years. Smith was initially relaxed. He did not think that the review could lead to any extension of political liberties. But as time passed, he began to worry about what might happen if there were a change of government. He decided it would be safer to accelerate the review by appointing the reviewing commission while he could still make the appointments. 'My present view, therefore, is that . . . we shall in any event, playing for safety, be driven to nominate the Commission in the middle of 1927 . . . We can play with the time as we want.'[1] He dismissed the need to wait the full ten years with typical flippancy: 'Wise men are not the slaves of dates.'

He took care in appointing the Commissioners. He packed it with carefully chosen nominees. Its chairman was Sir John Simon, a politician firmly on the right of the Liberal Party. There were to be no Indians on it. The decision to have an inquiry solely by foreigners into India's capacity for self-government was made against the advice of many, and Congress inevitably called upon Indians not to cooperate with the Commission and organized demonstrations against it. When they reached India, the Commissioners were met with banners reading 'Simon go back'. The Muslim League had said that it would cooperate. In order to bring Congress to heel, Birkenhead ordered that any meetings between Simon and 'representative Moslems' should be publicized in order to 'terrify the immense Hindu population by the apprehension that the Commission is being got hold of by the Moslems and may present a report altogether destructive of the

Hindu position'. In the event, the Muslim League divided, and a part joined in the Congress boycott.

The Commission's report, largely written by Simon himself, was published in two installments on 10 and 24 June 1930. It rather quaintly said that 'The British parliamentary system . . . has been fitted like a well-worn garment to the figure of the wearer, but it does not follow that it will suit everybody . . . British parliamentarianism in India is a translation and in even the best translations the essential meaning is apt to be lost.' The report, as Birkenhead had intended, was, from the point of view of Indian politicians, negative rather than positive. But we needn't take time to dwell on it. It had been overtaken, even before it was delivered, by an initiative on the part of the new viceroy, Lord Irwin.

Irwin confuses newcomers to British–Indian history because he has so many names. He started out as Edward Wood. Before he inherited his father's title, because of the convention that the viceroy should be a peer, he was created Baron Irwin of Kirby Underdale, and it is as Irwin that he is generally known in relation to Indian history. When his father died in January 1934, Irwin became *Viscount* Halifax, and in May 1944 he was created 1st *Earl* of Halifax.

He came to India with great goodwill towards the native population. Indeed, he probably had more genuine sympathy for Indian aspirations than any of his successors until Wavell. His conciliatory approach was criticized as 'Irwinism' by fellow Tories who opposed his policies. Even so, coupled with that goodwill and sympathy, there was the assumption that India should remain within the imperial fold.

Irwin had a degree of respect for Motilal Nehru, father of the future Prime Minister, Jawaharlal Nehru. He considered the old man to be subtle and resourceful, not unreasonable, yet as committed to independence as Gandhi. The viceroy had much less time for Nehru *fils*, Jawaharlal.

The Times pointed out that Irwin had no experience with Oriental problems and, as far as the public was aware, had never displayed any special interest in Indian affairs. That may be true, but it was perhaps no disadvantage to him: he approached the problem of the subcontinent with a fresh mind. He rejected the notion of an essentially *long-term* trust that was to be redeemed some day in the distant future. He said that Birkenhead, the Secretary of State, had in mind a timetable of 600 years.[2] After studying the problem for about three years, Irwin concluded that the timetable should be a short to medium one.

Irwin was decent, not meretricious. Birkenhead's put-down was fairly typical: 'How much better in life and how much more paying it is to be blameless rather than brilliant.'[3] As Irwin's views evolved, he found himself increasingly at odds with his first Secretary of State. But Birkenhead had correctly predicted the turn of the tide. The Conservative Government was replaced at the 1929 election by a minority Labour Government. Even before then, Birkenhead had left the India Office.

He was replaced briefly by Lord Peel and then by William Wedgwood Benn, a brave man who had fought in the First World War, first in the Yeomanry and then in the Royal Naval Air Service. He was a very different man from Birkenhead, and he and Irwin, although in different parties, worked well together.

*

The future of India under British rule was bleak and obscure in view of the limited promises in the Montagu Declaration. Irwin sought to clarify and improve matters. The Irwin Declaration, which eclipsed poor Simon and his commission, was the combined effort of a Labour Government (always more favourable to Indian aspirations than the Conservatives) cohabiting with a high-minded Conservative viceroy. The purpose of the Declaration

was 'to restore faith in the ultimate purpose of British policy'.
It was confirmation that the progress of India's constitutional
development, starting with the Montagu declaration of 1917,
would lead to the achievement of dominion status. The motive
behind the Declaration was Irwin's divergence from Birkenhead
and his wrecking policy. He saw through the Simon Commission.
He knew well, as the Conservative MP Rab Butler did, that
Birkenhead had 'appointed a small Parliamentary Commission,
composed exclusively of the conventional and the then obscure,
and chaired by the highly legalistic Liberal Sir John Simon'. Irwin
wanted positive progress and not negative blocking, and this was
why, at the cost of humiliating Simon and strangling the outcome
of his commission's labours at the moment of its parturition, he
moved the debate forward.

Irwin had in fact advanced far ahead of what his close friend,
the Conservative leader Stanley Baldwin, had intended. It was only
when the *Sunday Times* leaked the news of the Declaration on 13
October 1929, that the detached Baldwin realized how far apart
he and his shadow cabinet colleagues had become from Irwin. He
had made a serious mistake by letting Irwin get on with things in
his own way. He tried to get off the hook by saying that he had
only approved of Irwin's initiative in his personal capacity, not
as party leader. The shadow cabinet was strongly against Irwin's
Declaration. After a meeting on 23 October 1929, Lord Salisbury
wrote to Baldwin, 'I need not say what a shock it was to learn that
the Declaration was to be made before anything had been laid
before the Country, though we had appointed a commission for
this purpose . . . [I]t is cold comfort to me to be told that you—
most honourably—were careful not to commit any of us. What a
dislocation! Poor Conservative Party!'

Baldwin tried to pull Irwin back. Like other members of
his party, he was worried about the vague 'dominion status'
that appeared in the Declaration. This phrase was bound to

be interpreted in India in a manner that neither Irwin nor the government had intended. There was also a question of constitutional propriety. The King told Baldwin that the Simon Commission and its report should not be upstaged by a declaration by the viceroy. Irwin stuck to his guns and Baldwin to his; to his credit, Baldwin said that he would support the policy of this Labour Government (the Conservatives, remember, were in opposition now) and endorse the Declaration.

*

The Declaration was made in the form of an official communiqué in the India *Gazette* on 31 October 1929:

> In view of the doubts which have been expressed both in Great Britain and in India regarding the interpretation to be placed on the intentions of the British government in enacting the Statute of 1919, I am authorised on behalf of His Majesty's Government to state clearly that in their judgement it is implicit in the Declaration of 1917 that the natural issue of India's constitutional progress as there contemplated is the attainment of Dominion status.

What did this mean? The whole purpose of the Irwin Declaration was to clarify the Montagu Declaration. No one had known for twelve years what it *had* meant. But what did *Irwin*'s declaration mean? Crucially, what was meant by 'Dominion status'?

The meaning and evolution of the word 'dominion' are complicated and amorphous topics.* Really, all that matters is that

---

* See Reid, W., *Keeping the Jewel in the Crown: The British Betrayal of India* (Birlinn, Edinburgh, 2016).

the word was so imprecise that it could mean entirely opposite things, depending on what was wanted—or feared.

In 1869, Sir Charles Adderley divided the British Empire into national settlements such as Canada and Australia, which were bound for self-government as a matter of right, and, by contrast, 'occupations for use', which were, as the label suggests, entirely utilitarian and to be disposed of when they no longer served their purpose. There the Crown governed absolutely: 'stations merely occupied for war, depots of trade and subjects of inferior race are fitly so governed'. India fitted into neither category. It would neither be abandoned nor move towards self-government.

*

Even the 'National Settlements' of Canada and Australia were in an ambivalent position. When Churchill wrote *My Early Life* in 1930 (at the height of his battle over India), he referred to Australia and Canada as now being called dominions simply 'in the hopes of pleasing or at least placating them'.[4] Although it was vaguely assumed that they would achieve self-government at some point, they weren't in a position to press for it since they depended for their defence on the Royal Navy. With tiny and insignificant fleets until just before the First World War, they could not claim to be in charge of their own defence or foreign policies. Thus they entered the First World War and ended it more or less on the instructions of the London government. Foreign affairs were reserved for the grown-up parliament, the imperial Parliament. In 1895, the Colonial Secretary had sent a dispatch to the overseas governments to emphasize that they were to have no pretensions in this regard. 'To give the colonies the power of negotiating treaties themselves . . . would be equivalent to breaking up the Empire into a number of independent states.'[5]

And even in domestic matters, although the Dominions were regarded as self-governing and certainly regarded themselves as such, their independence was limited. In terms of the Colonial Laws Validity Act of 1865, the British Parliament could set aside any colonial legislation that was incompatible with British constitutional practice or English common law.

In the Great War, the contribution of Canada, Australia and New Zealand to the allied cause was immense, and their status had to be addressed. An important Imperial Conference was held in 1917, but it left unfinished business in the matter of clarification of the constitutional position of the Dominions. When war with Turkey over Chanak appeared likely in 1922, Lloyd George sent a telegram to the Dominion governments asking for their troops in the expected war and even allowed news of his request to appear in the press. This time, unlike 1914, the Dominion premiers made it clear that they were of an independent mind. At an Imperial Conference in the following year, it was agreed that the Commonwealth countries, as they were being called at the time, had the right to negotiate and sign treaties.

The status of the white Dominions continued to be clarified in a series of limited, *ad hoc* initiatives, including the Balfour Report of 1926 and the Statute of Westminster of 1931. The Balfour Report concluded by saying that there was no point in attempting an imperial *constitution* (how very British) but that the components of the Empire could be described as 'autonomous communities within the British Empire, equal in status, in no way subordinate one to another in any respect of their domestic or external affairs, though united by a common allegiance to the crown, and freely associated as members of the British commonwealth of nations'. This statement left a number of questions unanswered. In particular, did 'free association' mean that the Dominions could withdraw from the Commonwealth if they wanted?

London was not greatly worried by the fact that the question was unanswered. The Commonwealth was a white man's club, and its members could be relied on to sort out their differences quietly and hang together. The die-hards in Britain were equally clear that India could *not* be relied on. Not the least of their concerns was the fact that an independent India had serious defence implications. India provided defence for the Suez Canal and for the connection of Britain's Middle-Eastern territories with the Far East. Churchill referred to this in a BBC broadcast in January 1935, emphasizing the risk in that theatre from the Japanese.

Irwin's critics really needn't have been too worried. One of his advisers conceded that there was a lot of fuss about nothing at all, explaining in the legislative assembly that there were different *degrees* of dominion status. Southern Rhodesia, for instance, was given as an example of a limited dominion. In any event, was Irwin referring to dominion status as it had been at the time of the Montagu declaration in 1917, or had he taken into account—or was he even aware of—the implications of the Balfour Declaration and what might be contained in the not yet enacted Statute of Westminster?

*

Indian nationalists knew what they wanted. As far back as 1906, Congress declared that its object was 'the attainment of a system of government for India similar to that enjoyed by the self-governing dominions of the British Empire'. The same formula was jointly adopted ten years later by Congress and the Muslim League. An All-Party Conference in 1926 under Motilal Nehru recommended that India should have the same constitutional status within the British Empire as the white dominions, 'with a parliament having powers to make laws for the peace, order and good government of

India, and an executive responsible to that parliament, and should be styled and known as the Commonwealth of India'.

Irwin was an honourable man and a man of high religious principle, but he was no firebrand. Before making his Declaration, he read a memorandum from the Indian Home Department, which pretty much said that a commitment to dominium status meant nothing because the practical route to dominion status would be such a long and difficult one, involving as it did reaching first the goal of full responsible government in the context of a huge, scattered and illiterate electorate. There were 'immense obstacles in the path of full responsible government'.[6]

*

However high-minded, principled and limited Irwin's intentions had been, he created immense turmoil. Birkenhead and Reading, a former secretary of state and a former viceroy, were lawyers. They read the words of the Declaration with lawyers' attention to detail, aware of the significance of the Balfour Report and the Statute of Westminster. They were appalled. 'How,' they asked, 'could India, with its communal differences, its many languages and religions, its Indian states and British Indian provinces, and last but not least, its inability to defend itself, become a Dominion after the manner of Canada, Australia and South Africa?'[7] Their hostility was shared by the die-hards, the backwoodsmen of the Conservative Party in Parliament and in the country.

Indian lawyers, and many leading members of the Congress Party *were* lawyers and indeed had been trained and sometimes practised in Britain, equally understood the precise significance of words that Irwin had never intended to be read with such precision. Their demand for independence was whetted by the promises they had been given. Millions more Indians, the millions of followers of Gandhi, were convinced that the promises they had swallowed of independence after the war were now being renewed. But India's political leadership, in Delhi for the announcement of the Declaration, among them Gandhi, Mrs Annie Besant and the Nehrus, were not impressed.

13

India Grips the Commons

So the debate over India was becoming a very live issue at Westminster. It threatened the leadership of the Conservative Party. The Labour Party, many of whose members had close connections with Congress, had long been determined to see India make significant constitutional progress. Now they had the support, albeit unenthusiastic, of the Conservative Party. Baldwin was an insecure leader of his party for the moment. The Tories were unimpressed by his lethargic style. He was under challenge and not expected to last for long (although his fortunes turned and he did last until 1937). He was determined to do one worthwhile thing before he was deposed. He was intent on advancing the cause of Indian constitutional progress. He was opposed by the right wing of the party and vulnerable to potential challengers, among whom Churchill was prominent.

The result was something akin to a civil war in the party. Lord Rothermere's *Daily Mail* wanted the promise of dominion status cancelled. 'British rule in India is irreplaceable. Our duty there is not to argue with base agitators BUT TO GOVERN'. Churchill wrote an important article for the paper in November

1929. He looked at what Britain had done for India. He thought that the Raj had rescued India from barbarism and was preparing it for 'civilisation'. Against the beneficial influence of the Raj, he contrasted the horrors of the Hindu attitude towards the 'untouchables'—60 million Dalits who would forever be downtrodden if a Hindu majority took power. Churchill always tended to see the world divided between good and evil. The Empire deserved to be preserved because it was a force for good. Birkenhead agreed: 'The appetite of the Indians would merely be whetted by the Declaration, which would lead them to further and more extravagant demands'.

Irwin was far too grand an aristocrat to be bothered by the storm. The *Daily Mail* said that he was part of the section of the Conservative Party 'which manifested dangerous leanings towards platonic flirtations with Socialism', an interesting concept. He affected surprise.

*

The tension in London was exacerbated by events in India. The demand for progress exploded. On his way in his private train to take up residence for the first time in Lutyens' new Viceregal Lodge, Irwin's private train exploded too. A bomb blew a hole four feet wide in the rails. Irwin wasn't particularly disturbed by the bomb; he said he was used to his Cona coffee machine blowing up.

While many Tories were horrified by how far the Declaration went, the reaction in India was that it did not go nearly far enough. Jawaharlal Nehru and Subhas Chandra Bose rejected gradualism and demanded immediate independence.

Part of Irwin's proposals involved a Round Table conference in London. This did not appeal to Congress. Jawaharlal Nehru was against political advancement by negotiation. Congress issued the

Delhi Manifesto, in which they agreed to attend the conference, but only in return for the release of political prisoners and on the understanding that the purpose of the conference was not to determine whether or when dominion status was to be reached but to draft a constitution for the Dominion. This was not acceptable to London, and Congress boycotted the conference.

In March 1930, Gandhi began his new civil disobedience campaign, which concluded with the famous Salt March to the sea, where he would make salt from the sea water, thus subverting the Government's salt tax. Reports of the civil disobedience campaign sustained Churchill's allegation that Britain was losing the will to govern. The home member of the viceroy's Executive Council complained that 'the Government may not be retaining that essential moral superiority, which is perhaps the most important factor in the struggle'.[1] It is interesting that he used the word struggle. Irwin was disappointed by the Indian reaction. He told Wedgwood Benn, 'Though I am, as you know, a pacifist by nature, I am not disposed to go all lengths to meet people who seem to be behaving with utter unreason.' Gandhi was arrested in May 1930. In his absence, one of his supporters, Mrs Naidu, plus 2500 volunteers raided the Dharsana salt depots. Jawaharlal Nehru was arrested, and those regarded as troublemakers were thrown into jails throughout India. The press was muzzled. The Working Committee of Congress was declared an unlawful association, and along with the All-India Congress Committee, it was outlawed. Even Motilal Nehru, the venerable President of the All-India Congress Committee, went to prison.

*

The First Round Table Conference met in London but, without Congress, ended in failure. In January 1931, Irwin released Gandhi and his supporters. The gesture was unpopular amongst provincial officers, local district officers and the army, and it was badly received by British opinion. The Right saw it as another contemptible example of Irwin's liberal weaknesses.

Even Gandhi did not respond particularly well to his release; his first act was to call for an inquiry into police excesses during the emergency. But he decided to engage, and he wrote a letter to the viceroy in tones that suggested that he was prepared to confer on the representative of the King–Emperor the privilege of an audience. This led to his being photographed between two soldiers of the viceroy's bodyguard climbing the steps of Lutyens' Viceregal Palace and Churchill's famous reaction in which he said how painful it was to 'see Mr Gandhi, a seditious Middle Temple lawyer, now posing as a fakir of a type well known in the East, striding half naked up the steps of the Viceregal Palace, while he is still organising a defiant campaign of civil disobedience, to parley on equal terms with the representative of the King–Emperor'. He was not alone in his views. He was supported by the *Daily Mail* and many leading members of the Conservative Party. He talked of Irwin 'doing obeisance before Gandhi' and said that it was 'like feeding cats' meat to a tiger'.

Irwin was undeterred by political criticism. He met Gandhi on no fewer than eight occasions after his release from prison. He wrote to his father, saying that 'it was rather like talking to someone who had stepped off another planet on to this for a short visit of a fortnight and whose whole mental outlook was quite other to that which was regulating most of the affairs on the planet to which he had descended'.[2] One of the Congress members who worked with Gandhi at this time wrote thirty years later to the second Earl of Birkenhead, the author of Irwin's official biography:

'Faith in a higher Power and sincere allegiance to moral principles bound Lord Irwin and Mahatma Gandhi together from the first time when they met and it lasted right through.

They became friends in a common cause though they began as consecrated knights in opposing camps. The Gandhi–Irwin Pact over the salt *Satyagraha* was a historic memorial of what two God-fearing men could achieve though history placed them in opposite camps.[3]

The pact meant the end of the salt boycott and the end of the civil disobedience campaign, and it allowed Gandhi to attend the Second Round Table Conference in London between September and December of 1931. In his dhoti and sandals, Gandhi attracted much attention—and catcalls from children: 'Hey Gandhi, where's your trousers'.* But nothing much was achieved. The third and last Round Table Conference took place from November to December 1932. Few of the main Indian politicians were present. The Congress Party boycotted the conference, as did the British Labour Party.

*

By now, the government in London had resolved that it would have to take the initiative in seeking a solution. The division between Congress and the Muslim League, not to mention the separate issue of the Princely States, had made it clear that no

---

* George V was very doubtful about receiving Gandhi. 'What, have this rebel fakir in the palace after he has been behind all these attacks on my loyal officers!' He also had reservations about having 'the little man' in the palace with 'no proper clothes on and bare knees'. The meeting took place, but the Secretary of State, Hoare, was alarmed to see the king looking resentfully more than once at the knees. When Gandhi was about to leave, the king warned him, 'Remember, Mr Gandhi, I won't have any attacks on my Empire!' Gandhi's manners were better than the king's. 'I must not be drawn into a political argument in your Majesty's palace after receiving your Majesty's hospitality.'

agreement would emerge from negotiations. It would have to be imposed. The government at this time was the National Government, a coalition of Conservatives, the official Labour Party and various elements of the Liberal Party, very much dominated by the Conservatives, with Stanley Baldwin and Neville Chamberlain, supported by a very significant Conservative majority of backbenchers, at its effective head. A White Paper on India was tabled in March 1933, and a joint, that is, all-party, parliamentary select committee under Lord Linlithgow studied the Paper from April 1933 to November 1934. The House of Commons approved the Paper, and the enormous Government of India Bill was framed. It would become law as the Government of India Act on 2 August 1935.*

This, then, was the background to Churchill's mischievous and malevolent campaign from 1929 to 1935. In the course of it, he succeeded in destroying his personal position in the Conservative Party, in setting up tensions between the three elements of the Indian polity, Hindus, Muslims and the princes, and in so doing, to his own immense satisfaction, ensuring that the legislation would never achieve the positive and desirable purposes that it was intended to attain.

---

* The scale of the legislative effort was unprecedented. About 2000 speeches were made in the course of the debates, amounting to around 1,55,00,000 words.

14

Churchill and the Bill

It is frequently said that Churchill adopted opposition to the India Bill simply to advance his career. That was not the case. He was already established, as his rivals were all too well aware, as potentially the next Prime Minister—if not indeed the next Prime Minister—and while, like Lord Lundy, he was easily moved to tears, there was little danger that he would be sent out to govern New South Wales.[*]

By espousing a minority campaign in India, albeit a campaign supported by much of his party in the country, Churchill did his career enormous damage and reinforced his reputation for disloyalty, ambition and—above all—lack of judgement. Baldwin claimed to have written a speech in which he would tell the story

---

[*] Hiliare Belloc's Cautionary Tale, *Lord Lundy, Who was too Freely Moved to Tears, and Thereby ruined his Political Career*, tells of the eponymous anti-hero, whose sensitivity was his political downfall. His Grandfather, the Duke, tells him that, 'We had intended you to be / The next Prime Minister but three: / The Stocks were sold, the Press was squared: / The Middle Class was quite prepared: / But as it is! . . . my language fails! / Go out and govern New South Wales!'

of Churchill's being born surrounded by fairies who conferred on
him every imaginable gift, charm, eloquence, wit and so forth.
One fairy thought that far too many benefits were being conferred
on the boy. Her gift was a lack of judgement.

In 1935, the Government of India Bill was enacted, and
Churchill's role in opposing this liberal measure had come to
an end—and come to an end satisfactorily in his view: he was
convinced that the Act in its final form was bound to block any
movement towards self-government for the foreseeable future.
But at a personal level, he was in the wilderness, unlikely as it
seemed to ever attain office again. Had it not been for the war in
1939—and for the peculiar political dynamics of the time—it is
almost certain that he never would have returned to office. The
attack on Indian reform all but hijacked his political career.

*

Churchill was in the United States in the autumn of 1929 when
the shadow cabinet learned about the Irwin Declaration. On his
return to Britain, he immediately wrote the *Daily Mail* article
already referred to, contrasting benevolent British rule with the
existence of institutions such as the caste system. It would be his
argument throughout the following years that the demand for
dominion status came from an unrepresentative minority who
had no concern for the 60 million Dalits. This argument, spurious
though it was, came across better than overtly reactionary malice. In
December, he tried again to speak about India to ordinary people.
This time, it was not the *Daily Mail* but the BBC that he sought
to use. Astonishingly, he offered £100 to the Director General, Sir
John Reith, in return for being allowed to broadcast a ten-minute
appeal on India. Having consulted Wedgwood Benn, Reith said
that he was unwilling to introduce 'American' methods into British
broadcasting. Churchill replied: 'I am sure the American plan would

be better than the present British methods of debarring public men from access to a public who wish to hear. You are certainly obstructing me.'[1] The relationship between Churchill and Reith never mellowed. Reith's hatred for Churchill was more irrational than Churchill's perception that Reith, 'Old Wuthering Heights' as he called him, had ambitions unsupported by his abilities.

In the course of the year that followed the Irwin Declaration, Churchill became more and more disenchanted with the shadow cabinet's position, not just on India but on the difficult issue of Free Trade *vs* Imperial Preference. Publicly and privately, he argued against tariff reform, and despite retaining a superficially genial relationship with him, he increasingly came to regard Baldwin as a weak and indecisive leader. He saw this lack of leadership paralleled in the diminution of Britain's place in the world. He was depressed that the sacrifices that had been made in the First World War appeared to have been for nothing. Britain was now, as he thought, a second-rate naval power, and her authority in the Middle East had diminished. He overlooked the fact that, as Chancellor, he had reduced spending on the Navy and, as Colonial Secretary, had discouraged consolidation in the Middle East. India was the focus of his campaign for national regeneration. It alarmed him to think that it was now perfectly on the cards that Britain would clear out of India altogether. That would be an explicit recognition of the end of Britain as a great power. In September 1930, Churchill observed that tribesmen on the North–West Frontier were attacking Peshawar, despite its large British garrison. This was a reflection of Britain's diminished authority in India.

He spoke and wrote incessantly about India, and in response to a rumour that he was considering retirement from public life (which he was not), he issued a statement on 28 September 1930, saying that he would certainly not do so while the question of India was still under debate.

Churchill's position on India then differed from that of the shadow cabinet well before he resigned. Baldwin was advocating a bipartisan approach, supportive of the government and dominion status. This was opposed by Beaverbrook and his *Daily Express*. Beaverbrook was putting up his own candidates against official Conservatives at by-elections. Though his relations with the Beaver were strained because of the latter's campaign for imperial preference, Churchill openly supported his friend in his attacks on the party of which he was one of the leaders. He was very close to the other press baron, Lord Rothermere, who encouraged Churchill to keep repeating his message: 'Frequent repetition is the only method by which [modern electorates] can be influenced . . . We have a splendid cause. If India is not held, there is nothing for England but bankruptcy and revolution.'[2] Churchill was ready to sacrifice his time, although he grudged the fact that preparing a speech cost him between £300 and £400 in lost journalism income.

The battle between Churchill and *his* press, on the one hand, and Baldwin and *The Times*, on the other, was mirrored by the battle between the Indian Empire Society, which had been launched in July 1930, largely at the instigation of Sir Michael O'Dwyer, whom we met as Lieutenant Governor of the Punjab at the time of the Jallianwalla Bagh Massacre, and the Conservative Central Office. J.C.C. Davidson, the Chairman of the Conservative Party, orchestrated a plan to support party policy and stiffen the back benches. He employed correspondence in the press, weekly 'talking' films, and the use of a picked team of young MPs with a gift for communication.

Despite that, Churchill felt that he was winning the argument and that the mood of the Conservative Party was with him. There is no doubt that the party was rattled. Churchill was due to speak at the Albert Hall on 18 March 1931; to pre-empt it and make his views known, Baldwin went to the length of asking Ramsay MacDonald, the Prime Minister, to adjust parliamentary procedure so that he could speak in a Supply Debate six days before Churchill's speech. In his speech, Baldwin argued that India should be apart from and above party politics. Indeed, the debate was an internal one within the Conservative Party and not a matter of division between the two parties. When Churchill came to make his Albert Hall speech, it was punctuated by outbursts as much from fellow Conservatives as from Liberal and Labour supporters. Baldwin's Commons speech, in which he attacked extremists 'at Home and in India' was much more moderate and widely regarded as a triumph, perhaps the best he had ever made.

Churchill's deviation from official Conservative policy became steadily more evident. He opposed the Round Table Conference that Baldwin supported. He hoped that its collapse would lead to an end to the moves towards dominion status. He made defiant public speeches despite pressure not to. In reaction to Gandhi's ascent of the steps of the Viceregal Palace, he attacked his own party's policy as well as the government's. In reply, Baldwin pledged his party's support for the Government.

It was on the following day that Churchill resigned from the Business Committee of the party, as the shadow cabinet was then known. Part of his reason for doing so was certainly his attachment to Free Trade. He also had to make some money. He had lost a lot in the American Stock Market Crash. He needed time to replenish his coffers. He was not receiving a ministerial salary, and he had recently bought Chartwell, which was costing an enormous amount of money—much to Clemmie's concern. When the Government lost the 1929 election, Churchill went off on a protracted speaking tour of the United States, and while he was there, he signed contracts worth £40,000 for magazine articles.[3] * But India was the real reason for the resignation. He said he had reached a 'breaking point' over Conservative support for

---

* In 1930 a senior cabinet minister, such as the Chancellor of the Exchequer, received £5,000 a year, including his allowance as a member of Parliament.

the Government's India Bill.[4] He was certain that India was going to be 'the greatest problem of British politics' in the 1930s.[5] He was much more flexible about the move to the imposition of taxes on non-imperial foodstuffs, following the Ottowa agreements of 1932. He could be flexible about other parts of the Empire, but not India.

Churchill was very confident that his line would appeal to the mass of the Conservative Party. It is doubtful if it truly gripped the rank and file. It was popular with the existing die-hards but didn't add to their numbers. And a lengthy period in which Baldwin had been weak and criticized as leader of the Opposition came to an end on 19 March 1930, when an unofficial candidate, challenging his authority, stood at a by-election in the Westminster St George's Division and was roundly defeated. From now until he resigned in 1937, Baldwin was unassailable, and Churchill remained in the cold until then, and indeed for two years after Baldwin's resignation.

At the height of the campaign by the Beaverbrook and Rothermere Press, Rothermere had told him that, in view of his Indian campaign, he could succeed to the leadership of the Party: 'If you go unswervingly forward, nothing can stand in your way.'[6] But Baldwin's victory at the Westminster St George's by-election put paid to that.

*

While Free Trade meant less to Churchill than opposition to Indian policy, that is not to say that it didn't matter. The two issues were linked. It is an interesting conjunction that on 14 October 1930, he both told Baldwin that he could not support the Conservative Party if it went to the country on a Tariff Reform platform and also formally joined the Indian Empire Society and sent in his subscription. On 12 December, exactly a month after the First Round Table Conference had opened, Churchill was the principal speaker at the Society's first public meeting at the Cannon Street Hotel. He claimed that even the moderate Indian representatives at the conference were demanding full dominion status 'with the right to secede from the British Empire'. He talked about the British Raj being replaced by 'the Gandhi Raj'. If that happened, then there would be tensions between the Hindu majority and the Muslims and the princes. He returned to the Dalits and said that the 60 million of them would be denied a semblance of human rights. On the following day, Irwin wrote to Geoffrey Dawson, the editor of *The Times*: 'What a monstrous speech Winston has just made.'

Dawson was in complete agreement. He had already said in a leader that Churchill was 'no more representative of the Conservative Party [than] the assassins of Calcutta' represented the Indians at the Round Table. Churchill was not discouraged and, in the following months, made many more speeches of the same sort. He found the whole process invigorating. On 8 January 1931 he wrote to his son, Randolph, who was in the United States: 'I am going to fight this Indian business *à outrance* . . . I am sure that events will justify every word.'[7]

Sir Samuel Hoare, the Tory spokesman on India and soon to be the Secretary of State for India, sought to ensure that the Tory representatives at the Round Table talks supported the shadow cabinet line. Churchill regretted the exclusion of Sir John Simon, whose negative approach he preferred to Irwin's positivism about dominion status. He maintained that Simon had been excluded to please Gandhi, 'this malevolent fanatic', and at the request 'of a handful of disloyal Indian politicians'. He urged Baldwin not to allow his friendship with Irwin to affect his judgement.

*

In a speech in the Commons on 13 May 1931, Churchill touched on an important element of the opposition to Indian independence: the trade implications of dominion status. He said that as a Dominion, India would have the right, like Canada, Australia and New Zealand, to embargo or exclude British goods and to distinguish between Indian producers and British importers. That, he said, was why the mill owners of Bombay and Ahmedabad had given their support to Gandhi. He claimed to be concerned that, without British control, labour and safety regulations in the Indian mills would go by the board. He also claimed that a boycott was being urged against British-manufactured goods by the tyrannical Congress Hindus. It 'enriches their wealthy friends and . . . ruins Lancashire'. As always, he went on to stress the dangers of sectarian division. Shouting across noisy interruptions, he told his own front bench, 'By your actions you have produced misery such as India has not seen for half a century. You have poisoned relations between the Mohammedans and the Hindus.'[8]

*

Early in 1933, after the collapse of the Round Table Conferences, the new Conservative-dominated National Government began to firm up its Indian policy and prepare the White Paper on the basis of an all-India federal scheme. Churchill had continued to campaign against the Government's proposals. He had hitherto kept a distance from the most extreme die-hards—elderly Tories, whose policies had been a caricature of all that was immoderate and illiberal. Churchill was different from the die-hards in at least four ways. He had been a Liberal, indeed of a fairly radical disposition. They did not like that. Secondly, he was not a protectionist, and they were. As Chancellor of the Exchequer, he had resisted protectionism and was still emotionally committed to Free Trade. Thirdly, he would ultimately have been quite content to bring down the Government. Many said that that was indeed his true intention. Most of the die-hards were ultra-loyal Conservatives. Finally, he was much cleverer than they were. In a debate on 12 March 1931, Churchill took pains to refer to his attack on Dyer in the House ten years earlier—indeed, Baldwin reminded the House of Churchill's liberal stance on the issue. But he was increasingly implored by the extremists on the Conservative benches to join them formally in their opposition to the Government's Indian policy. He succumbed to their advances, and he was very soon perceived to be at the centre of the opposition to the Government's policy. A meeting took place between all the MPs who had hitherto voted against the Government's India policy. Churchill said that this group would be a nucleus of opposition in the House of Commons. It formally became just that a couple of weeks later, calling itself the India Defence Committee and consisting of about fifty Conservative MPs.

*

J.C.C Davidson, the Chairman of the Conservative Party, told Churchill in the House of Commons smoking room 'that I thought that the British public was much more interested in the size of their pay-packet on Friday than by great oratorical appeals to their loyalty to the British Empire. I told him that they might cheer him, but they wouldn't vote for him. He didn't like it a bit'.[9] Davidson was right.

Churchill's opposition to government policy may have gone down well with the die-hards and their supporters outside Parliament, but to the majority of MPs on both benches, he was becoming an object of derision.

He was seen as obstinate and blinkered. He made unsubstantiated assertions. He claimed that officials in the Indian Civil Service were promoted depending on their willingness to promote government policy. Austen Chamberlain recorded in his diary how, on this issue, 'Winston stammered and blundered and for the rest of a very long speech had a steadily dwindling and offended audience. The fact of the matter is that on this subject he has become hysterical. It is impossible to discuss it with him.'[10] Attlee, the most prominent 'Indian' on the Labour benches, could see the damage Churchill had done to himself. 'If the Tories had a leader, they would like to oust MacDonald, but there is no one at present, Churchill having cut his throat.'[11] India had, it seemed, become an obsession for Churchill. Just as leaving the shadow cabinet to start his campaign made no sense in terms of political advancement, his continuation of the campaign was a cause that had nothing to do with opportunism. J.C.C Davidson said that Churchill cut very little ice with the Conservative Party. 'In fact, the die-hard Tories who opposed us [the government] over India never regarded him as a Conservative at all but as a renegade Liberal who had crossed the floor. He was regarded as unstable politically.'[12] His long-time ally, Beaverbrook, said that Churchill had set out on a farewell tour of politics.[13]

*

But Churchill's views on India were, in truth, not those of an unreconstructed die-hard. They were the outcome of how he read events since 1914 and their implication for him of national decline. This is brought out well in an exchange between him and Linlithgow in 1933. Linlithgow, chairman of the all-party committee on India, wrote to him in conciliatory terms, saying that he too only wished that the India of 1900 could be recreated in 1934 but that this was an impossibility. Churchill's reply made it clear that he was not trying to turn back the clock but was looking ahead. He did not see 'the future as a mere extension of the past . . . In my view England is now beginning a new period of struggle and fighting for its life, and the crux of it will be not only the retention of India but a much stronger assertion to her commercial rights . . . [W]e are justified in using our undoubted power for [India's] welfare and for our own'.[14]

Linlithgow tried to persuade Churchill to leave off his campaign, as much in Churchill's own interests as the Government's. He argued that the White Paper scheme, in some shape or form, would go through and that Churchill would be better off concentrating on opposing the Government's trade and tariff scheme instead. Churchill replied that his interest in India had nothing to do with personal ambition, that it was indeed the only thing that kept him active in politics, and that he would continue to oppose Indian policy, whatever damage it did to his career.

Whether they believed it or not, the Government promoted the view that Churchill's motives were purely selfish and that he and his associates were attacking party organizations in the constituencies primarily to smash the National Government. Sir Samuel Hoare, now the India Secretary, spoke for many when he claimed that Churchill's real objective was to force the government out. Churchill and his supporters were frequently called the Winston Crowd or Winston's Stage Army.

*

Churchill had to decide how the Winston Crowd would be represented on the joint select committee, which would consider the White Paper. He wrote to the Chief Whip, David Margesson. He acknowledged that the Government had to have an effective majority but claimed that he and his colleagues represented three-quarters, or at least half, of the Tory Party in the constituencies. The joint select committee was to be composed of both MPs and peers. He argued that if there were to be twelve government supporters, the opponents should have eight places, four from each House.

Would Churchill himself join the committee? At the end of March, Hoare wrote to him, asking him to do so. Churchill took some time to reply. He was aggrieved that the committee appeared to contain twenty-five supporters of the government's policy against nine opponents. He was in considerable doubt about what to do and consulted widely. Finally, on 5 April, he replied to Hoare, saying that he saw no point in joining a committee that was so stacked in favour of the Government: 'I will have neither part nor lot in the deed you seek to do.'[15] Many of Churchill's supporters were surprised by his decision, but he stuck to the argument that he could be more effective outside the emasculated committee than inside it.

15

Trade, Lancashire and the Committee of Privileges

By 1830, cotton goods accounted for half the value of British exports. The manufacturing of cotton goods was initially the main focus of the Industrial Revolution. Only later did iron and steel come to be the focus of British industry; cotton had primed the pump. By 1860, Britain, with 2 per cent of the world's population, was producing half the world's iron and steel and monopolizing 40 per cent of world trade in manufactured goods.[1]

India was as important a market for iron and steel products as it was for cotton. Britain suppressed native industries and made India dependent on the import of British-manufactured goods. But by the 1930s, India's economic relations with Britain had been turned on their heads. India cost Britain much more money than the income it produced. The cotton industry in Lancashire, in particular, suffered. Instead of enjoying a monopoly on supplying cotton goods to India, Lancashire had to watch as India manufactured her own cotton goods or bought them from Japan.

How significant was the Lancashire cotton lobby? Churchill probably used the lobby more than he was used by it. He stressed his historical connection with Oldham, his attachment to the area and his concern that increased moves towards Indian independence would adversely affect the interests of Lancashire's cotton industry. Thus, in select committee hearings, the Manchester Chamber of Commerce argued that India's ability to regulate her own trade should be restricted.

At a meeting of the joint select committee on 3 November 1933, the senior representative of the Manchester Chamber of Commerce, Harold Rodier, was asked whether Manchester had any alterations to suggest to the White Paper. He replied in the negative and repeated his 'no' when asked a second time. Four months later, in March 1934, there were rumours that there had been serious impropriety and that an earlier Chamber of Commerce submission, prepared in May and June 1933, had said in the strongest terms that the White Paper constitution would affect Lancashire badly: India's Finance Ministry could penalize importations from Lancashire in the interests of supporting the mills in Bombay and Ahmedabad. The original submission had been quite detailed in its arguments, and now, it was alleged, the Chamber had changed their evidence in the face of direct pressure from two senior members of the committee: Lord Derby, who represented Lancashire on the committee, and Sir Samuel Hoare, the Secretary of State himself.

Churchill had been leaked details of this interference by a director of Associated Newspapers Limited, part of Lord Rothermere's stable, and he made further investigations himself, speaking to the Foreign Editor of the *Daily Mail*. He came quickly to the conclusion that these two members of the committee had exerted pressure on a witness to change his evidence and that this represented a breach of the privileges of Parliament. He submitted the documents to the Speaker of the House of Commons and asked that a committee of privileges examine the issue. He was hopeful that the matter could be built up in the press into an enormous scandal.

Lord Derby was a man of prodigious significance in Lancashire, where he was often referred to as the Uncrowned King. He was in a position to influence the Lancashire delegation. Moreover, it is now thought that, unknown to Churchill at the time, there was further evidence that never came to light that Derby *had* indeed acted improperly. There was also damaging correspondence from Hoare to the viceroy, Lord Willingdon, which revealed the pressure that was being put on the Lancastrians. Had all this been available to Churchill, the outcome might have been very different.

Hoare and his advisers had to spend weeks refreshing their memories about the events to which Churchill's allegations related. Hoare spent two days giving evidence and never forgot the resentment he felt as he waited outside the House of Commons Committee Room to be summoned for his cross-examination, 'as if I were a prisoner outside the courtroom in the Old Bailey'.[2]

The resort to the committee of privileges was incautious and reinforced the view that Churchill was capricious and lacking in judgement. The inquiry was, in truth, hardly a model of open justice. The die-hards were not represented, and Churchill was denied the opportunity to cross-examine and question witnesses. The committee absolved the government on the technical basis that the joint select committee had not been a judicial body and was therefore not bound by the rules that Churchill alleged it had broken. The complaint was dismissed.

Churchill should have accepted the situation, but he argued the case in the House, appearing bitter, obsessed and unbalanced. After him, Leo Amery spoke. The careers of Leo Amery and Winston Churchill had been intertwined from an early point. They had both been pupils at Harrow. Churchill, thinking that Amery was his contemporary or even a junior, pushed him into the school swimming pool. Amery was, in fact, his senior, and the consequences could have been serious. Churchill attempted to defuse the situation by saying that he had not realized Amery's seniority because he was so small. (Amery was indeed quite small; it was said that if he had been half a foot taller and his speeches half an hour shorter, he might have been Prime Minister). Realizing that this hardly improved matters, he went on to say that his own father, who was a great man, was also very small. Amery was amused and let the matter drop. But perhaps he had never forgotten the episode. In the course of his speech, he set a trap. He used the Latin quotation, *'Fiat justitia ruat caelum'.*[*] It's a convention in the Commons that speeches should be in English. Churchill fell into the trap. He asked for a translation. Amery had it ready; he said that it meant, 'If I can trip up Sam [Hoare] the government's bust.' It was an effective ruse, touching on the prevalent conviction that Churchill's primary interest was to seize the leadership of the party. Much more seriously, it made Churchill look silly. That was the end of the affair with the committee of privileges.

*

After that debacle, Churchill continued to concern himself with Lancashire. He spoke in the Manchester Free Trade Hall on 26 June and, a few days, later published an attack on Derby in the *Sunday Dispatch*, alleging again that he had forced the Chamber of Commerce into silence about the grievances they feared. Derby wanted to respond to the charge, but Baldwin persuaded him to stay silent. The Conservatives recognized that Churchill had a substantial following in the county and in working class areas. Hoare wrote that Winston 'and his crowd are arranging a series of

---

[*] 'Let justice be done, even if the heavens fall.'

mill meetings at which they hope to stir up trouble'.[3] Churchill's son, Randolph, also did a lot of speaking in Lancashire, and on 6 May 1934, he proposed a motion at the conference of the Junior Imperial League opposing the White Paper. His motion was defeated by just 210 votes to 159.

In early January 1935, Randolph decided to stand as 'an anti-India Bill' Conservative candidate against an official Conservative candidate at a by-election in the Lancashire seat of Wavertree. Churchill had not been consulted and thought Randolph's decision very unwise, likely simply to split the Conservative vote and let the Labour candidate in. But there was nothing he could do. He contributed financially to his son's campaign, allowed his daughters, Sarah and Diana, to go to help Randolph, and promised to attend on the eve of the poll. The India Defence League executive equally thought that they should have been consulted but decided to support Randolph. Churchill's prediction was correct. Randolph received a vote of 10,575 and the official Conservative candidate 13,771. The Labour Party candidate was elected with a vote of 15,611. Another black mark for the Churchills in the Whips' office.

At the end of January, before the Wavertree vote, Sir Samuel Hoare presented the India Home Rule Bill to the Commons. On 29 January, Churchill broadcast on the BBC. He said, '[W]hat is this India Home Rule Bill? I will tell you. It is a gigantic quilt of jumbled crochet work. There is no theme; there is no pattern; there is no agreement; there is no conviction; there is no simplicity; there is no courage.' The following sentence appears in two versions: It is sometimes rendered, 'It is a monstrous monument of shame built by pygmies.' It's generally thought, however, that the fourth last word was 'sham', and that makes sense. Churchill was meticulous in his choice of words, and the Bill was, on his argument, inherently flawed by the fact that a federal framework for India could never transcend the fissures between the different communities; it purported to provide something that was incapable of delivery.

As one is drawn into the bitter internal dispute within the Conservative Party, as the increments of vehemence pile up on each other, one develops a resistance to the bilious rhetoric, and it is possible to fail to see quite how astonishingly hostile Churchill was to his own party. He really couldn't have thought that he and his supporters were likely to defeat the Bill. He hoped in the committee to make it ineffective by wrecking interventions, but it is difficult to think that he would ever recover the respect and affection of his own party members. Hoare wrote to the viceroy, Willingdon, two days after the broadcast:

> I listened to Winston on the wireless. As you will have seen he made the most extreme speech that he has hitherto made. I hope that it was too extreme for the BBC hearers who are on the whole rather a quiet lot. In any case it shows that he is as truculent as ever. It is, therefore, greatly to be hoped that Randolph does really badly and that the effect of his failure will depress Winston before the committee stage comes on.[4]

The second reading of the Bill took place in the first week of February. Churchill entertained some members of the India Defence League's parliamentary committee to dinner, including Sir Michael O'Dwyer, General Dyer's superior at Amritsar, to discuss coordination of opposition to the Bill. On 11 February, Churchill made the final opposition speech in the second reading debate. He was quite frank and said that he and his fellows would establish in their speeches the idea 'that we are there forever'. There was no question of dominion status, of India moving on as the white colonies had done, or of India taking its place as a great independent nation. The Bill passed its second reading by 404 votes to 133. Labour had tabled an amendment that explicitly committed the Government to conferring dominion status on India. Eighty-four Conservatives voted against the Government.

The committee stage opened on 19 February and lasted thirty days. The clauses were challenged one by one. Churchill was aggrieved that the Government kept their supporters on standby so that amendments could be defeated if they went to a vote. Churchill's men chose, for the most part, not to press the amendments. He wanted to wear down the Government's supporters without giving them the satisfaction of defeating him. The point in the legislation that was most at risk was the federal notion. Here, Churchill and his supporters spread the story that the scheme was being worked up by way of shadowy deals between the Government and certain well-bribed princes.

But on 25 February, when the princes met in Bombay, they rejected the Federation. This was exactly what Churchill wanted. He leapt into action. Just a matter of hours later, Churchill told the committee, that in light of developments, the Bill would have to be abandoned. The Government said no, that the princes would just have to do what they were told. On this occasion, the matter went to a vote. Churchill was defeated by 283 votes to eighty-nine. This represented the largest number of votes he was able to muster at any stage in the parliamentary process. He was not dissatisfied; he thought that whether or not the government had won the vote, the Bill was scuppered by the princes' decision. Indeed Hoare and his colleagues did consider whether the Bill would have to be abandoned.[5] Hoare had been in an embarrassing position on the committee. *Churchill* had been privy to what was going on in India and knew about the princes' vote as soon as it was taken, while Hoare was clearly ignorant. The government's position was that if the princes made the government drop the Bill, there was not the least chance of them introducing another one. The government might fall, but there would be no more Indian legislation for years to come. For that reason, the legislative process continued, but it had been a pivotal moment. Although the government was to get the legislation on the statute book, because of the princes' decision, federation, the object of that legislation, was never achieved or even remotely close to achievement.

*

Clementine Churchill was away at this time on a six-month cruise to the East Indies and Australia on board Lord Moyne's yacht, *Rosaura*. Churchill wrote to her a day or two after the princes' bombshell. He told her that he was in the House all day long, two or three days a week, speaking three or four times a day, always without notes, 'and I have I think got the House fairly subordinate . . . I seem to be able to hold my own and indeed knock the Government about to almost any extent'. He described the government's supporters as cowed, resentful and sullen. But his main news was about the princes. He wrote with some excitement about the collapse of the government's plans. Some years before, the princes had been the principal architects of the federal scheme, but here they were rejecting it. This frustration at the smooth progress to dominion status and a federal Parliament filled him with delight. He felt that all the main players in the Indian political scene, not just the princes, had rejected the Government's plan. 'This is a political fact of capital importance. It wrecks the federal scheme against which I have been fighting so long.'[6] That was no doubt written in a moment of unreflective exuberance, but it was pretty near the mark. The princes' attitude, along with the cumbrous legislation for the protection of minorities, rendered the Bill unworkable.

Churchill's delight over his creative destructiveness was spoiled again by Randolph, always capable of making a mess of things. Undeterred by his failure at Wavertree, he found another by-election, this time in the south London constituency of Norwood, where he wanted to stand against the official Conservative candidate, Duncan Sandys. Just to make his plans even more crass, Duncan Sandys would be marrying Churchill's daughter Diana later in the year. This time, Randolph didn't present his father with a *fait accompli*. He told his father what he was planning to do. They had a violent disagreement, and he stormed off in anger. In the event, Randolph did not himself stand but promoted the candidature of Richard Findlay. At the by-election on 14 March, poor Findlay came last in the poll, losing his deposit. Duncan Sandys was elected.

Churchill still hoped that the Government might drop the legislation in view of the princes' opposition. Hoare wrote to the viceroy on 15 March: '[S]o far as the princes' resolution goes, we are still walking on a volcano. Winston and his friends are honestly convinced that they have destroyed Federation and their joy over it is really repulsive.'[7]

By the last week of March, the committee was looking at some fairly technical points. Churchill didn't bother attending assiduously now, and the government was able to rattle through some sixty clauses in no time at all. By this stage, he was increasingly relaxed about the outcome. Even if the bill were enacted, he felt it was now fairly irrelevant. He wrote to his wife on 13 April: 'Of course the Government will get their beastly Bill through, but as the princes will not come in, all the parts I have objected to will remain a dead letter.'[8]

He was not upset—far from it—by the fact that the machinery of government would be worse and the interests of the ordinary Indian would not be well served.

The committee stage continued, with the opposition within the Conservative party keeping below ninety out of a total Conservative potential of 473. The third reading of the Bill took place on 4 June. Churchill had given a dinner at Claridge's on 31 May for those who intended to speak against the Bill again. In the final vote, there were only 122 against the Bill, eighty-four of them Conservatives. The Bill was now an Act of Parliament.

For all the nervous energy that Churchill had injected into his opposition to the Bill, he took the outcome, which he had expected, with equanimity. He was never a man to hold grudges, and very speedily, indeed, he set about reconciling himself with the Conservative leadership. To an extent, he had already turned the focus of his attention to the European situation, and he thought that in any event, he had little to worry about from the final form of the Bill that had initially offended him. Lord Linlithgow, an old friend, although they had differed over the Government's proposals, was appointed viceroy in August. When Churchill wrote to congratulate him, he said:

> We apprehend increasing communal ill-will, and steady deterioration in all services . . . As long as the princes are not nagged and bullied to come into Federation, you need not expect anything but silence or help from us. We shall count more in the new Parliament than in this fat thing.[9]

Churchill was always capable of magnanimity. After the bill had been enacted, he invited G.D. Birla, one of Gandhi's supporters, to have lunch with him at Chartwell. When he arrived, Birla found Churchill in the garden wearing a workman's apron, which he had not changed for lunch. Afterwards, Churchill showed him the bricks he had laid and the building work that he had accomplished. He told Birla that Gandhi had risen in his esteem by standing up for the Dalits. He discussed Indian agriculture and spoke of his desire for an improvement in the lot of the masses. He didn't care whether they were loyal or not to Great Britain. He didn't mind about education, but he wanted the masses to have more butter. He wanted to go back to India for a six-month stay before he died. In Birla's account, it was a slightly rambling and maudlin discourse, but it may have been sincere. Birla certainly thought it was.

Many years after the enactment of the India Bill, Hoare looked back on the opposition that Churchill led. This is what he said:

> As I was one of the principal participants in the battle over India that raged from the day on which [Churchill] left the business committee [of the parliamentary Conservative Party, because they had accepted Hoare's support of federation] in 1931 to the final passage of the India Act in 1935, I am not an impartial judge of his action. Nonetheless, I may perhaps make two comments. From the point of view of India, the consequences were altogether bad. His formidable opposition embittered a constitutional discussion that should have been kept free of recrimination. It delayed by many months and perhaps years the passing of the Act . . . if the Act had reached the statute book in 1933 instead of 1935, I am convinced that it would have been in effective operation before the war started. Even more serious than delay was the atmosphere created by years of parliamentary wrangle . . . with the inevitable result that Indians came to believe that instead of giving them the fullest possible opportunity for obtaining responsible government, we were intent upon tying them up in a straitjacket.[10]

*

The enactment of the India Bill marked the end of this section of Churchill's involvement with the subcontinent. He turned to other issues. One was the support of Edward VIII in the abdication crisis of 1936. The entire British establishment and political opinion in the Commonwealth were entirely against the idea that the Prince of Wales should marry an American woman after her second divorce and remain on the throne. However, as ridiculous as it may seem almost a century later, it was at the time utterly unthinkable that the head of the Anglican Church could be married to a woman who was, in the view of the Church, already married to another man. Edward's idea that the marriage could be morganatic was irrelevant and fanciful.* Churchill had never particularly admired the Prince of Wales: there was indeed little enough to admire. But his romantic soul and perhaps his archaic views on monarchy appear to have been captured, and he campaigned on behalf of Edward, even seeking to rally a 'King's Party', with echoes of eighteenth-century politics.

This bizarre frolic consolidated the reputation he had acquired for perverse misjudgement, and the other occupation of his post-1935 years, opposition to Germany and concern over German rearmament, did just about as much damage. Hindsight changed everything, but at the time, he was thought to be continuing to tilt at windmills. Members who would listen spellbound to his great wartime speeches a few years later poured out of the chamber when he rose to his feet to talk about the dangers of Hitler.

*

---

* A morganatic marriage is the device used, most famously, by the Archduke Franz Ferdinand, who was murdered at Sarajevo in 1914, to marry Sophie Chotek, which allowed a person of royal or aristocratic birth to marry a commoner, by providing that the titles and belongings of the privileged partner would not pass to his wife or offspring. The marriage itself is just as real as any other marriage and would have been subject to the same rules of the Church. Its specialty is merely related to the rights of succession.

He would return to India when he became Prime Minister in 1940. Indeed, back in the Cabinet in 1939 as First Lord of the Admiralty, he had already started to talk about the role of Britain in India. What he talked about was the three-legged stool on which Britain could sit indefinitely. The legs of this stool were the Hindus, the Muslims and the princes. The fashioning of these three independent components was the fruit of his time in opposition to the India Bill. The Government of India Act 1935 was the last serious and structured attempt by Britain to create a framework that might eventually provide a mechanism for delivering Indian self-government and ultimately dominion status to an undivided subcontinent. The Act, which in the event, was rushed through ahead of independence in 1947, was a compromise, cobbled together in the face of communal dissension and something approaching civil war. The flaws in the 1935 Act were not all of Churchill's making, but he had been a damaging distraction. He did nothing to discourage the creation of potential conflict between Hindus and Muslims, and he certainly welcomed it if he did not actively foment the opposition by the princes. The great objective of British Indian policy was to keep the subcontinent united; indeed, if that had been achieved vast numbers of lives would have been saved and all the agony of inter-communal division would have been avoided. How far Churchill was responsible for making federation impossible cannot be assessed, but at the time of the passing of the 1935 legislation, he certainly congratulated himself, as we have seen, on having made it unworkable.

When, as Prime Minister, he came to direct policy in his last period of involvement in Indian affairs, from 1940 to 1945, he made full use of the separation of the communities. He continued to profess concern for the Dalits, claiming that they were ill-served by the political classes. Equally, he asserted that nothing must be done that would be to the disadvantage of the Muslim minority.

He played this card repeatedly in the last five years. The more the interests of the minorities were emphasized, the less chance there was of a union based on compromise.

16

Inside Churchill's Language

Churchill was in the wilderness until 1939. He came back to office in that year as First Lord of the Admiralty and, in the following year, became Prime Minister. He would therefore again have responsibilities for and a practical interest in India. His responsibilities in relation to the complicated situation in India when Britain was at a vulnerable point in her fight for survival tested him in new ways.

In the meantime, however, India was forgotten; his preoccupation was with the threat from Nazi Germany. Events that proved he was very much in the right during these years should not lead us to think that that was how he was seen by his party at the time. On the contrary, he seemed wrong-headed and almost eccentric.

Before we turn again to his engagement with the subcontinent, it is appropriate to consider his mindset and his attitude towards races other than his own. We can only judge whether the charge of racism is valid by judging him against the standards of his time.

We then need to consider the values that formed a man of his age
and background.

*

I might as well face up at once to what may be a minor part of
the charge against him but which still does enormous damage to
his reputation, and that is his language. He said some appalling
things, which it pains me to record. Some of them read as
racism fired off by a scattergun: 'I hate people with slit eyes and
pigtails.' 'Hottentots' were likely to throw white people into
the sea. In 1920, he told Duff Cooper that 'Gandhi ought to
be lain, bound hand and foot, at the gates of Delhi and then
trampled on by an enormous elephant with the new viceroy
seated on its back.'[1]*

This abusive language was certainly linked to the idea of the
superiority of white peoples. On 16 December 1900, in the course
of the South African War, he became aware of a report that there
had been fighting in the northern Cape between a commander of
Boer Raiders and 'Cape Boys', men of mixed blood. He wrote to
Joe Chamberlain, saying that he was disturbed:

> We have done without the whole of the magnificent Indian
> Army for the sake of a 'White man's War'; surely it is unnecessary
> to employ Cape Boys . . . Personally I'm conscious of a feeling
> of irritation that Kaffirs should be allowed to fire on white men,

---

* Churchill was almost always very rude, indeed, about Gandhi and
regarded him as evil. Gandhi was backed at times by Indian mill-owners,
who could see that with Independence, India could close her markets,
to their advantage and at the cost of Lancashire. Was Churchill's view
of Gandhi informed by his connections with the Lancashire cotton
interest? Probably not.

and I am sure that those who live in S.A. will feel this much more strongly.[2]

But alongside a general distaste for other races, there was a particular dislike of Indians. Particularly Hindus. He could talk of 'Baboos', Indians, that is, describing them as gross, dirty and corrupt. In 1942, he said to Leo Amery, then Secretary of State for India: 'I hate Indians. They are a beastly people with a beastly religion.' This remark needs qualification. When the Cripps Mission, discussed below, failed and Congress unleashed the Quit India Movement, declaring that it would only offer passive resistance to a Japanese invasion, Churchill was furious. He thought that Gandhi and the Hindus, as opposed to the Muslim League, which had supported the war, were stabbing Britain in the back when help was most needed.[3] Many of Amery's comments about Churchill's racial views have to be taken with a pinch of salt. Amery's Cabinet contributions were long-winded and boring and Churchill mischievously liked to interrupt them with unacceptable racist jokes that would stop him in his tracks.

In February 1922, he told a conference of ministers that he was strongly opposed to the idea that India would gradually be handed over to the Indians. 'He believed that opinion would change soon as to the expediency of granting democratic institutions to backward races that had no capacity for self-government.'[4] When Irwin was viceroy, he recognized that the problem was partly due to the influence of Churchill's youth. He suggested that Churchill's views on India were like those of 'a subaltern a generation ago', and that he might like to bring himself up to date by meeting some Indian activists who were in London at the time. 'I am quite satisfied with my views on India. I don't want them disturbed by any bloody Indian.'[5]

In his second administration, from 1951 to 1955, he had to face increasing concern on both sides of the House about

Commonwealth immigration. It was very small, at 3000 arrivals in 1953 and 11,000 in 1954, but that was enough to cause concern, particularly as his Home Secretary, David Maxwell–Fyfe, discovered that a substantial proportion of the immigrants lived on welfare. There were many people, of course, who took a liberal view on the matter, and others took a legalistic view that came to the same conclusion: in late 1948, the British Nationality Act had given British Citizenship to all subjects within the Empire. But there were racists too. And Churchill, for all his capacity for magnanimity, had sympathy with their views. He learned that a fund was being set up by public subscription on the occasion of his eightieth birthday. He said he didn't want the sum raised for charity 'just to bring home some coloured gentleman from Jamaica to complete his education'.[6] He said the continued immigration would create 'a magpie society' which 'would never do'.[7] In January 1955, he told the Cabinet that 'Keep Britain White' would be a good slogan.[8] But these views were far from being particularly his; they were shared, alas, by a large element of the supporters of both political parties and by people of all ages and classes. Even Violet Attlee, the wife of the Leader of the Labour Party, admitted after a reception at which black people were present that she found it very difficult to like them, even though she knew she should. In 1968, scores of thousands of dockers in mass protest went on strike and marched in support of Enoch Powell, the Tory MP and former Cabinet member who had just made his notorious racist 'Rivers of Blood' speech. Shamefully, these views have far from disappeared today, even if they are less openly articulated.

*

In Churchill's youth, and indeed throughout most of his life, people did use language that would be regarded now as quite unconscionable. The inhabitants of the different nations in the United Kingdom, or indeed of the provinces at a distance from London, were referred to in terms which were on the face of it, extraordinarily offensive but which were accepted as the currency of chaff. In Parliament, Churchill and his contemporaries would stretch the rules of the House to refer to members of opposing parties in the most savage of terms. After exchanges that might have been expected to separate the combatants' families for generations, they would go off for a drink in the bar. When Churchill and others thought that opponents were beginning to get a little out of touch with each other during the intense controversy over the Parliament Act in 1911, he and F.E. Smith formed the Other Club in order to avoid division caused by vitriol. But Rule 12 provided that: 'Nothing in the rules or intercourse of the Club shall interfere with the rancour or asperity of party politics.'

Churchill could make offensive remarks and jokes about Jews, as was common at the time. All the same, a disproportionately high number of his friends were Jewish. His admiration for the Jewish people went beyond these personal links. He believed in 'the genius' of the Jews, whom he described as 'the most formidable and remarkable race that ever appeared in the world'.[9] He had worked closely with Jewish groups in Manchester in his time as a Liberal MP, and there he became a friend of Chaim Weizmann, the future Zionist leader and President of Israel. He supported the Zionist cause and was genuinely moved by what he learned about Nazi genocide. He is listed as one of the Righteous Among the Nations on the Wall of Honour in the Garden of the Righteous at Yad Vashem in Jerusalem. That said, his pro-Zionism is not so much an indication of a lack of racism as an acknowledgement of a belief in racial hierarchy.

*

Churchill was human. I've said elsewhere that the scale and range of his abilities were matched by a profound sense of humanity and magnanimity. But he was not perfect. He unalterably believed that the British race was superior to the races in the black colonies, that Britain had a civilizing duty, and that it was neither in the interests of Britain nor of the subject races that it should be assumed that power should automatically and always be transferred from the former to the latter. I said earlier that Churchill chose his language with great precision, and so he did when he was writing or speaking for the record; on other occasions, however, he could also use it carelessly. That was because he was capable of being downright silly and often peevish and petulant. In the course of one of their long and exhausting battles, Sir Alan Brooke, the Chief of the Imperial General Staff for most of the war, was failing to get Churchill to adopt a coherent strategic view, a planned succession of moves. In frustration, he pointed out that if Churchill was going to the barber's, he would decide on his route before he left his front door. Churchill infuriatingly said, 'No, I wouldn't.' That was of a piece of saying that he hated Indians and that they were a beastly people.

He was a product of his times, as we all are, and his views were formed in days that were, by the 1930s, fairly distant and permeated by assumptions that were by then discredited. He was to an extent conscious of this. We have seen that in *My Early Life*, he described himself as 'a child of the Victorian era'. Much later in life, in 1952, he reflected to his doctor, Charles Wilson, 'When you learn to think of a race as inferior beings it is difficult to get rid of that way of thinking; when I was a subaltern in India the Indians did not seem to me equal to the white man.'[10] Lord Moran wrote of Churchill's attitude towards the Chinese: 'Winston thinks only of the colour of their skin; it is when he talks of India or China that you remember that he is a Victorian.'[11]

But 'Victorian' is sloppy shorthand. Many Victorians, including Churchill's headmaster, were liberal in their views of the Empire.

*

When he was in India as a young man, it was not uncommon for the British to find themselves better disposed towards the Muslims than the Hindus. To that, Churchill added an admiration for the warrior qualities that he perceived among the Muslims. The martial races were seen as loyal and dependable, and the non-martial races were seen as corrupt and lazy, 'baboos' and 'boxwallahs', spineless shopkeepers. It may be no coincidence that it was on the much-caricatured baboos that Churchill depended for the loans that kept him going as a young officer. He certainly appreciated the qualities of the martial races and celebrated them in *My Early Life*. In 1899, in *The River War,* there are critical references to Islam, expunged from the second edition. The First World War reinforced his views: 'During the Great War, the Moslems of India confounded the hopes of their disloyalty entertained by the Germans and their Turkish ally and readily went to the colours. The Punjab alone furnished 180,000 Moslem recruits.'[12] We shall look more closely at this categorization of the different communities in the next chapter.

17

Boxwallahs and Martial People

All this talk of 'martial races' and the like is pretty strange stuff. What was it all about, and why did Churchill and his contemporaries buy into it?

Some nationalist writers have suggested that the caste system was a creation of the British. That is emphatically not the case. There is debate about just how old and how pan-Indian the system is. It is certainly not uniform across the subcontinent, but it is very old. Its existence can be seen in the collections of scripture known as the Vedas of 1500–1000 BCE, and the importance of caste is stressed in the Bhagavad Gita, an element in the epic of the Mahabharata.

So some sort of caste system existed long before the British period and, with regrettable consequences, has continued since the British left. Today, the Constitution of India seeks to encourage support of the 'weaker sections' of the community, which are defined by caste, and in doing so, it explicitly recognizes the existence of the system.

Caste is an immensely complicated topic in its own right
and worth pursuing.* But this is not the place to do so, nor even
to attempt to define an elusive and dynamic notion as it moved
towards a concentration on *jati*, the kinship group, and *varna*,
a categorization based on occupation. For most of a century,
the subject has attracted anthropologists in perhaps greater
numbers than any other issue. The fruits of their research are
detailed and, to a remarkable extent, contradictory. Happily, this
essentially political book does not require us to sieve through
the anthropological soup. A few comments will, however,
help to explain the notions that informed Churchill and his
contemporaries and their outlook.

*

All societies have dominating cadres and dominated élites and
subject classes. The élites seek to perpetuate their privilege by
making the social layers impermeable. This is as true of eastern
societies as it is of those of western Europe and its feudal system.
But the boundaries blur, and dominant sections of society bend
them to reinforce their security. The caste system in India was
far from static and was constantly evolving in its nature and its
geographical distribution. Britain's predecessors, particularly
the Mughal Emperors, used the system creatively for their own
political ends.

That said, from at least the eighteenth century onwards, the
British were fascinated by notions of caste. It had an exotic, almost
romantic appeal. Europe noticed caste, talked about it and wrote

---

* See Susan Bayly, *Caste, Society and Politics in India from the
Eighteenth Century to the Modern Age* (Cambridge: Cambridge
University Press, 2001).

about it. Indeed, the very word 'caste' is not of Indian origin but comes from Latin via Spanish and Portuguese. For the British, it also had convenient administrative attractions—not least in that it fitted neatly into the divide and rule policy.

The caste system was infinitely more complicated after British rule than before. All the notions about martial races and indolent boxwallahs, urban and obese, were not of Churchill's invention. The categorization of Indian society was an obsession of the British. The British utilized it for recruitment to various levels of the Indian Civil Service.

So the British did engage with caste. From the days of the East India Company, Britons and other Europeans preferred to deal with people of Brahmin or other elite origin. The Company was concerned that its regulations would not be respected if they did not acknowledge Brahmin pre-eminence. But eventually the Company concluded that Brahmins should stick to their priestly functions. Their enthusiasm for *jati* and *varna* was thought to mitigate against their loyalty to their European masters, and the last Brahmin Peshwa was deposed in 1818.* By now, 'manly, thrifty and hardworking husbandmen' were thought to be more dependable than devious Brahmins.[1]

The company carried out extensive surveys from the 1820s onwards, which came to constitute repositories of 'caste law'. Initially, the categorization and ranking between 'castes' or 'tribes', was not very significant, but the process, a grading of the moral superiority of different groups, developed as the century went on. It was fuelled in a number of ways. The first was what has been described as 'a whole host of mammoth all-India data surveys'.[2] There were a series of gazetteers, decennial all-India censuses from

---

* The Peshwa was the latterly hereditary prime minister of the Maratha Empire. The expansion of Maratha rule had partly been due to the fact that it favoured Brahmin families.

1871 onwards, statistical reports and a huge series of *tribes and castes* surveys from 1891.

*

A virus entered this vapid research with the developing study of race, particularly in Germany. It fed into the raw data that these surveys and censuses produced. With it came an added fascination with Darwin's theories of natural selection. Darwin's theory was dynamic. On the face of it, other anthropologists, such as Francis Galton, held that human abilities and attributes were determined and thus *fixed* by inheritance. But, in fact, Galtonians sought not just to identify types through the dubious science of psychometrics but also to manipulate evolution by a combination of eliminating undesirable breeding and encouraging genetic enhancement.*

By the time Churchill arrived in India—but not much before—some sort of 'scientific' basis for a categorized system had established itself. 'Orientalists', beguiled by the East and its apparent exceptionalism, surrendered themselves to the exotic, and the British were seduced by its charms to the extent that rather than manipulating the caste system to their advantage, they seemed to have become its servants. An outstanding efflorescence of 'Orientalism' was the preoccupation in the 1830s with the *thuggee* cult, a highly colourful belief in a widespread conspiracy involving fanatics who worshipped a bloodthirsty goddess, strangled travellers and paid bribes to the Company to be allowed to operate. While, of course, there were lots of criminals and gangs of criminals, the coordinated and organized activities of the *thugees* were a matter of fiction.

---

* These debates were followed in journals like the *Journal of Anthropology*, the *Transactions of the Ethnological Society of London* and *The Anthropological Review*.

Less dangerous but equally synthetic was the widespread contrast between the manly mountain people and the thieves and criminals on the plain. This distinction fitted with the eighteenth-century European approval of the noble savage and the nineteenth-century adaptation of Rousseau's notion to embrace the equally noble Highlander.

*

The mechanism for the elaboration of the caste system was the census. Some sort of census was obviously necessary as a tool of government. The initial ones in the British period were very rough and ready. They were not synchronous, and frequently cut corners by, for instance, multiplying habitations by an arbitrary number of hypothetical residents. From about 1865 onwards, the procedure became more systematic, more synchronized, and attempted to cover the whole of the country. This initiative was in large part the result of the 1857 uprising. Part of the reaction was a commendable desire to understand India better in order to avoid further troubles, but the process was shot through with a desire to categorize and stratify society. It was sometimes said that the caste system was the cement that held 'the myriad units of Indian society' together. In reality, it prevented these different elements from coalescing, particularly against the British who, in such small numbers, felt acutely vulnerable to the subject masses.

The census categorized occupation, caste, race and tribe, indifferent to any overall system but always aiming to attach labels. It has to be said that the process was assisted by the enthusiasm of individual interest groups that petitioned to be listed as separate identities and, once listed, frequently petitioned for reclassification. The classifiers, the British officials of the period, were increasingly influenced by bogus theories of anthropometry and scientific or biological racism. The commissioner for the 1901 census, H.H.

Risley, a man like Galton who whipped out his callipers at the sight
of an interesting cranium and held that racial characteristics could
be established by the measurement of noses, said that the pride of
the Brahmins rested on the scientifically provable fact that they
had 'preserved the Aryan type in comparative purity throughout
Northern India'. As the leading proponent of ethnology in the
British Empire until his death in 1911, Risley regarded caste as
'an elemental force like gravitation or molecular attraction', a
regulating factor in Indian life'.[3]

The concomitant of this categorization was the attribution
of generic qualities to the different groupings. From the point
of view of preserving British rule and avoiding another rising,
it was particularly important that the Indian soldiers on whose
support the Raj rested were dependable. Accordingly, particular
importance was attached to identifying who could be relied upon.
The conclusion was that the military should look to people who
were accustomed to living rough, hunting and defending their
communities in rugged mountainous conditions. They were 'the
martial races', and army policy was to recruit from them. This
arbitrary classification was immensely offensive and condescending:
the martial races were regarded as loyal and fearless, but rather thick
and lacking the intellectual and leadership qualities that would
direct them to challenge their officers. Avoiding independent-
minded and intelligent soldiers led to a shortage of troops in both
world wars. The theory was in part based on an analysis of those
who had fought for or against the British during the 1857 uprising,
but its theoretical basis was, of course, nonsense. The martial races
may have come from unsophisticated, rural backgrounds, but
they were neither stupid nor lacking in initiative. Those British
officers who fought alongside them in innumerable engagements,
including the battles in the First and Second World Wars where
the Indian Army was an indispensable element, invariably came to
respect their men as much as they loved them.

Just as the martial races were written off as brave but uneducated and backward, the educated and sophisticated people of the plain were regarded as seditious and unreliable. The martial races were virile and manly. The others were effeminate and weak. This notion fed into the dismissal of the Hindu commercial classes as corrupt and unscrupulous baboos and boxwallahs. Churchill was not the only man—very far from it—to feel that there was more to admire in the men of the hills.

In Britain, too, the rugged Highlanders who fought valiantly for the defence of Britain in disproportionately large numbers were regarded with approbation, and there are many pictures showing rugged, kilted Scotsmen and men from the Punjab fighting shoulder to shoulder. But the Highlanders were not subjected to cod-ethnological theories—or at least not a great deal—and their cousins in the lowlands were not regarded as spineless and unreliable.

18

The Imperial World

I have tried to contextualize and thereby explain some of Churchill's language and views. I am well aware, however, that the sensitivities of today's readership (with which, incidentally, I do not in the least disagree) will make it very difficult, if not impossible, to hear what he said without offence. I wonder what we take for granted today that our grandchildren will regard as unacceptable. Some of these assumptions I can guess at; what worries me are those of which I am unaware.

But at the end of the day, what matters is not Churchill's casual rudeness and throwaway offensiveness but rather the deeper elements on which his thinking rested. The first of these was the significance to his generation of the Empire. He was born in 1874. A hundred years earlier, America was not yet independent, and the British Empire was still amorphous and being shaped. His roots were, therefore, in the early days of the Empire.

When the East India Company was founded in 1599, England (there would be no Britain for over another 100 years) was part of a cold, wet island, divided by its channel from a hostile Europe. It lacked the rich agricultural ground on which the inhabitants of mainland Europe could rely; they regarded it as a crude and uncivilized place. It had been invaded at regular intervals before 1066, and the invasion did not stop then. There were successful invasions in 1216, 1326, 1399, 1471, 1485 and 1688.[1] There were further Jacobite invasions in the seventeenth and eighteenth centuries. Invasion was expected on a daily basis at points during the Napoleonic Wars. The internal stability of England was precarious throughout the sixteenth and seventeenth centuries, and it was against this precarious political and economic background that Hobbes wrote *Leviathan* in 1651. The nation lacked a great deal of self-respect.

*

Having an Empire made all the difference. Britain acquired one in the eighteenth century. The American colonies had been there for 100 years already, but they didn't quite count. They had just been Englishmen abroad. After they had slipped out of the imperial nexus, Canada, Australia and New Zealand were in much the same position, Britons away from home. In the second half of the nineteenth century, it was recognized that they would largely be allowed to look after themselves, and they were treated like adolescents who had left home but still relied on their parents from time to time.

The eighteenth century was the great era of romantic imperial acquisitions, with its dramatic intensity focused on the Seven Years' War, 1756–1763. There were flamboyant derring-do cameos, such as Wolfe's army rowing up the St Lawrence to the Plains of Abraham to capture Quebec. Later in the century, Nelson provided more propaganda for the cause.

This was the period when Britain, and in particular England, responded to the rhythm of martial success. The great patriotic melodies all date from these years. *Rule, Britannia!* was written in

1740, the National Anthem in 1745 and *Hearts of Oak* in 1760. British chests swelled. *Great* Britain—the grandiose epithet dates from 1707—was no longer insular and insecure. It saw itself in the imperial tradition of Greece and Rome. The adjective 'Augustan' that was applied to this period of its history was a link with the Emperor Augustus of Rome rather than simply an allusion to the names of Hanoverian monarchs. The traditions of classical Rome were consciously adopted. The fact that the middle and upper classes were educated in the language and literature of Greece and Rome consolidated a sense of continuity with the ancient world. Britons, even more than other Europeans, felt themselves to be part of the classical tradition.

The courtyards and corridors of the India Office and Colonial Office (later the Foreign and Commonwealth Office and now the Foreign, Commonwealth and Development Office—the name gets longer as its responsibilities get less) display statues of generals and administrators dressed in togas and classical accoutrements.

> [A] Grand Durbar Court, made for the reception of Indian dignitaries, features allegorical statues in a style that is supposed to be half classical and half Indian; elsewhere, Spiridione Roma's painting, *The East Offering its Riches to Britannia* [depicts] . . . a dark-skinned character representing India willingly offering a pale Britannia all her jewellery and treasures, turning violent looting into an act of peaceful benevolence.[2]

The establishment were the heirs of Greece and Rome.

The arts were indeed powerfully affected by the Empire, particularly literature. The Anglo–Saxon tradition was obliged to accept an increased importation of Latin words, idioms and even rules of grammar. Parliament, formerly a fairly no-nonsense assembly of squires and practical men, became an arena in which statesmen weighed the affairs of Empire in orotund flourishes. The busts of politicians represented them as heroes of antiquity, lightly dressed for a northern climate in togas designed for Rome.

British exceptionalism was reaffirmed by the Napoleonic Wars, when the country stood out against continental aggression and finally defeated Bonaparte at sea by its own efforts and led the campaign that defeated him on land. Now Britannia not only ruled the waves but played a prominent role on the European land mass, a crucial player in the Congress System, and was thus an arbiter of the fate of great powers and their peoples. The self-confidence it engendered is difficult to share now, but it was powerfully felt at the time. It was famously expressed by the Foreign Secretary, Lord Palmerston, in a debate on British foreign policy in the House of Commons in June 1850:

> I therefore fearlessly challenge the verdict which this House . . . is to give . . . on the question . . . whether, as the Roman, in days of old, held himself free from indignity, when he could say *Civis Romanus sum* [I am a Roman citizen]; so also a British subject, in whatever land he may be, shall feel confident that the watchful eye and the strong arm of England, will protect him against injustice and wrong.

This sense of confidence could be jingoistic and aggressive* but was not necessarily so. Decent, moderate and pacific people, even politicians, could take a quiet satisfaction in owning a significant fraction of the world.

---

* 'Jingoism' comes from a song sung at the time of the Russo–Turkish War, 1877–1878: 'We don't want to fight but by jingo if we do / We've got the ships, we've got the men, we've got the money too. / We've fought the bear before and while we're Britons true / The Russians shall not have Constantinople.'

In 1895, Churchill's headmaster at Harrow, J.E.C. Welldon, said that 'the Victorian era marks the consummation of the British Empire'. He identified the nineteenth century, as opposed to the seventeenth and eighteenth, as the period in which the Empire became the possession of the state rather than of individuals or corporations. The nineteenth century was, he said, marked not by the expansion of the Empire, but by the consolidation of 'the spirit of Empire'.[3]*

This was the world into which Churchill was born and in which his early assumptions and prejudices were formed. Looking back, it can be seen that by the late nineteenth century, a decline was setting in, but only relative decline, not absolute decline.

*

What about India? The acquisition of India was very much an eighteenth-century phenomenon. A lot happened in the seventeenth century after the granting of the charter to the East India Company in 1599, but much more happened in the succeeding hundred years.

The Indian subcontinent was enormously rich at the beginning of the seventeenth century. India's share of world GDP was about 30 per cent and Britain's about 3 per cent. The relationship was reversed in the course of the eighteenth century, by which time, by any standards, it was now Britain that was enormously

---

* In 1898, Welldon was appointed Bishop of Calcutta. Churchill didn't think that sounded an attractive appointment: 'The East, without wife, woman, sport, war, authority or friends seems to me to be a vy bad bargain'—Churchill to Curzon, quoted in Toye, R., *Churchill's Empire: The World that Made Him and the World He Made*, St. Martin's Griffin; Reprint edition (2011). Later, when Welldon was back in Britain, he criticized Churchill's campaign against the extension of self-government for India implied in the Government of India Bill of 1935.

rich. India, and it was India with which the East India Company principally occupied itself, had an advanced steel industry from a very early point. It also had a flourishing textile industry. Britain dismantled the steel industry and suppressed the export of textiles, substituting their manufacture in Britain for their export to India.

Enormous fortunes were brought back to Britain. 'Loot' is a Hindi word. The scale of these fortunes beggars belief. The legislature colluded and did nothing effective to discourage what was happening. After all, a quarter of the members of the British Parliament had stock in the East India Company. Robert Clive, the first British Governor of the Bengal Presidency, amassed huge wealth after the Battle of Plassey in 1757. In modern equivalents, he received about £22 million and the company about £232 million. This was the beginning of what was known as the 'Shaking of the Pagoda Tree'. When he was accused of feathering his own nest, he said that he was being treated like 'a common sheep-stealer . . . I stand astonished by my own moderation'.

The effects of all of this were bad for India. The country was despoiled. The agrarian economy collapsed, and a move to an industrial economy was thwarted. Britain taxed India heavily. The costs of maintaining the British presence were paid for by the Indians and not by the British.

The effect on Britain was immense, but corrupting, not beneficial. The Nabobs, self-made men from provincial England, came back from India laden with plunder and bought themselves seats in Parliament by acquiring rotten boroughs. This change in the economics of class was resented, though it provided the fluidity and dynamism that were the basis of Britain's industrial and manufacturing activities in the nineteenth century. The money brought back kick-started and sustained the Industrial Revolution. The inflow of money provided an element of gearing that underlay the growth in the slave trade.

In recent history, the activities of the East India Company were described as the 'supreme act of corporate violence in world history'.[4] But it was not only in hindsight that the British role in India was criticized. There were many who found it distasteful at the time. Horace Walpole exclaimed, 'We have outdone the Spaniards in Peru!' The great Earl of Chatham deplored what was happening. The political scientist Arthur Young regretted the fact that a deniable corporation was 'fighting battles and dethroning princes'.

In 1770, William Bolts, an adventurous and enterprising trader, argued that Bengal should be taken over by the British state.[5] This didn't happen for almost ninety years; although the link between the Company and the British government could be usefully denied when it was politic to do so. In practice, the United Kingdom Parliament was not uninvolved in the management of the Company, repeatedly acting in response to Company excesses and inefficiencies by passing regulating acts. Acts of 1712, 1730 and 1742 were attempts to limit the Company's independence, but they also worked to secure revenues for the crown. By 1773, Parliament had created a governing council of five members, of whom the majority were government appointees. From then on, the Governor General of Bengal was appointed by London. Acts of 1784, 1786, 1793, 1813 and 1833 followed, and so on until the final abolition of the Company. By the end of the eighteenth century, the UK Parliament was indeed becoming more delicate in its tastes. The great bravura of the eighteenth century was coming to an end and was being replaced by Victorian respectability and sensitivity, and the emphasis was changing from despoiling India to a sense of responsibility for its material and moral welfare.

This was a step in the right direction, although the patronizing assumptions implicit in the new approach now seem insufferable.

The historian Thomas Babington Macaulay, whose work the young Churchill studied in Bangalore, was intimately involved with India. He resigned his seat in the House of Commons to go to the subcontinent from 1834 until 1838 as a Law Member of the governor-general's council. He was involved in the formulation of the Criminal Code and in Indian education. Macaulay's aim for India was that perhaps, sometime in the future, it might have quasi-independence. But that was distant and problematic. The main thing was to 'improve the nature of India and Indians', by forming 'a class . . . of persons, Indian in blood and colour, but English in taste, in opinions, in morals and in intellect' as he put it in his 1835 minute on Indian education. 'A single shelf of a good European library [is] worth the whole native literature of India and Arabia.'[6]

He believed passionately what would nowadays be unacceptable: that the route to improvement for Indians lay in adopting the English language and assimilating European culture. On 10 July 1833, before he went to India, he made a famous speech in the House of Commons on the second reading of the India Bill of that year. He set out his views on the development of India and ended with his vision of how Britain might finally retire from the subcontinent:

> It may be that the public mind of India may expand under our system till it has outgrown that system; that by good government we may educate our subjects into a capacity for better government; that, having become instructed in European knowledge, they may, in some future age, demand European institutions. Whether such a day will ever come I know not. But never will I attempt to avert or to retard it. Whenever it comes, it will be the proudest day in English history. To have found a great people sunk in the lowest depths of slavery and superstition, to have so ruled them as to have made them

desirous and capable of all the privileges of citizens, would indeed be a title to glory all our own.

If the British period in India—at least in its initial 200 years—amounted to crippling the subcontinent's development, taxing its inhabitants close to the point of starvation, looting its assets and forcing it to buy materials that it could more reasonably have produced itself; and if the proceeds of the wealth that was torn away from India were used to prime the pump of the slave trade in that notorious triangle, which involved taking goods to West Africa, slaves to the West Indies, and sugar, rum and tobacco to Britain, Britain has little to be proud of. Of course, there were good deeds and good people, and more of both as time went by, but the fact remains that terrible things were done. We should not, of course, rewrite history and judge it by the standards of later times. But what was done was scarcely acceptable by the standards of its own time. Just as in relation to the Holocaust, there was a deliberate closing of the eyes and a turning away of the head. But there was an awareness of the evils. Governments increasingly interfered in the operations of the free market because of evident excesses. Clive was criticized for the wealth he brought back from India, and Warren Hastings was impeached. Despoliation could not be ignored. The Nabobs returned from the subcontinent with vast wealth. They built in a palatial style and on an enormous scale. The great Georgian houses of England were created with wealth snatched from India. But there was a creative amnesia.

*

Churchill's family was not directly involved in the seventeenth or eighteenth centuries in India or the West Indies. The great Duke of Marlborough, Churchill's most famous ancestor, benefited from the slave trade, but his successors did not. Marlborough and his astute wife, Sarah, invested heavily in the South Sea Company. Marlborough himself was senile by the time the Bubble was about to burst, but his shrewd wife got out in time, at the top of the market, making a profit of about £1 million. The family spent the money; the fifth duke was particularly profligate and had to sell many assets. By ducal standards, the family was hard up until the ninth duke married into American wealth and wed a Vanderbilt. All the same, they, and the society into which they fit, were all implicated in the transfer of wealth from India and its investment in the trade. They were, like others of their class, part of a prosperous system that was funded directly or indirectly from sources that should be regarded as tainted. They were part of that eighteenth- and nineteenth-century Britain whose financial well-being had been elevated by the spoils of Empire. In the eighteenth century, slave-related businesses contributed the same proportion of British GDP as the professional and support services sector today.[7] I repeat that Churchill and his family were not personally implicated in the evils of Imperialism. My point is simply that this period of history was in his DNA, in the ballast of his settled assumptions.

*

The landscape in which the upper classes lived was formed by Indian wealth. The Churchills lived in particular splendour, not in a house but in a *palace*. Blenheim Palace was the nation's gift to Marlborough for his victories in the War of the Spanish Succession, but most of the great houses of the eighteenth century were paid for with repatriated loot. They were not only built with what Sathnam Sanghera describes as 'the vast amounts of wealth Britons siphoned from India during Empire';[8] they were also frequently built in a style, real or imagined, that referred to Indian exoticism. The Nabobs, the men usually in early middle age who returned from service with the East India Company with huge fortunes, built houses that were almost as palatial as Blenheim. Their seats in Parliament were resented as upsetting the natural structures and true virtues of English life. Thus the elder Pitt, Lord Chatham, complained that

> The riches of Asia have been poured in upon us and have brought with them, not only Asiatic Luxury, but, I fear, Asiatic principles of government. Without connections, without any natural interest in the soil, the importers of foreign gold have forced their way into Parliament by such a torrent of private corruption as no hereditary fortune could resist.[9]

Hypocritical, perhaps: his own grandfather, Thomas 'Diamond' Pitt, the son of a cleric, went out to India in 1674 at the age of just twenty-one to work for the East India Company. He broke the rules, like everyone else, and traded on his own behalf, making so much money that when he returned to England just fourteen years later, he could buy himself a seat in Parliament. Seats in Parliament were frequently principally a means to gain yet more money and within the year, he returned to India as President of Madras. He got his nickname because of the 410-carat diamond, 'The Regent Diamond', which he acquired as an uncut stone in 1701. He sent it back to England hidden in one of his children's shoes. It became one of the Crown Jewels of France. True to form, some of the proceeds from the sale of the diamond were invested in the purchase of a country house in Berkshire.

Thus Shashi Tharoor, for instance, argues that 'Britain's Industrial Revolution was built on the destruction of India's thriving manufacturing industries.'[10] Certainly, a large number of people made fortunes in India. Clive is probably the most notorious. He calculated that he was worth the equivalent of £702 million in today's money. But others did pretty well too. A Select Committee set up to investigate the East India Company's abuses concluded that between 1757 and 1775, Company employees received bribes worth about £4 billion in today's money on top of about £1 billion from their private enterprises, and all of that on top of their salaries.

All of this supports the Indian wealth drain theory. It has been estimated that in the ten years from 1783 to 1793, there was an annual outflow from the subcontinent of £1.8 billion in today's money.[11] The wealth drain is linked to Industrial Revolution 'pump priming'. The Industrial Revolution and the slave trade were all the more profitable because of the availability of capital to inject into their development. Some economists challenge these arguments. It depends to an extent on definitions and on how income and expenditure are allocated. Some Indian tax revenue did not go into the coffers of the East India Company and was used within the subcontinent, for instance, for schooling. How much of the cost of the Royal Navy should be debited to India? What period should the analysis cover? But a spreadsheet of income and expenditure does not take account of the structural manipulation of the Indian economy—the fact that Britain suppressed the textile and metal industries in order to work at home with the raw materials it purloined from India.

*

Disraeli said in 1872 that 'it has been shown with precise, with mathematical demonstration, that there never was a jewel in the crown of England that was so costly as the possession of India'. That is a very doubtful proposition. But certainly by the last years of the Empire, when Churchill was fighting his rear-guard action, India was a net cost. During the Second World War, indeed, it became a creditor.

From the beginning of 1940, the Indian Government was responsible for its own 'ordinary' defence expenditure, together with just part of the cost of Indian troops fighting outside the subcontinent. London was responsible for the rest of the cost and was required to pay in sterling. This created a huge sterling debt to the Government of India. The existence of this debt was not greatly discussed in public, as Linlithgow, the viceroy, had begged the War Cabinet not to attempt to alter the arrangements because of the political consequences that would follow. In 1939, India owed Britain £356 million. By 1945, Britain owed India £1,260 million, a fifth of the UK's gross national product. The existence of the debt was of great concern to the Cabinet and potentially capable of precipitating a run on the pound. 'Are we to incur hundreds of millions of debts,' Churchill asked the War Cabinet, 'for defending India in order to be kicked out by the Indians afterwards?'

The London Treasury was concerned that at the end of the war, India would be in a position to ruin an already depleted Britain. The situation was repugnant to Churchill. Secretary of State Amery told Linlithgow that

> Winston harangued us at great length about the monstrous idea that we should spend millions upon millions on the defence of India, then be told to clear out, and on top of all that, owe India vast sums incurred on her behalf. I tried, without much effect, to make him understand that a great deal of this expenditure was for goods supplied to the Middle East.

For once, Linlithgow did not agree with Churchill. His sympathies were with the Indian Government.

*

The situation was very different in the eighteenth century. The subject is best approached not by consulting global figures but rather by looking at the huge number of individual experiences, which demonstrate that for many Britons, India was an opportunity to plunder on an immense scale and to bring the loot back to their homes. While generalizations are open to challenge, individual histories are more revealing. They are so marked, independent and numerous that, cumulatively, they demonstrate that lots of people made a lot of money from India and used it further to promote the imperial campaign.

*

Churchill was then emphatically influenced by Britain's eighteenth-century history. In his bungalow on the North–West Frontier, he read his Macaulay and Gibbon, and in them he read the history of that century. He was influenced by the former's Whiggish interpretation of its history. He admired and adopted the magnificent Gibbonian style, flowing and orotund. From both, he absorbed the conception of history's grandeur. In the pages of the Annual Register, he found the style and assurance of the Augustan age.

The romantic dash of eighteenth-century military and naval exploits appealed to him. His staff in the Second World War were amused by the hortatory missives he sent off to his generals and admirals when he observed what seemed to him to be unnecessary caution in the prosecution of the war. In a variety of permutations, he would address them with words such as, 'Glory awaits the commander who will seize the initiative, embrace risks and danger and engage the enemy to his confoundment.' Generals were instructed to race to the relief of strategically unimportant but symbolic stations like Tobruk. Admirals were enjoined to seize minor islands in the Dodecanese, occupied by a handful of hapless Germans. Poor Alan Brooke, the Chief of the Imperial Staff, despaired of his master's enthusiasm, at the expense of coherent strategy, for daring hit-and-run raids on parts of the European continent, 'breaking windows with golden guineas', as Charles James Fox had said William Pitt had done during the Napoleonic Wars.

It was hardly surprising, though, that the Empire, the eighteenth-century Empire, mattered. During the Second World War, in response to prodding from President Roosevelt, who wanted to see India independent, Churchill was speaking from the heart when he said, 'I have not become the King's First Minister in order to preside over the liquidation of the British Empire.'

*

Against this backdrop, can we address the paradox that Churchill, starting as an inherently liberal and tolerant young man, whose instincts were with the rebel Boers, who said that 'there should be no barrier of race, colour or creed', who deprecated Kitchener's triumphalist conduct after his victory at Omdurman, who censured Dyer for what he had done at Amritsar, who as Colonial Secretary positively rushed the newly acquired bits of the Ottoman Empire into a quasi-independence for which they were palpably not ready and who was so supportive of the secession of Southern Ireland from the British Empire that Baldwin thought he might be a suitable Secretary of State for India, even viceroy, became despite all this to be implacably opposed to the idea of Indian independence and fought to thwart it in a mean-minded way, so alien to his usual generosity of spirit?

The reason was, above all, that India was different. The white Dominions, as I have said, were just Englishmen abroad and more than a little boring too. Many other imperial possessions were purely utilitarian. For cost reasons, they were small, a worldwide scattering of capes, straits, settlements, coaling stations and garrisons. They were functional but dispensable. India, on the other hand, was a conspicuous ornament. It and its associated territories, Sri Lanka and Burma, were exotic. They were the source of immense riches in their time. Their economic value amounted to the assault of the subcontinent. But the romance remained. Churchill was a romantic. India remained in his mind—the India he had gone to as a very young man.

He was his father's son, the son of that Lord Randolph Churchill who had referred to India as 'that most truly bright and precious gem of the crown'.[12] Randolph had a strong Indian connection. Recuperating after the exertions of the 1884 Reform Act, he spent three months in the winter of 1884–1885 touring India. Such a visit was very unusual for senior politicians at the time. It can't have been a particularly recuperative stay. He studied the nature of British rule in India in some detail, travelling around the country and staying with senior officers. He came back with a sense of the precarious nature of British rule, depending as it did on the control of vast numbers of Indians by a very small number of Britons. His prescription for the continuation of the Raj was based on force rather than love. He was emphatic that Britain should not show 'the faintest indications of relaxing our grasp'.[13] He intervened constructively at the time of the Panjdeh incident, when Russia entered Afghanistan. It was largely as a result of this intervention that, when the Conservatives came to power in 1885, Randolph became Secretary of State of India. He remained there for seven months and enjoyed his time. He supported the annexation of Upper Burma by the viceroy, Lord Dufferin, and although he was famously opposed to military expenditure, he persuaded Parliament to vote a special credit for the defence of India. The Conservatives were only in power until February 1886, but Randolph Churchill remained interested in India thereafter.

He was indeed genuinely interested—slightly surprising for such an essentially meretricious man. He had taken pains when he was in India to meet Indians and visit them in their own homes, saying that he thought it remarkably foolish of English administrators to eschew Indian society. He liked India, as his son was never to do. He was praised by the Indian press.

As Secretary of State, he was much less liberal than he looked likely to be. The Indian National Congress held its first meeting in 1885, and when a delegation of Indians came to see him in London, he treated them with exceptional courtesy but with studied silence about what the future might hold. The delegation gave their support to his Liberal opponent in Central Birmingham, John Bright. They found him much more responsive to their ambitions. Churchill, by contrast, sneered at the 'ignorance and credulity' of the Indians. '[T]o secure the return of Mr Bright [the Liberals] had to bring down on the platform of that great Town Hall three Bengalee Baboos.'[14] * Randolph lost the election despite the annexation of Upper Burma, an initiative designed to appeal to his Birmingham electors.

*

Winston Churchill neither broke the filial tie nor did he want to. When he crossed the floor of the House on 31 May 1904, he sat in his father's old seat. On 8 March 1905, he spoke to his own motion, 'that in the opinion of this House, the permanent unity of the British Empire will not be secured through a system of preferential duties based upon the protective taxation of food'. He complained that Chamberlain had forgotten India, but he had not. He used his father's words about the bright and precious gem. He was determined to keep that jewel in the Crown. He said that without India, Britain would amount to no more than Belgium. For a man of his age and his background who had imbued himself

---

* A Baboo (or Babu, as it is spelled in India) was a clerk: the word was always critically employed, implying pettifogging obstructiveness.

with the glorious history of the eighteenth century, that was a quite unendurable perception.

*

The relative decline in Britain's position in the world that occurred in the last quarter of the nineteenth century was observed only by a few, but it *was* observed by them and was not only evident in hindsight. Kipling's *Recessional* was written in 1897 and envisaged the supersession of Britain's power by that of the United States:

> Far-called, our navies melt away;
> On dune and headland sinks the fire:
> Lo, all our pomp of yesterday
> Is one with Nineveh and Tyre!

In these years, there was a great deal of interest in what is called Social Darwinism: the theory of natural selection projected into the world of human behaviour, embracing the notion that societies advance through aggression, conflict and strength, weakening and declining if they cease to assert themselves. In Britain, there was a widespread view among some thinkers that the country had become too comfortable and effete. Some of the responses to this diagnosis were pretty unappealing, creating a cocktail of fascism, eugenics and aggression. Many who eschewed these extremes still felt that for material and moral progress, nations had to go through the beneficial experience of war and that there was a necessity for occasional bloodletting.

Churchill was affected by this thinking. With people who were essentially forward-thinking and progressive, he wanted to improve the national stock by eliminating the 'socially unfit' and avoiding 'the multiplication of the Feeble-Minded'. To this end, he was in favour of the compulsory sterilization of an initial batch of 1,00,000.[15]

One man who wrote in the spirit of Social Darwinism was William Winwood Reade. His most influential book was *The Martyrdom of Man* (1872). It may be recalled that this was one of the books that Churchill studied with particular care as a young officer in Bangalore. In the opinion of Paul Addison, one of his most perceptive biographers, it was a book that particularly influenced Churchill. Reade was the nephew of the novelist Charles Reade. He tried to follow in his uncle's footsteps and wrote some unsuccessful novels. He then focused on exploration, research, history and anthropology. He corresponded with Darwin, who used some of his research material in *The Descent of Man*. *The Martyrdom of Man* was the outcome of these areas of interest. In it, William Reade attacked conventional religion and sought to establish a secular framework for mankind, and to argue that Darwinian progress could be made if men were guided by pure science. In its time, the book was influential. Cecil Rhodes said that it had made him what he was. The most recent politician to acknowledge the effect of the book was Michael Foot.[16] *The Martyrdom of Man* was often referred to as a secular bible, and it was described to Churchill by his colonel, Colonel Brabazon:

> [It] was Colonel Brabazon's great book. He had read it many times over and regarded it as a sort of Bible. It is in fact a concise and well-written universal history of mankind, dealing in harsh terms with the mysteries of all religions and leading to the depressing conclusion that we simply go out like candles.*

---

* Brabazon was a well-read colonel who pronounced the letter 'R' as 'W'. In the mess Churchill on one occasion quoted,

God tempers the wind to the shorn lamb, as Churchill recalled in *My Early Life*. 'Brabazon asked, 'where do you get that fwom?' I

In 1920, Churchill, reacting to the threat of Bolshevism, talked of a 'world-wide conspiracy . . . designed to deprive us of our place in the world and rob us of victory'. Positive action was needed to resist this 'malevolent and subversive force'.[17] This period marked the onset of his Darwinian campaign. Long before the controversy about the India Bill—immediately after the First World War, in fact—Churchill was taking a gloomy view of the outlook for the world and for the British Empire. In 1914, he was only forty, but he had a clear and, as it turned out, spectacularly wrong conviction that he would, like his father, die young. Perhaps as a result, he tended towards a premature middle-aged reflectiveness. The loss of very many friends in the course of the war may have contributed to this consciousness of the passing years and the brevity of life. In September 1921, he wrote to his wife: 'Another twenty years will bring me to the end of my allotted span even if I have so long. The reflections of middle age are mellow.'[18]

These reflections seemed sombre rather than mellow. Amateur psychologists (and some professional ones)* make too much of Churchill's 'Black Dog'. His bouts of depression were reactions to turns of events: the frustration of his political ambitions or, as here, the concurrence of setbacks.

He had shared with his generation the experience of being nurtured in the uncomplicated Whiggish narrative, nationalist jingoistic and triumphalist. He talked of the self-confidence of

---

had replied with some complacency that, though it was attributed often to the Bible it really occurred in Sterne's *Sentimental Journey*. 'Have you ever wead it?' he asked, in the most innocent manner. Luckily I was not only naturally truthful, but also on my guard. I admitted that I had not. It was, it seems, one of the Colonel's special favourites.

* See Storr, A., in Churchill: *Four Faces and the Man*.

'the palmy days of Queen Victoria', and in an early draft of his war memoirs, he wrote: 'Children were taught of the Great War against Napoleon as the culminating effort in the history of the British peoples, and they looked on Trafalgar and Waterloo as the supreme achievements of British arms by land and sea.'

Another Great War destroyed this illusion for Churchill. He thought that the war had been badly fought by Britain and never believed that victory in 1918 restored Britain's place in the world. On the contrary, he saw increasing threats. He saw them in revived Irish activity at home, in European instability, and in a collapse of settled values and stable institutions.

When he was at the War Office, he set out a gloomy memorandum narrating at length the various ways in which civilized values had been ignored. 'Every outrage against humanity or international law was repaid by reprisals . . . Bombs from the air were cast down indiscriminately. Poison gas in many forms stifled or seared the soldiers.'[19]

In a speech on 11 November 1922, he talked about the disappointment the twentieth century had so far been. He saw chaos in every part of the globe. He mentioned China, Mexico, Russia, Ireland, Egypt and India, where 'we see among millions of people hitherto shielded by superior science and superior law a desire to shatter the structure by which they live & to return blindly & heedlessly to primordial chaos'.

His confidence in the inexorable progress and security of the British Empire had been destroyed forever. For the rest of his life, he feared for the future. At the end of that life, he feared for the safety of the world in an atomic confrontation. For now, his fears were for Britain. It had to be more than another Belgium. It had to resist decline.

19

In Power Again

Churchill came back to office as a result of the failure of Neville Chamberlain's foreign policy and the fact that he, Churchill, had been the principal critic of that policy. He did not come back because the party wanted him back—on the contrary, Neville Chamberlain thought that he would talk too much and impede the dispatch of Cabinet business—but because his newspaper proprietor friends manipulated support for him amongst their readers. Anonymous donors paid for massive posters carrying the words 'Bring Winston Back'.

In September 1939, he returned to the Admiralty, filling the office he had held from October 1911 to November 1915. It's widely believed that the Board of Admiralty sent out the signal, 'Winston's back'. There's now some doubt about whether such a signal was ever sent. If it was, it didn't convey a message of delight. Churchill had not been liked in his first period at the Admiralty, and he wasn't in his second. On 10 May 1940, he succeeded Chamberlain as Prime Minister. The only other candidate was Lord Irwin, whom we last met as viceroy. Now, as Lord Halifax, he was Foreign Secretary. Halifax could have had the top job if he had wanted it. Churchill had only a small following in his own party; most of the Conservatives would have preferred Halifax. So would the King and Queen. Chamberlain certainly would have. The Labour Party would probably have been prepared to serve under Halifax and find a way around his membership of the Lords, but he didn't have the stomach for the job—literally, he had felt physically sick at the prospect of becoming Prime Minister. Churchill had promised Brendan Bracken, his most loyal supporter, that he would remain silent at the meeting, and when Chamberlain asked him if, in the circumstances of the war, it would be acceptable that a Prime Minister should be in the Lords (as Halifax would have been), Churchill remained silent for, as he put it in his memoirs, a period as long as the two-minute silence that took place on Remembrance Sunday. The silence was broken by Halifax, who ruled himself out.

Chamberlain thought that Churchill wouldn't be there for long. He was pretty sure that *he* would be asked to return as soon as the brief need for a wartime warrior Prime Minister was met. But the war was not the brief conflict that Chamberlain had expected, and Churchill remained Prime Minister until 26 July 1945. He was a largely absent Leader of the Opposition when India became independent via the Indian Independence Act passed by the Parliament on 15 July 1947.

The purpose of this chapter is to set up very briefly the scaffolding of the political engagement between Britain and India in the period from Churchill's return to office in September 1939 to the final granting of independence in July 1947.

*

It was the last thing Churchill would have wanted, but the war had brought Indian independence to the forefront of politics. The government that he formed was a coalition in which the Labour Party was a powerful element. Labour politicians had for a long time been broadly favourable to India's aspirations towards some kind of independence. That is not to say that all Labour politicians were in favour of outright independence in the foreseeable future. Most felt that the conditions were not yet right for that. But there were close links between the Labour Party and Congress and a very distinct feeling of sympathy. The leader of the Labour Party and de facto Deputy Prime Minister from 1940* was Clement Attlee. Attlee had attended Haileybury, more fully 'Haileybury and Imperial Service College', which had originally been founded to train recruits for the East India Company and continued, well into Attlee's time, to prepare high-minded boys for work in the imperial service.† Attlee did indeed have a real interest in India. He had been a member of the Simon Commission, and therefore he had continued to keep abreast of developments. He had been the Labour Party's India expert.

Among other Labour Party politicians (though temporarily expelled from the party for doctrinal deviancy) with a strong interest in India was Sir Stafford Cripps. Cripps, if he is remembered at all today, is remembered for his supposed asceticism, an image that partly derives from his austerity as Chancellor of the Exchequer during 1947–1950 and partly from the lifestyle required by his chronic colitis. There certainly was a hint of astringency to him, and it gave rise to a lot of jokes: 'Wherever Sir Stafford has tried to increase wealth and happiness, grass never grows again.' On the

---

* In 1942, he was officially appointed Deputy Prime Minister de jure, the first time the official role had existed.

† 'To the student at Haileybury, the abiding subject of interest was the expansion and maintenance of British Rule in India.' This was how the school was described in 1893 (Haileybury Archives 10/2). Attlee went to the school in 1896.

other hand, Churchill referred to him in his tribute in the House
of Commons on Cripps's death in very different terms:

> His friends—and there were many—among whom I am proud
> to take my place, were conscious, in addition to his public gifts,
> of the charm of his personality and of the wit and gaiety with
> which he enlivened not only the mellow hours but also the hard
> discharge of laborious business in anxious or perilous times.

One of his colleagues wrote, 'He is the nearest to a saint I have
ever met. He was a man of complete selflessness and devotion to
humanity. I hope and believe that I am a better man for having
known him.'[1] That humanity found its expression in many ways,
not the least of which was his commitment to India.

Cripps's aunt was Beatrice Webb, and he was much influenced
by his stepmother, Marion Parmoor, a Quaker who supported
the India Conciliation Group. Cripps became a friend of Nehru
before the war. In 1937, he described his friendship with Nehru
as the greatest privilege of his life. Nehru and his daughter Indira
stayed at Cripps's country home, Goodfellows. They wrote to
each other as 'My dear Stafford' and 'My dear Jawaharlal'. He
made three important visits to India in pursuit of what was to
some extent a personal commitment to achieve a just settlement
of the Indian question. The second of these, known to history as
the Cripps Mission, will be explored later.

*

As a result of the Labour Party's interest in the subcontinent,
Indian affairs preoccupied Churchill's 1940–1945 administration
much more than he would have wished. By 1945, when the
Conservatives lost the General Election, it was pretty well
accepted amongst realistic politicians on either side of the House

that India would become truly independent within the next ten years. It is a beautiful irony that Indian independence was brought far, far closer under Churchill's Prime Ministership than at any other time.

It goes without saying that the acceleration of the move to independence that took place under him did so despite and not because of his views. So far as India is concerned, the essence of the years 1940–1945 was of events and personalities conspiring to promote the cause of independence while Churchill, with some help from the viceroy, Linlithgow, did everything he could to scupper progress.

*

One or two other actors in this act of the drama. The first is Franklin D. Roosevelt. He's here in part to represent liberal opinion in the United States generally. But he's also here very much in his own right. From his very first meeting with Churchill in the course of the war, when the two leaders met on their warships in Placentia Bay, off Newfoundland, in August 1941, President Roosevelt took an interest in Britain's Empire, which Churchill found unnecessary and intrusive. According to his son, Elliott, who accompanied his father for the conference, Roosevelt described Churchill afterwards as, 'A real old Tory, of the old school', with 'eighteenth-century methods' of running the Empire.[2] Elliott Roosevelt is woefully unreliable, and his comments have to be read with considerable caution, but that description does sound like an authentic FDR appraisal.

As the two leaders shuttled back and forth between each other's ships, a document began to emerge that would become known as the Atlantic Charter. At this precarious and critical stage of the war, Churchill had hoped that the conference might result in a ringing declaration of support from the United States. All he got was the Charter. The Charter was not an innocent and idealistic statement of common intent; it was a severely political document, designed to limit potential actions by the British Government and reassure American critics of an end to the Empire. Article One disclaimed territorial ambitions. Articles Two and Three said that territorial changes were to be in accord with 'the freely expressed wishes of the people concerned', and Article Four defended the 'right of all peoples to choose the form of Government under which they live'. Subsequent articles attacked imperial preference.

Churchill's reaction to what the economist John Maynard Keynes called these 'lunatic proposals' was that America was 'trying to do away with the British Empire'. He handled the matter well, but he was worried about what he had signed. He wrote to his Secretary of State for India, saying that Article Three was presumably only intended to apply when there *was* a transfer of power: It could not be intended 'that the natives of Nigeria or of East Africa could by a majority vote choose the form of Government under which they would live, or the Arabs by such a vote expel the Jews from Palestine'.[3]

America's preoccupation with India wasn't confined to Roosevelt. After the Quebec conference in 1943, a guest at a lunch that Roosevelt gave for Churchill was Mrs Helen Ogden Mills Reid, the vice-president of the *New York Herald Tribune* and a hostile critic of British India. She raised the matter of India with Churchill. He replied. 'Before we proceed any further, let us get one thing clear: are we talking about the brown Indians of India, who have multiplied alarmingly under benevolent British rule? Or are we speaking of the Red Indians in America, who, I understand, are almost extinct?'[4] There was no further discussion of India by Mrs Reid.

Churchill had to be more circumspect with Roosevelt. For victory and survival, American aid was essential. The immense effort that Churchill put into his telegraphed pleas for help reflected just how important it was. They ran through many drafts and the urgency of his requests still bleeds from the pages. Look, for instance, at this paragraph from his request of 31 July 1940, for decommissioned American destroyers: 'Mr President, with great respect I must tell you that in the long history of the world this is a thing to do *now* . . . . I know you will do all in your power, but I feel entitled and bound to put the gravity and urgency of the position before you.'[5]

Roosevelt generally replied genially but negatively to these agonised cries for help in the darkest of days in 1940, following the fall of France. On this occasion, he did supply some ancient vessels, but only in exchange for British bases in the West Indies.

Both Churchill and Roosevelt were indeed genial men. When they were together, they joshed each other and appeared to enjoy one another's company, although later in the war, Roosevelt rather cruelly ganged up with Stalin to embarrass and even humiliate Churchill. Churchill respected Roosevelt, although I have never discovered any evidence of real affection for him, and there is some evidence of dislike. But his dependence on the President was immense. He declared that 'no lover ever studied every whim of his mistress as I did those of President Roosevelt', and though his declaration that he had not become the King's First Minister in order to preside over the dissolution of the British Empire was made in response to Roosevelt's demands that he should do just that, he was obliged at least to appear to work towards a time when India would be free to cast off the oppressive shackles of the Empire.

*

The other personalities in the drama were closer to home. The Secretary of State for India throughout Churchill's first administration was Leo Amery, whom Churchill had pushed into the swimming pool at Harrow and who had humiliated Churchill over the Latin tag in the committee on privileges debate. Amery may have forgotten the first incident but Churchill had not forgotten the second.

Linlithgow, the viceroy, wrote to Amery, saying that Churchill's appointment as Prime Minister had been interpreted in India as indicating a prospective move to the right in the government's policy. Amery gave the impression that *he* would be a progressive influence. Linlithgow, although very far from progressive himself, wanted Amery to quieten things down for him by restraining the extreme tendencies of the Prime Minister. Amery was in reality no radical firebrand, but perceptive Indians could see the difference between him and Churchill. He was satisfied that India must have a responsible government. That was, of course, a long way from independence.

At first sight, Amery was an odd appointment. He and Churchill had differed significantly over the years, and never more so than in India. The reason Churchill appointed him Secretary of State all the same was, in fact, that he didn't think India would be a live issue during the war.

Neither did Amery. He, more than anyone else, had tended the sacred flame of Joseph Chamberlain's memory. He carried forward the great Joe's commitment to Empire, 'The final object of patriotic emotion and action' as Amery described it.[6] He had been born in the north–west provinces of India. Eight years after his mother returned from India to Britain, she divorced her husband, who moved from India to another part of the Empire to take up farming in Canada. As Joseph Chamberlain's protégé, Amery's vicious and effective attack on Joe's son, Neville Chamberlain, in the Norway debate in May 1940 was all the more devastating; he famously told him that he had sat long enough for all the good he did. More than any other single person, he could be seen as being responsible for putting Churchill in Number 10. He expected a substantial reward, probably one of the service ministries. He considered the India Office such a backwater that he was initially inclined not to accept it.

But the matter of India became critically important throughout the war, and Amery found himself much busier than he had expected to be. Although he believed in the Empire, his vision was of an overarching, enabling, democratic institution in which the different parts of the Empire all benefited from their association. He was in favour of Indian political advancement. There was, accordingly, continuous tension between him and Churchill. They got along well enough on the whole, but Amery was repeatedly frustrated by Churchill's archaic views. He said that Churchill knew as much about India as George III had known about the American Colonies. His attempt throughout his time at the India Office was to try to make the 1935 Act work and to create a responsible and democratic government. Churchill sought to achieve quite the opposite.

*

Churchill was assisted in his endeavour by the fact that he inherited as viceroy Lord Linlithgow, the next actor we should look at. We last met Linlithgow as Chairman of the All-Party Select Committee. Victor Alexander John Hope, Lord Linlithgow, 'Hopie', after his family name, had been appointed viceroy on 18 April 1936. He was an agreeable aristocrat, principled, kindly and well-meaning with a compendious knowledge of the music hall. He enjoyed popular songs and, in particular, singing them with his family. His sense of humour was not elevated, his favourite comedians were Bud Flanagan and 'Monsewer' Eddie Gray. He was a Scottish countryman who derived much commendable enjoyment from the observation of nature. His son acknowledged that he was not a clever man. But even Linlithgow identified the obstacles to progress as Indian political stupidity and British political dishonesty.

Lord Wavell, his successor as viceroy, described him as 'a wise, strong man and very human, really'. The 'really' is significant; others referred to his 'cold exterior'. The editor of the Calcutta-based but then English-owned *Statesman* found this 'cold, cautious, self-assured aristocrat . . . outwardly . . . an inscrutable rather unpleasant figure: stiff, unsmiling; physically very large* . . . and in some indefinable way uncouth'. Nehru accepted his 'integrity and honesty of purpose', although he was 'heavy of body and slow of mind, solid as a rock and with almost a rock's lack of awareness'.[7]

He was an honourable man. He worked hard by his lights, although not nearly as hard as the viceroys who succeeded him, Wavell and Mountbatten. He had time to visit remote parts of the subcontinent, both for fact-finding and sightseeing, with a reasonable amount of hunting, sport and butterfly-collecting thrown in. The 1935 Act created all the requirements for stasis. It set the princes, the Muslim League and Congress in architectural opposition to each other. Linlithgow was the ideal man to preside over stagnation. He did not have vision. He was an old-fashioned administrator. He and his family went into dinner each night as the viceroy's orchestra played 'The Roast Beef of Old England'. He put little effort into the case for federation. The outbreak of war put an end to the project, and there is a sense that he was relieved to have an excuse.

Even at a late stage, Churchill had dreamed that 'we might sit on top of a tripos—Pakistan, princely India and the Hindus'.[8] Linlithgow thought much the same. Britain could 'carry on with some scheme of government imposed by ourselves with, of course, the inevitable corollary that we shall remain there to hold the balance'. He thought that British rule would last for

---

* He was six feet and five inches tall, about the same height as Lord Irwin. Amery was seventeen inches (43.18 cms) shorter than Linlithgow.

at least another generation.[9] When it was said in Cabinet that there was a risk of a growing cleavage between the Muslim and Hindu populations, Churchill 'at once said: "Oh, but that is all to the good."'[10]

Linlithgow was thus an ideal man for Churchill to work with, ensuring that no progress would be made on the road to independence. Churchill got along with him so well that he renewed his appointment as viceroy. He spent seven years in the office, longer than any other viceroy or governor general since the time of Lord Dalhousie, ninety years earlier.

*

When Linlithgow finally had to go, he was replaced by Field Marshal Lord Wavell. A lot of people were considered before Wavell was appointed. Attlee, Rab Butler, Sam Hoare, Lord Cranborne, Harold Macmillan (rejected as 'unstable') and Anthony Eden. Eden would have had the job if Churchill had been prepared to let him go. Amery even suggested himself; Churchill thought that was very decent of him but that he was too old. At first sight, Wavell seemed ideal. Churchill hadn't thought much of him in the Middle East and didn't think that he was very useful as a Commander in Chief in India. He had already tried to dump him on Australia as the Governor General. Wavell would be dull and dependable and could do no great damage, and appointing him as viceroy would mean that Claude Auchinleck, who had also been removed from command in the Middle East, could go back to his former job as Commander in Chief, India, the job Wavell was leaving. Just a few days later, however, Churchill read Wavell's biography of Allenby, whose military career had been followed by an appointment as High Commissioner for Egypt and the Sudan, where he had proved to be of an independent and progressive mind. It was clear from the book that Wavell too had progressive views, and Churchill realized, when it was too late to do anything about it, and for all that he was a military man, that the new viceroy might prove to be more radical than most politicians.

'The letters and reports of Archie Wavell,' said Patrick French, 'stand out among the thousands of official British documents preceding the transfer of power in India. He dealt with realities. If the British were going to Quit India, how would they do so in practice? If the demand for Pakistan was conceded, what would be the boundaries of the new state?'[11]

Wavell's policy was not informed by preconceptions. As a military man, he proceeded by analysing the situation, formulating plans to address the circumstances and then implementing that plan. He pretty well ignored the politicians. The politicians didn't like him. Churchill had misunderstood the man he appointed. He had said on one occasion that it might be his own fault, but he thought that Wavell was rather like the chairman of a golf club or a Conservative Association. He was very wrong. Wavell is highly regarded by military historians. He was intellectually formidable, although he did not parade this fact. In 1938, he gave the Lees Knowles lectures at Cambridge on 'Generals and Generalship'. Rommel carried a copy of the lectures with him throughout the North African Campaign. Wavell was a scholarly soldier. He had been under consideration for the Chichele Professorship of Military Studies at Oxford when war broke out. Eventually, he was the Chancellor of one university and had honorary degrees from six others.

Wavell said that Churchill hated India and everything to do with it. His regard for Amery was limited: he had 'a curious capacity for getting hold of the right stick but practically always the wrong end of it'. Wavell, on the other, hand knew India. He had served there in 1903, and when he moved from North Africa to become Commander in Chief in India in 1943, he automatically became a member of the viceroy's executive council, and for two years, the viceroy's right-hand man. Even before he became viceroy, he had the benefit of close observation of the workings of British rule. He had a better apprenticeship for supreme office in India than any other viceroy. He believed that India should be independent. Before he took up his new post, he prepared himself at the India Office by researching British policy, and he realized that his approval of independence was not shared by the government. He said, 'We were proposing a policy of freedom for India, and in practice opposing every suggestion for a step forward.'[12]

It was inevitable that this pragmatic realist would run into trouble with the politicians, and he did. He was sidelined and sabotaged by Churchill, which is hardly surprising. What was less predictable was that Churchill's successor, Clement Attlee, treated the viceroy equally badly. Attlee had been an effective officer in the First World War, but he emerged from that conflict with a strong prejudice against senior commanders. Whether or not that was the reason, he treated Wavell extraordinarily badly, ignoring his contributions to policy and discourteously not choosing to consult him even when the viceroy was in London.

By the end of his time in India, Wavell was seen by his critics as pessimistic, weak and having run out of steam. But it was he who decided that India should be granted independence within eighteen months. He acquiesced in the conclusion that there would have to be partition; he didn't like it, but he was resigned to it and advised the government accordingly. He advocated not scuttle but an orderly withdrawal against an eighteen-month timetable.

All that was pretty much what his successor, Mountbatten, decreed, yet Wavell is regarded as feeble and unsuccessful and Mountbatten as decisive and successful. The reason may just have been to do with appearances. Mountbatten had charm, good looks and charisma. Wavell was tongue-tied, shy and restrained.

At times, his reticence amounted almost to an inability to speak. He 'tended to grunt, murmur and bump into things, caught off balance by his bad eyesight and poor hearing'.[13] His difficulty in communication was exacerbated by the fact that he had only one eye (he had lost his left eye at Ypres in 1915 and was almost totally deaf in one ear).

Because of his one eye, King George VI described Wavell as 'an oyster', even though he had sacrificed the eye for King and country. It is intriguing to picture the meetings between the awkward, stuttering George and the one-eyed, deaf and silent Wavell. The king found the smooth and urbane Mountbatten, his close relative, more congenial company.

*

And Mountbatten is remembered as a dashing and successful last viceroy. In reality, despite hard work and prodigious efforts, he was unsuccessful. He followed the Wavell prescription for a fast move towards independence and then, pretty well off the cuff, accelerated it even further to a date plucked out of the air. Such planning as he made for precipitate independence was largely based on policies already formulated in Wavell's time, and he made no great efforts—perhaps there was little he could have done—to avoid the frightful bloodshed, displacement of millions and the tragedy of Partition, except to get off the scene as quickly as possible in order to avoid apparent responsibility.

*

These are then the main players in the drama of Churchill's last war against India. Now we look at different acts of the drama.

20

War: The August Offer

On 3 September 1939, Neville Chamberlain delivered his self-pitying broadcast to the British people, telling them what a personal disappointment it was for him that Britain now found itself at war with Germany. At this point, Linlithgow made the greatest mistake of his viceroyalty. On the very same day as Chamberlain, Linlithgow also made a radio announcement. It was a very brief one, and it was made without consultation with the Indian leaders and without their agreement. He told the Indians that they too were at war with Germany.

Linlithgow was technically entitled to do what he did. The Government of India Act had been amended just a few months earlier to allow him to do it. But it was an enormous political mistake that would intensify the constitutional struggle of the Congress leaders for the rest of British rule. The reaction was perhaps even more serious than he could have imagined, but he didn't need hindsight to see that it was foolish and unnecessary. Congress had probably been more strongly against fascism than Britain had been. But the party had passed various resolutions, making it perfectly clear that acquiescence in a declaration of war was not to be taken for granted. Indications had been given of how Congress would view a unilateral declaration. The party had reacted strongly, for instance, when Indian troops were sent to Aden, Egypt and Singapore before the outbreak of war. Linlithgow had debated with the Secretary of State, the Marquess of Zetland, what would happen if Congress members resigned from office. Emergency legislation was passed, which conferred executive authority on the central government. So Linlithgow was well aware of what the consequences of the unilateral declaration would be. The effect of the declaration was, at a much lower level, similar to the Jallianwala Bagh Massacre in creating an unbridgeable chasm between the political regimes in England and India.

In 1939, now First Lord of the Admiralty but not yet Prime Minister, Churchill's thoughts, as usual, ranged far beyond the limits of his departmental responsibility. He looked, for instance, at Ireland, alarmed by de Valera's commitment to neutrality and keen to recover the three Irish 'treaty ports', originally retained by Britain in 1921 but subsequently returned to Ireland. Anthony Eden, at this time Secretary of State for the Dominions, was uneasy about this. He was equally uneasy about Churchill's attitude towards India.

Just a few weeks after war had been declared, Churchill wrote a memorandum on 'Employment of Indians or Colonial Natives in the Royal Navy.' He started by saying that there should be no discrimination on the basis of race or colour. Everything would depend on merit. His tongue was, however, in his cheek: 'I cannot see any objections to Indians serving on HM ships where they are qualified and needed, or if their virtues so deserve rising to be Admirals of the Fleet. But not too many of them please.'[1]

What concerned Eden was that, in Churchill's view, the outbreak of war had put an end to any talk of Indian reform. This determination, which chimed in with the views of the stolid conservative viceroy, was to be Churchill's default position when he became Prime Minister in 1940. Throughout the war, Churchill was determined not to make any concessions to India. Anything conceded during the war would have been given away when Britain's bargaining position was very weak. By the end of a successful war, Britain would be able to impose her will.

This sustained policy did enormous damage to Britain's relations with India. Churchill's alienation of the Indian political establishment from the very outset of the Second World War destroyed constructive cooperation and forced the Indian political classes into a hostile and suspicious posture. The outcome would be the scuttle of 1947, a crude partition of the subcontinent that gave rise to the cruelty and suffering that continue to this day. In that process, 15–18 million people were displaced. More than 3 million were missing or dead. Hundreds of thousands of women were raped or abducted. Britain portrayed Partition as an undesirable and anomalous expedient accepted because of the failure of Hindus and Muslims to work together. But that failure was the outcome of a policy, deliberately adopted by some, including Churchill, of dividing in order to rule. In any event, as Priya Satia has pointed out, 'by the 1940s "partition" was part of Britain's decolonisation toolkit'.[2] It was used not only in the Indian subcontinent but also in the Irish solution. It had frequently been talked of in relation to Palestine before Britain handed the Palestine problem over to the United Nations.

Things could have gone quite differently. In 1939, even the pacifist Gandhi was prepared to give moral support to Britain. Congress, too, was prepared to support the war, subject to conditions that could have been met, and the Muslim League did in practice support the war. The Marquess of Zetland, Secretary of State until Amery, pressed Churchill to put forward constitutional proposals that would placate Congress. Churchill's response, in February 1940, while still not Prime Minister, was to ask whether it was reasonable that Parliament or the War Cabinet should be involved in these complicated issues while fighting a war. He urged Linlithgow to offer nothing new. The War Cabinet Minutes of 2 February 1940:

> The First Lord said that he did not share the anxiety to encourage and promote unity between the Hindu and Moslem communities. Such unity was, in fact, almost out of the realm of practical politics, while, if it were to be brought about, the immediate result would be that the united communities would join in showing us the door. He regarded the Hindu/Moslem feud as a bulwark of British rule in India.

In the course of the war, he repeatedly expressed concern for the Muslim minority, but his real concern was to keep the communities divided.* His remarks to the Cabinet disclose his unquestioning assumption that the perpetuation of British rule in India was to be government policy. He had commended himself for ensuring that the 1935 Act was unworkable, and now, approaching the office of Prime Minister, he would be in a position to ensure that that was the case. By the time he was out of office in 1945, his stubborn commitment to negativism had made it certain that there would be no seamless, peaceful, amicable transition to independence.

On 24 March 1940, the Muslim League, meeting in Lahore, took the momentous decision to say that the Muslim areas should

---

* While Churchill certainly exaggerated concern about the Muslim minority to justify doing nothing, it is worth recalling that in 1926 he wrote to Clemmie: 'reading about India has depressed me for I see such ugly storms looming up . . . Only a Muslim-majority state in the northern part of the Indian sub-continent would protect Muslim minority rights if and when the British left'.

become independent of the Hindu areas. The step was deprecated by British politicians and administrators, who had always seen the creation of a single India and its preservation as a single country as a great achievement of British Rule—indeed, almost as the justification for it. But Churchill's reaction to the Lahore resolution was to welcome the demonstration of self-reliance and self-assertiveness on the part of the League. Sir John Simon said that: 'Winston rejoiced in the quarrel which had broken out afresh between Hindus and Moslems, said he hoped it would remain bitter and bloody and was glad that we had made the suggestion of dominion status which was acting as a cat among the pigeons.'[3]

On his appointment as Prime Minister in May 1940, Churchill replaced Zetland as Secretary of State with Leo Amery, figuring, as will be recalled, that Amery would be presiding over a department that would hibernate throughout the war. Amery made his first statement as Secretary of State in the House of Commons on 23 May 1940. He envisaged a role for India in the Commonwealth that would amount to something more than the 1935 Act formula. What it would be was not spelled out. Originally, he planned to say that India would play a 'predominant' role in determining its new role, but the Cabinet turned that down to 'vital'.

Cripps began to urge on Amery the germ of the mission that he would take to India in 1942: the idea of independence post-dated to the end of the war. At the same time, Linlithgow wanted some practical changes to the way India would be governed during the war. He suggested an expanded viceroy's Council with a War Advisory Committee that would include representatives of the princes—even if the Muslim League and Congress wouldn't join in. In the interests of conciliation, he also wanted to say that the government aimed for dominion status within a year of the end of the war. Amery was entirely in agreement with this. He had, however, to take Churchill with him, and when Churchill found out what had been going on, he was furious. Amery was taken aback by the general lack of support from the Cabinet. Churchill's secretary, Jock Colville, referred to a 'blood row' over the germinating policy. Only the Labour members of the Cabinet were behind Amery.

Churchill felt so strongly that in July 1940, although he was absorbed in the most hectic period of his leadership as invasion was apprehended day by day, he told Amery that: 'He would sooner give up political life at once, or rather go out into the wilderness and fight, than admit to a revolution that meant the end of the imperial crown in India.'[4] He now began what he would do for the rest of Linlithgow's viceroyalty: he insisted on seeing all the telegrams going between the Secretary of State and Delhi. Amery reasonably took the view that effectively, private correspondence was being censored. He thought hard about resigning, only not doing so because the country was at war. Churchill cabled Linlithgow:

> Secretary of State has shown me the telegrams which have passed on secret and in personal file and for the first time I realised what has been going on. I must ask in the public interest and in justice to you to show these telegrams to the War Cabinet and two or three other colleagues who have great Indian experience and whom I have consulted . . . . The Cabinet has left it to me to draft for your consideration an alternative statement in harmony with the only policies to which we are at present committed.[5]

Churchill was making it clear that he would be at the centre of Indian policy for the rest of the war, and that he was not there to expedite the arrival of dominion status.

A declaration of intent was to be made, and unhelpfully, Churchill insisted on being involved. He watered down Amery's original ideas very considerably. No timetable whatsoever would be associated with any move to dominion status. The 'representative' Indians who would be added to the executive council were essentially tame, collaborating Indians. There was little that was decisive in the offer—other than the provision, directed at Muslims, that no structure would be permitted, which was unacceptable to 'large and powerful elements in India's national life'. Churchill, always drawn to the martial qualities of the Muslims, was aware that a third of the Indian Army was Muslim. For every reason, Muslim opinion had to be taken into account.

Amery complained to Linlithgow,

> The whole terrific fuss which he has made, culminating in my showing him every telegram that passed between us, was really irrelevant and unnecessary. The trouble is that he reacts instinctively and passionately against the whole idea of any government of India other than that which he knew forty years ago.[6]

The outcome was the Declaration of 8 August 1940, usually known as the August Offer. It contained no definite commitment to dominion status, merely an enlargement of the viceroy's Council. There was no promised timetable, and there was to be no transfer of responsibilities. Any progress that may have been hinted at was also subject to the critical proviso about 'large and powerful elements in India's national life'. Gandhi recognized this as the divide and rule formula, and it was used for the rest of Churchill's time to obstruct progress. The August Offer is more important for that negative element than for anything positive.

Congress rejected the August Offer in its totality, and the Working Committee of the Muslim League rejected it in part. Meanwhile, Linlithgow asked for powers to arrest Congress leaders whenever he wanted to and to declare the whole body an illegal entity. This was an approach Churchill liked: Linlithgow was due to retire in April 1941, but in October 1940, Churchill asked him to stay on for a further year.

Gandhi proposed civil disobedience. The Indian Government prohibited the printing or publishing of any matter calculated to foment opposition to the prosecution of the war. Nehru was sentenced to four years' imprisonment. Churchill was happy to sit on the rejected August Offer, content to say that Britain had done her best but to no avail. After the rejection of the August Offer in 1940, the proposal to enlarge the executive council was shelved.

The United States was, however, increasingly critical. India was largely under direct rule by the viceroy and this did not sit well with the battle for democracy. In May 1941, Linlithgow and Amery decided they *would* enlarge the executive council, bypassing Congress and taking in useful individuals. Churchill responded to Amery angrily:

> [Y]ou say, 'Linlithgow's proposals are the least with which I can continue to hold the House of Commons'. This ought not to be the criterion for governing India. I may add that *I* should find no difficulty in riddling these proposals in Debate to the satisfaction of the overwhelming majority of members, whether of the Right or of the Left.[7]

The emphasis of the 'I' is mine: Churchill was telling Amery that he could manage perfectly well without him. But Amery wouldn't have been easy to dispose of. He had the support of Attlee, Sir John Simon and John Anderson in the cabinet.

*

In the year after the August Offer, India's military contribution to the war was important and helpful. The Indian Army grew very substantially as recruits joined the forces. This had repercussions that played against Churchill's policy. The expansion of the Indian Army meant that its officer corps contained a much larger proportion of Indians than formerly. The scale and scope of recruitment also meant that soldiers no longer came from non-political sectors of the population. Finally, the cost of India's war effort, which rose to £1 million a day and was payable by London, increased Britain's massive debt to India.[8] The Indian Army had been commanded almost entirely by British officers trained in Britain until the Indianization process that started in the 1920s, and even then it was still substantially commanded by such men. It was, however, entirely distinct from the British Army, although, to confuse matters, the British Army sometimes served in India. The purpose of the Indian Army historically had been to support the British Army, as it had done in the First World War. From 1942 onwards, it was however very much involved in the defence of India and in the war in Burma.

21

War: India at War

In 1942, the military situation in the east had become grave. The Japanese captured Singapore in February 1942 and advanced through Burma, taking Rangoon in March, apparently ready to attack India itself. The outcome was critical: India was the crucial link between Britain's Middle East and Far Eastern possessions. Linlithgow was alarmed. His fears were shared by General Chiang Kai-shek, the President of the Chinese Republic, who agonized over India's vulnerability to a Japanese walk-in that would leave China exposed. He and Roosevelt were convinced that the political alienation of the Indian masses left India open to Japanese propaganda and annexation.

The defeat in Malaya, the capture of Singapore and the loss of Burma carried a powerful propaganda message: the suggestion that Britain's Eastern empire in all its glory and magnificence had been a sham, the product of illusion, capable of collapsing overnight. This perception added to the sense of India's vulnerability. The option of sitting tight until a victory that may never come and making no concession while the enemy threatened was no longer an option. Thus the Cripps Mission—the product of an awareness of the need to defuse political tension in India. We shall analyse the Cripps Mission later. At a military level, Churchill continually pressed for a counteroffensive. His initial desire was to recover Rangoon by the end of 1942. Wavell came under great pressure.

Tension developed between Churchill, on the one hand, and the Chinese and Americans, on the other. Churchill's desire was to recover the south, the area around Rangoon. His allies thought his principal concern was to safeguard what they regarded as imperial territories and colonial possessions. *They* were more concerned about the north, which was the essential supply route to China. The Americans wanted to bulldoze a route through the mountains from the north of Assam, and while this was being built, aircraft were being used to fly equipment and supplies across the Himalayas, 'the Hump'. They maintained that the British did not have their hearts in this project and were interested only in recovering lost Empire and restoring national pride. In his war memoirs, Churchill said that, of course, Britain wanted to recapture Burma, but not through the hostile north. He said, 'Our whole British–Indian imperial front would . . . advance across the Bay of Bengal into close contact with the enemy, by using amphibious power at every stage.'[1] One can see Roosevelt shuddering at the use of such a phrase.

*

In February 1942, Roosevelt asked Averell Harriman to convey a personal message to Churchill, asking him what his policy on India was going to be. Harriman was aware that he was treading on thin ice and that his boss's approach was simplistic. Roosevelt's position on India was inconsistent, uninformed and largely based on American prejudice against European colonialism. In addition, the United States was opposed to Britain's position on imperial preference as opposed to unrestricted Free Trade. Harriman thought that Roosevelt's approach to India was less sophisticated than Stalin's. Stalin understood something of the complex nature of Indian society, riven by religious and caste differences. One of Roosevelt's strangest notions came from Professor Aleš Hrdlička of the Smithsonian Institution. Hrdlička, on the President's orders, was researching a project known as 'racial crossing' something that smacks unpleasantly of Nazi eugenics. Some racial crossings were good, and others were bad. A good one would be to cross-breed and develop 'an Indo-Asian or Eurasian or (better) Euroindasian race' as a counterbalance to the hated Japanese. Churchill's views on India may have been open to censure, but at least they were comprehensible.

The outcome of the 1943 Burma campaign in Arakan was disastrous. The commander, Noel Irwin,* blamed his troops and said they were not yet up to tackling Japanese troops in the jungle. The Command psychiatrist of Eastern Command found that by the end of the campaign 'the whole of the Indian 14 Division was for practical purposes a psychiatric casualty'.[2] Irwin was sacked, and his command was given to Bill Slim. There are many reasons for the failure of the campaign, but Churchill saw it as indicative of the poor state of the army in India, by which he meant the Indian Army. He had never thought much of the Indian Army and he was reinforced in this view throughout the war. He told John Curtin, the Australian Prime Minister, that the Japanese advance was rapid because they had faced only small numbers of 'white' troops 'the rest being Indian soldiers'. In fact, the best of the Indian soldiers had been transferred to the Middle East, and many of the 'white' officers were raw and inexperienced. The invidious comparison was omitted when this letter was quoted in Churchill's history of the war.[3]

---

* Nothing to do with Lord Irwin.

Ultimately, Auchinleck and Slim miraculously improved morale and inspired and led their troops to a glorious victory over Japanese armies that were not invincible, though they did hold many advantages. The Forgotten Army came to believe in itself and proved itself capable of quite outstanding resilience.[4] Its victories in the war in the east were among the very greatest of the achievements of the allied forces, but Churchill made very little of them at the time or later. It is difficult not to conclude that his reason is that the victories were won overwhelmingly by Indian soldiers.

*

Something has been said above about Churchill's dismissive attitude towards Indian troops in the context of the First World War. From the outset of the Second World War, he continued to be dismissive. At the time of the evacuation of the British Expeditionary Force from Dunkirk, as he turned his thoughts to recreating a British Army, he tended to see Indian reinforcements as pretty inadequate makeweights. He wanted them all the same for the Middle East. He thought the Indian Army wasn't doing anything worth speaking of and could at least be added to the British strength in the Middle Eastern Theatre.[5] He was equally critical of African troops.[6] 'Native' troops were never truly to be trusted.

The apparent ease of Japan's invasion of Burma told Churchill how right he had been, and all of this informed his appreciation of the reconquest of Burma. In his war memoirs, he finds it almost impossible to acknowledge that the reconquest was indeed effected by the Indian Army. His language has been interestingly analysed.[7] He frequently referred to the 'British–Indian Army' or to 'British Indian Divisions'. Cat Wilson has studied the historiographical background of Churchill's writing on India in the Second World

War in detail, in the same way that David Reynolds studied it in more general terms. She concludes:

> Churchill's use of the term 'British-Indian Army' speaks volumes about what he thought of the Indian Army. He saw the Indian Army as essentially British, albeit including Indian soldiers and although he was not the only person to think this, he was one of an ever-decreasing number.[8]

Allied Land Sea Forces South East Asia (ALFSEA) Eleventh Army Group was ostensibly British, but 87 per cent of the men were Indian and there were almost as many African colonial soldiers in the Fourteenth Army as British. The Japanese thought the Africans were the best jungle fighters in the army. It is difficult to avoid concluding that Churchill played down the achievements in Burma because the victory there was not won by white troops.

It is true that at the outset, the Indian Army needed a lot of work to bring it up to the required standards of efficiency. Many senior commanders noted that. They were not the only troops, however, that needed work. General Sir Henry Pownall said that at the outset the Indian troops were inferior to the Japanese, but he also said that the Japanese were superior to the British and Australians. The standard of the Indian Army improved, as did the standards of the British and Australian armies. In describing the retreat from Burma in the face of the Japanese invasion, Churchill implies that the problem lay in the poor moral fibre of the Indian troops, which could only be corrected by the injection of a powerful white leader. 'If we could not send an army we could at any rate send the man.'[9] The man would be General Alexander. Other galvanizing Anglo–Saxon heroes would be Wingate and Mountbatten. There is some irony in the fact that a great white officer did indeed galvanize military action in this theatre, but it was General Slim, to whom Churchill never warmed, and not the Prime Minister's meretricious heroes. And 'the man' may have been British and white, but most of the men he led were not.

Churchill had watched the retreat from Burma critically. He blamed the Indian Army and its 'Sepoy Generals' and was always more eager to praise his dashing protégé, Alexander, rather than Slim, who saved his army in a long fighting withdrawal and was later the man who recaptured Burma.[10] 'Nothing persuaded [Churchill] that the Indian Army was anything other than an armed constabulary able to do much more than undertake limited operations against second-tier enemies.'[11]

His restless irritation is reflected in a memorandum he sent on 24 July 1943 to his Chief of Staff, General Ismay, recommending spectacular promotion for Orde Wingate, a relatively junior officer whose exuberant personality endeared him to Churchill in the same way as T.E. Lawrence and Mountbatten. Wingate's technique of jungle penetration had impressed Churchill, but others questioned his judgement, noted his eccentricities* and concluded, like Churchill's doctor, that he was on the borderline of insanity. Churchill wrote: 'I consider Wingate should command the army against Burma. He is a man of genius and audacity, and has rightly been discerned by all eyes as a figure quite above the ordinary level . . .'[12]

The July 1943 memorandum has been described as an example of Churchill's capacity for impetuous folly.

Churchill never recognized how changed the role of the Indian Army was. It was no longer simply an imperial reserve. It was required to protect the eastern seaboard, Sri Lanka and

---

* He ate raw onions and garlic, which he wore round his neck, gave orders straight from the shower, dressed only in a shower cap, or sometimes naked on his bed, while he brushed his body hair with a toothbrush.

the Assam and Bengal lines of communication. In a matter of months, the Indian question had changed from seeking to sit tight and maintain the status quo at a political level, to fairly desperately seeking to defend the subcontinent's military against threats from without.

*

The effect of the reverses in Malaya, Singapore and Burma, with 1,00,000 British, Indian and Australian servicemen going into captivity, had an effect on the political classes in India. It energized the campaign for independence. But it did not have that effect on ordinary Indians, who made haste to join the huge and entirely volunteer Indian Army. They were not deterred by nationalist demonstrations or the Quit India campaign.

The focus of interest from London remained the political vulnerability of India rather than the readiness of the Indian people to join their army and fight in the most appalling conditions and with outstanding bravery to save India from the Japanese. They did so shoulder to shoulder with British and Australian soldiers, but the achievement was overwhelmingly theirs, and it was an achievement that was not recognized or celebrated by the London government. These Indian soldiers recognized an affinity for Britain. Britain did not have a reciprocal perception. Two and a half million young Indians volunteered to join the Indian armed forces during the war. By 1945, the majority of officers in the Indian Army were Indian, 5000 compared to 4500 British.[13] These were well-informed young Indians who were not deterred from entering the army by nationalist views. The volunteers were very far from confined to what Britain had liked to call the 'martial races', particularly the peoples of the Punjab. They came from all over India, including the areas that the British had liked to characterize as effeminate and idle, the south and the east.

22

War: Two Cripps Missions

The 1939 Mission

The extent to which Cripps worked with the government on his first jaunt, in 1939, is surprising. The government was still predominantly Conservative. Cripps, for that matter, was not even technically Labour—he'd been expelled from the party. He sat as an Independent.

Yet his mission in 1939, originally intended to extend to Russia and China, was widely discussed with Halifax, the Foreign Secretary. Indeed, Cripps had interviews with Sir Findlater Stewart, the Permanent Under-Secretary at the India Office. He even had the backing of the Secretary of State, the Marquis of Zetland and Amery. Churchill, still First Lord of the Admiralty but not yet Prime Minister, was very much against any Crippsian bridge-building; he and most of the Cabinet were hostile. He said in Cabinet that he welcomed 'the Hindu-Muslim Feud as the bulwark of British rule'.[1] The viceroy, Lord Linlithgow, was equally unenthusiastic.

When Cripps got to India and met Nehru, his old friend played down the inter-communal problems. But Cripps found the communities separated by the 1935 legislation, and Congress now taking a much more independent view than in the past. Liaquat Ali Khan, the secretary of the Muslim League, took a pessimistic view not just as a result of the inter-communal split but on the broader ground that he felt that western democracy was just not suitable for India.

Cripps went to see Gandhi in a mud hut in his ashram. Linlithgow, unlike Irwin, had avoided meeting Gandhi. During his long viceroyalty, he only met Nehru on two occasions. Cripps reported to Linlithgow on the outcome of his visit on 24 December 1939. Linlithgow made no comment. Cripps described his reaction as 'sphinx-like'.[2]

His mission was entirely unproductive. It had been bound to be. He came as an unofficial visitor, entrusted only with a hint that if India toed the line during the war, it might expect to become a dominion after it. He found his relationship with Nehru less cordial than before. Nehru was coming to be very sceptical about promises from Britain. He told Cripps that his proposals had not carried matters forward; he told others that Cripps had failed to understand the nature of the Indian problem.[3]

Cripps didn't help matters when, on a stopover in New York on the way home, he told reporters that it was class interest that caused the Muslim League to talk about a separate Muslim State. He would return to India with *the* Cripps Mission in 1942, but for the moment, his stock was falling. Linlithgow discouraged Zetland from further initiatives: 'It is no part of our policy, I take it, to expedite in India constitutional changes for their own sake,'[4] a sentiment that was entirely in line with the position of Churchill, who was Prime Minister within a few weeks.

The 1942 Mission

The entry of Japan into the war at the end of 1941 made the stability of India more important than ever. In January 1942, even Sir Tej Sapru Bahadur, the constructive leader of the Indian Liberal Party who had supported Linlithgow's unilateral declaration of war, said that another British initiative was called for. Churchill was in Washington and was for doing nothing. But with the support of the War Cabinet, Attlee said that while he was aware of the complex situation in India, he thought that the Japanese entry into the war made it essential that the Indian problem be addressed. When Churchill got back to London, Attlee argued that someone should be sent to India with the power to negotiate. There was a deadlock for a time. Attlee didn't get his way, with Amery arguing that this was no time for playing around with the Indian Constitution. Amery was supported, of course, by Churchill and Linlithgow.

In July 1942, intelligence reports suggested that Congress was preparing a trial of strength. Churchill was always convinced that Congress had nothing to do with the true India. He told the Commons in September 1942, 'The Indian National Congress does not represent all of India. It does not represent the majority of the people of India. It does not represent the Hindu masses. It is a political organization built around the party machines and sustained by manufacturing and financial interests, opposed by all Muslims and the millions of interests that were the subjects of the princes.[5] Churchill had never liked Congress or the city-based Hindu politicians. Congress, for its part, increasingly saw Britain as a failed regime. The semi-detached Labour left-winger, Aneurin Bevan, tried to put a wedge between Churchill and his Labour colleagues. He asked whether the Prime Minister's 'silly language' was endorsed by his Labour colleagues. Churchill said it was.

Japanese aircraft were already bombing India's eastern coast, and Japanese propaganda claimed that Indian soldiers had mutinied. Thousands of Indian soldiers had indeed defected to the Japanese, who were recruiting them into the Japanese-sponsored 'Indian National Army', the INA. In April 1942, the Congress Working Committee asserted that Britain had forfeited any moral right to rule. The United States continued to use its influence. America was now in the war, and their forces had been arriving in India since the beginning of 1942. By the end of the war, there were half a million American troops in the subcontinent.

This dimension meant that Churchill had to go through some contortions to satisfy American sensibilities. On 4 March 1942, Amery told King George VI that Churchill was prepared to make an overture to India in order to get American support and support from China as well, much though he disliked such a démarche. Churchill even considered going to India himself. The nature of his reception is an intriguing subject for speculation. In the event, the task was given to Sir Stafford Cripps. Churchill thought that Cripps and Gandhi, both vegetarians, would get along well.

Cripps was an utterly sincere man. He meant the mission to work. Quite how he thought that he could get past Churchill's opposition is not easy to imagine. In Cabinet and elsewhere, Churchill expressed himself very forcefully on the subject of retaining India. Roosevelt sent his close confidant, Harry Hopkins, as a personal envoy to Britain to assess Churchill at an early stage in the war. Churchill was well aware that every word he said to Hopkins would be reported to his boss. But even those sensitive ears were assaulted by Churchill with a 'string of cuss words [which] lasted for two hours in the middle of the night on the subject of India'. Churchill later excused his language to Amery, referring to 'the relief that really bad language gives in anxious times'. The language must have been really bad; it would be interesting to know what he said.

This renewed intervention by Roosevelt was critical. The
United States' attitude was of great importance. When Churchill
was writing his war memoirs, F.W. Deakin, perhaps the most
important member of the syndicate responsible for the memoirs,
urged Churchill to recall the degree of influence America was
exerting on Britain at this time in regard to the Indian situation.
Deakin felt that Churchill could not simply refer, as he was wont
to do, to Indian agitation, a lack of wartime spirit and a lack
of martial drive. He urged Churchill to reveal the extent of his
correspondence with Roosevelt and the pressure from American
anti-imperialists. Deakin was sure that the correspondence would
be published in any event someday, and he urged Churchill to
take a pre-emptive move.[6] Churchill didn't comply, but it was
certainly as a result of this pressure from the United States that
Cripps was sent to India. When the volume of the memoirs that
dealt with this period was published in 1951, Churchill was
seeking to return to 10 Downing Street, and one of his unique
selling points was his reputedly special relationship with the great
English-speaking republic. Despite the need for diplomacy later,
in 1942 he was very critical of Roosevelt's interference, as well he
might be. Roosevelt expressed his views to Churchill very forcibly
in a telegram that referred to the end of the 'master and servant'
relationship in Asia. This was the background when Cripps
offered to visit India.

*

Between his 1939 visit to India and his 1942 mission, Cripps
had spent eighteen months in Russia as British Ambassador. In
doing so, he improved his standing enormously. By the time
he left, Russia had become Britain's heroic ally, and Cripps
was embraced in popular affection along with Russia itself.
He seemed to have single-handedly defended Stalingrad and

Leningrad. In an opinion poll of December 1942, when asked who should succeed Churchill if anything happened to him, 37 per cent were for Eden, with Cripps just three points behind at 34 per cent. Six months earlier, there had only been 1 per cent support for Cripps. Churchill appreciated the threat. Indeed, Amery suspected that part of Churchill's reason for sending Cripps off to India was to get rid of a 'dangerous young rival'.[7] Churchill invited Cripps and Lady Cripps to lunch at Chequers on his return from Russia and greeted them, 'Well, Stafford, how have you returned, friend or foe?' Cripps's reply was: 'I am a friendly critic or a critical friend.' He became Lord Privy Seal and Leader of the House.

For the moment, the initiative in Indian affairs had passed to Cripps. Amery was aware of this and needed to resist the Cripps effect. On 2 March 1942, he asked Churchill to help him resist pressure from Cripps and Attlee. He tried to ensure that Linlithgow, too, was supported against the enthusiasts.

Attlee understood Cripps's mindset. He had been present at a weekend party at Cripps's country house, Goodfellows, in June 1938, as were Nehru and the Indian politician Krishna Menon. The men of the British left who were present included Aneurin Bevan, Richard Crossman, Leonard Barnes (a Labour politician who was particularly opposed to colonialism) and Harold Laski. The Labour politicians were as usual sympathetic to Congress and felt that the India Act did not accord a sufficiently important role to the Party. Later in his life, when Attlee reflected on events and wondered why Churchill had agreed to the mission, his mind went back to that weekend. He wrote,

I had a good many stiff contests with Churchill on India. It was a great surprise when he embraced the idea of the Cripps Mission. The lines on which Cripps was empowered to go went beyond anything previously considered by any government. It embodied in fact some of the main ideas discussed by Cripps, Nehru and myself [at that weekend at Goodfellows].[8]

The reason that Churchill agreed was a combination of domestic politics and the events of the war. Churchill's national standing was at a low point at this stage. There was a campaign in the press to supplant him with Cripps. He had been obliged to reconstruct the War Cabinet in February 1942, when Attlee's position was strengthened; he became Deputy Prime Minister and Secretary of State for Dominion Affairs. Secondly, with the Japanese attack on Pearl Harbor on 7 December 1941, India had become strategically critical. And not only was the United States leaning on Britain, but nationalist China was an important ally, too, with a particular geographical interest in the area. Its leader, Chiang Kai–Shek, was sensitive about Indian aspirations and concerned that if they were ignored, the subcontinent might defect to Japan. Amery told the King that 'Winston . . . hated the idea of giving up all his most deeply ingrained prejudices merely to secure more American, Chinese and left-wing support. [It was like] 'a virtuous maiden selling herself for really handy ready money'. The King was so amused that he told a story that Amery did not think was suitable for the ears of his secretary.[9]

*

There had been earlier signs that the evolution of Indian policy could not just end with the August Offer. By early 1941, Attlee and Amery were aware that Britain could no longer just sit tight. Cabinet minutes for 5 February concluded that 'it was dangerous to stand on the present position without making every effort to see whether some way out of the constitutional deadlock cannot be found'.[10] This thinking would eventually express itself in the Cripps Mission.

But the changed significance of India in the war was the principal reason for Churchill's sudden initiative in February 1942. On 11 February, Amery sent a telegram to Linlithgow: 'Take the strongest *peg* you can before continuing.' Churchill was going to broadcast to India, announcing that an Indian Council of Defence was to be set up, with its members elected by proportional representation on a provincial basis. The princes would also be represented. This body would send delegates to the Peace Conference after the war (which never took place) and frame India's post-war constitution. Amery said that Linlithgow shouldn't be offended by Churchill's precipitate initiative: '[You] know his sudden ways'. These 'sudden ways' had even initially envisaged for a Prime Ministerial visit to India. Linlithgow was spared that visit, but he was not spared the Mission by Stafford Cripps.

Churchill did not proceed with the broadcast or the visit to India, but on 26 February 1942, he did set up an Indian committee of the Cabinet. The committee was established at Attlee's instigation, the outcome of his frustration over Churchill's die-hard views.

The committee would remain in existence for five and a half years. It consisted of Churchill, when he attended, Sir John Simon, Sir John Anderson, the Lord President of the Council, and Sir James Grigg, Secretary of State for War, together with Cripps, Attlee and Amery. Attlee took the Chair when Churchill was not present. Amery was not impressed by Churchill's performance in the committee. He noted 'Winston's complete inability to grasp even the most elementary points on discussion.' Surely unfair. Amery said that someone who didn't know who the Prime Minister was 'would have thought him a rather amusing but quite ga-ga old gentleman who could not understand what people were talking about'.[11]

Not only Amery was dismissive of how Churchill performed from time to time, Cadogan, Permanent Under-Secretary at the Foreign Office and an uninhibited critic of his masters, described him as 'simply drivelling' at meetings, spewing forth 'irrelevant, redundant talk'. Dalton, Minister for Economic Warfare, talked about 'an infinitely rambling discussion by the War Cabinet' about how a telegram to Gandhi was to be worded, and the Chief of the Imperial General Staff, Alan Brooke, said that Churchill seemed to be content to let Indians starve but still wanted to use the country as a base for military operations.[12]

Churchill certainly did feel himself out of sympathy with the mood that currently surrounded him. But he could not ignore pressure from the United States, however much he resented it. He told the Canadian Prime Minister: 'We have resigned ourselves to fighting our utmost to defend India in order, if successful, to be turned out.'

He was particularly loathe to make concessions when India was militarily under threat. This was not the time, in his view, for a new political initiative. It was his perverse view, too, that the Indian troops were fighting so well because of their allegiance to the King–Emperor and that a fighting race would never tolerate the rule of 'the Congress and the Hindoo Priesthood machine'.[13]

Although Attlee was regarded, and regarded himself, as the pre-eminent Indian expert in the Labour Party, it should not be thought that his views on India, although informed, were radical. He was afraid of 'a brown oligarchy'.[14] He had, after all, been educated at Haileybury, the training ground for servants of the Raj, and he fell in love with any institution that he entered. Lord Listowel was a man from an impeccably aristocratic background who ended up on the Labour front bench in the Lords. He said that his illusions were shattered when he found that the Labour Party members on the India Committee were 'no more radical than their Conservative colleagues and that Attlee as Chairman was a muted echo of his master's voice'.[15] Indeed, when the Cripps mission failed, Attlee blamed the Indian leaders for their intransigence.[16]

*

The India Committee prepared the brief that Cripps would take to India. They did so in the face of Churchill's obstructionism and Linlithgow's opposition. Linlithgow wanted to stand firm on the 'solid platform of the Act of 1935'.[17] Even Amery wanted to go no further than repeat the 1940 August Offer. Cripps and Attlee wanted something much more innovative. Attlee wrote to Amery:

> [N]ow is the time for an act of statesmanship. To mark time is to lose India. A renewed effort must be made to get the leaders of the Indian political parties to unite. It is quite obvious from his telegram [in which Linlithgow had said that he did not want to move from the 1935 Act] that the viceroy is not the man to do this. Indeed, his telegram goes far to explain his past failures . . . He is obviously thinking in terms of making minor concessions while resting on the status quo . . . my conclusion therefore is that a representative with power to negotiate within wide limits should be sent to India now, either as a special envoy or in replacement of the present viceroy.[18]

Linlithgow countered by making a number of conciliatory and unremarkable proposals. In light of that, on 1 March 1942, Churchill proposed to broadcast yet another declaration. It was not one he particularly wanted to make. For the first time, it would have been proclaimed officially that an Indian Dominion could secede from the Commonwealth. Secondly, any province could stand apart from the union and still achieve its own dominion status. Roosevelt was told about this proposed declaration on 4 March.

On 5 March, the full War Cabinet met, and Churchill told its members what was proposed. There is no official record of the meeting, but according to Sir Alexander Cadogan, Permanent Under-Secretary at the Foreign Office, Churchill was strongly negative about any initiative. The meeting was heated, and there was talk of resignations. Churchill's 1 March proposal had been the high-water mark of conciliation. Now he was convincing himself that he could resist American pressure. According to Rab Butler, 'We had a great meeting of all members of the government . . . The Conservative reaction, i.e., the view that some British interest must be retained in India, appears to be on top of any other influence. There will therefore not be a statement in the immediate future, and when it comes, it should not sell everything away'.[19] Linlithgow had been strongly against the 1 March proposal. He, the Commander in Chief, Wavell, and the Governor of the Punjab said that the proposal would imply acceptance of a separate Pakistan, with serious political repercussions in the Punjab.

The notion of a division of India would be resisted until it was manifestly inevitable. The India Office and people like Rab Butler regarded the preservation of Indian unity as central to British policy. For reasons that are not entirely obvious, bringing together the disparate components of the subcontinent into a single nation was regarded as an outstanding British achievement that should not be undone. The Commonwealth High Commissioners, for their part, were unhappy that India would have a constitutional right to secede from the Commonwealth.

By 6 March, Amery was letting Linlithgow know that the fate of any declaration was in the balance, and there were critical and dramatic meetings between that date and 9 March 1942. There was a lot of continuing talk about resignations. Cadogan thought that if Churchill did not give way, Cripps would resign. On the other hand, if a declaration were made, then Linlithgow might resign.

The India Committee convened over the course of the weekend. Cripps was at Chequers on Sunday as the debate went on. The resignation of the viceroy—or indeed of Cripps—would have brought down a government already shaken by the greatest military catastrophe of the war, the fall of Singapore.[20] Churchill's government was at its weakest in 1942. If Churchill had been deposed, Cripps would almost certainly have succeeded him, but in the event, Cripps saved Churchill. On that Sunday at Chequers, he produced a draft statement that said that instead of persevering with the inflammatory declaration, a member of the War Cabinet would go out to India to discuss a scheme and see whether it would receive a generous measure of acceptance. He volunteered to be that minister.

*

Cripps's offer to go to India was accepted by the War Cabinet just an hour before a telegram arrived from Linlithgow saying that he would resign if a declaration were issued. Churchill told him that they had already decided not to publish the declaration but to send out a minister 'to see whether it could be put across on the spot'. 'It' meant the substance of the unmade declaration. Churchill was pretty upset about Linlithgow's threat to resign and accused him of a lack of patriotism: 'Do not . . . think of quitting your post at this juncture.'[21] Amery was a little more genial: 'So, old friend, whatever else happens, you must see this thing through.' He confirmed that Linlithgow's resignation could well have broken up the government.

The four days of debate had been a battle between the progressives, who were for making a declaration, and the resisters, Churchill, Linlithgow and Amery, who were not. The outcome is usually represented as a victory for Cripps and Attlee. But in truth, the die-hards had won. Linlithgow was still viceroy, and Churchill was still Prime Minister. And Churchill could reasonably hope that Cripps's mission would be unsuccessful. He could be certain that he would do his best to make sure that it was. Churchill's victory was important. If a declaration had been made, the British Government would for the first time have sanctioned the idea that India would be entitled to independence *and* secession from the Commonwealth. The possible division of British India would have been acknowledged. The full Cabinet discussion on 5 March, the one referred to by Butler, revealed the extensive hostility to these concessions.

Instead of these certainties, there was the uncertain outcome of how Cripps's proposals would be received in India, where the conflicting desires of different interest groups would test what he had to offer in a much more complex way than the simple push and pull within the British Cabinet. Linlithgow was aware of this. He told the Reforms Commissioner, H.V. Hodson, that he acknowledged that Cripps was coming to India out of sheer public spirit. He wouldn't be coming if he simply wanted to be viceroy or prime minister. Linlithgow acknowledged that Cripps thought he could sell policies to India that they wouldn't take from anyone else. He foresaw, however, that Cripps would have difficulty with the divisions in the Indian communities and might find himself faced by opinions that hardened 'more and more against his offer—like hawking rotten fish'. He was confident that the only support Cripps would encounter would be from Congress and the Hindus. He said that the Indian Government's position must 'avoid at all costs any suggestion that we are standing in his way'.[22]

This book is about Churchill's influence on and interference in Indian policy. It is not a history of the Independence Movement, much less a narrative of the detailed but fascinating twists and turns of Cripps's mission. It can certainly be said that the failure of the mission was not due to Churchill alone. Cripps found himself unwelcomed by Linlithgow. After an initial stay at the viceroy's house, Cripps and his entourage were based at 3 Queen Victoria Road, Delhi. Linlithgow referred to the entourage as 'the Crippery' and Cripps himself—predictably—as 'Sir Stifford Crapps'. None of that was terribly surprising. What was more of a disappointment for Cripps was that the former bonhomie of his relationship with Nehru had disappeared. Nehru, looking at the string of British defeats in the early months of 1942, responded to news of the Cripps Mission by asking, 'With whom are we going to negotiate? With an Empire which is crumbling to dust?' Now he was sceptical of the distant promises which Cripps brought with him—a 'post-dated cheque,' as he said, 'drawn on a crashing bank.'

Hitherto, Cripps and Nehru had cultivated each other as useful contacts and had found themselves broadly in agreement. Now, in direct negotiation, they had discovered more about each other. Cripps had never accepted that Nehru was in many ways a radical and extreme spokesman for Congress. Equally, Nehru found that Cripps was constrained by imperatives, which meant that there were many points on which he was unable to compromise. Above all, the British Government could not surrender control of India's defence in the middle of a Far Eastern war.

Gandhi was more predictably difficult. He was opposed to the idea of partition as well as to the fact that Britain's promises were all pitched into the future. He dismissed Cripps as a mere 'globe-trotter' and claimed that when he had looked briefly at the declaration, he had said to Cripps, 'Why did you come if this is what you have to offer? If this is your entire proposal to India, I would advise you to take the next plane home.' The negotiations were tiresome. Indian politicians understandably wanted to look at detailed commitments rather than broad policy. This led to misunderstandings and changes of position. Cripps was accused of a lack of candour.

The problem was that Cripps was attempting to sell an evolutionary scheme: that was the best he could offer. The politicians he met wanted cut-and-dried detail. Apart from defence, one of the larger issues was the matter of the Executive Council. Would it function like a twentieth-century British cabinet, or would its powers be circumscribed by a powerful viceroy? Would the viceroy be a constitutionally limited monarch like George VI, or would he act like George III? Linlithgow was for George III. There is doubt about precisely what Cripps said about the relationship between the Council and the viceroy, but essentially, he was offering a broad constitutional position that India could then develop in the same way that British constitutional law and practice had developed. His interlocutors were perhaps entitled to view this approach with suspicion.

But if Churchill was not solely responsible for the foundering of the mission, he did his best to make sure it would not work. Behind Cripps's back, he kept up a secret correspondence with Linlithgow and fomented the failure of the mission. For all the capriciousness of his policy in India, after all his experience in opposition to the 1935 Act, he knew as much about Indian politics as anyone. He was aware that an imprecise promise, if indeed it amounted to as much as that, could safely be made and would anyway be unlikely to be accepted.

Cripps had been sent out on Saturday 14 March 1942, without any precise instructions. He was not a plenipotentiary, merely an emissary with 'full power to discuss with the leaders of Indian opinion the scheme upon which the War Cabinet is agreed'. There *was* no agreed scheme—just a declaration that had been killed off. He was constrained by his instructions to make sure that defence and good government were not compromised and to bear in mind the crucial importance of the military situation. Churchill told Linlithgow that Cripps was limited to discussing the draft declaration, but his role was both more extensive and much vaguer, and Amery sought to bring that home to Churchill.

Churchill's bad faith went further. He had no intention of honouring promises made against the exigencies of war. He told Amery that when the war was over, he would consider himself to be under 'no obligation to honour promises made at a time of difficulty'.

While Cripps struggled on in India, Churchill, informed by his private communications with Linlithgow, was entirely in the loop. By 2 April, he felt that quite enough had been done by way of concession. He personally drafted a cable that the War Cabinet approved, saying that the mission had demonstrated Britain's good faith. 'We all reached an agreement on it before you [Cripps] started, and it represents our final position.' He queried whether Congress was really genuine in its negotiations and stressed that 'there could be no compromise on defence, (which must remain a viceregal responsibility) without Cabinet agreement'.[23]

The mission was falling apart. When Cripps made a vague, implied threat of resignation, Amery's initial reaction was fear about what would follow if Cripps did resign. He prepared a draft message, but Churchill rejected it at once. It was 'too conciliatory to Cripps and [expressed] a confidence which he, Winston, no longer feels'.[24] The India Committee rejected a suggestion that the viceroy's powers should be restricted and reminded Cripps that he had never been given authority to negotiate. All he was supposed to do was try to gain acceptance with 'minor variations or elaborations' of what the British Government had already offered. Churchill's attitude hardened in the last days of the mission. At a meeting of the India Committee, followed by a meeting of the War Cabinet, he reported on what he had been told by Harry Hopkins, Roosevelt's personal representative in London. Hopkins was less than frank and misrepresented the extent to which Roosevelt was intriguing through his representative in India, Colonel Louis Johnson. As a result, the Cabinet—even Attlee—became very critical of Cripps. He was sent two messages, one objecting to proposals that he had put to Colonel Johnson and the other rebuking him in more general terms for negotiating behind the back of the viceroy. It was only now that Cripps discovered

that Linlithgow had been reporting back to London in cables that
he hadn't seen, despite the fact that he had shown the viceroy all
of his. His credibility had been blown, and the War Cabinet was
coming solidly behind Linlithgow.

The cable that Churchill sent to Cripps was clear and
condescending:

> We feel that in your natural desire to reach a settlement
> with Congress you may have been drawn into positions far
> different from any the Cabinet and Ministers of Cabinet rank
> approved before you set forth . . . We are concerned about the
> viceroy's position . . . You speak of carrying on negotiations.
> It was certainly agreed between us all that there would not be
> negotiations but that you were there to try to gain acceptance
> with possibly minor variations or alterations of our great offer
> which has made so powerful an impression here and throughout
> the United States.[25]

'Not generous,' said Cripps's aide when he read Churchill's cable.

Immediately after this, Amery heard that Congress was not
going to buy a deal. He said,

> That certainly gets Cripps out of a pretty awkward tangle
> for I don't think he'd have liked facing his Congress friends
> with definite Cabinet instructions to make clear to them that
> there could be no nonsense about a convention [limiting the
> viceroy's powers], but that if they came in it must be under the
> existing constitution and that if they differed from the viceroy
> they could only resign.[26]

Amery was quite clear about what prompted Churchill to allow
the mission. 'The pressures outside upon Winston from Roosevelt,
and upon Attlee & Co from their own party, plus the admission

of Cripps to the War Cabinet suddenly opened the sluice gates.'
Amery told Linlithgow on 10 March 1942: 'It would be impossible
owing to the unfortunate rumours and publicity, and the general
American outlook, to stand on purely negative attitudes and the
Cripps Mission is indispensable to prove our honesty of purpose
and to gain time for necessary consultations.' In other words, the
mission was a public relations exercise. Its outcome was never in
serious doubt.

On 10 April, Cripps sent a cable to Churchill, telling him that
a deal had been rejected, not on the narrow matter of defence,
but on wider grounds. 'There is clearly no hope of an agreement,
and I shall start home on Sunday.'[27] He had been in India for just
nineteen days.

When Amery heard of the failure of the mission, he heaved
a sigh of relief and told Linlithgow that its only point so far
as Churchill had been concerned had been its good effect on
America: 'For the rest he isn't interested, really disliking the whole
problem as much as before.'[28] Amery's reaction to the failure
revealed his own lack of sincerity: 'On the whole I think we are
well out of the wood. We can now go ahead with the war with a
clear conscience.'[29]

*

That was pretty much the end of Cripps for the time being. The
tide had turned. Cripps proposed to resign. Churchill asked him to
wait until the outcome of the North African landings was known.
In the event, the landings coincided with the second Battle of
El Alamein. Suddenly, Churchill was triumphantly ascendant.
Approval of the government's conduct of the war, which had
been only 41 per cent in September 1942 shot to 75 per cent in
November. Churchill's approval climbed to over 90 per cent and
Cripps declined to 51 per cent. The year 1942 had been one in

which Churchill was almost always vulnerable. He faced two votes of confidence in the Commons and was aware that his hold on power was tenuous. But now and for the rest of the war, he was finally secure.

Keeping FDR in the loop, Churchill was delighted to send a copy of the letter from Cripps narrating that the negotiations had failed. Roosevelt certainly had a personal interest in Indian independence. The interest was shared surprisingly widely by ordinary Americans, of whom between 70 and 80 per cent declared in an opinion poll of 1942 that they were aware of British negotiations with India.[30] Arcane matters of foreign policy rarely matter to American voters, and the degree of interest is surprising. It should not be confused, however, with an enthusiastic commitment to independence. In 1943, only 20 per cent thought it should be granted immediately, and by 1945, less than half of those polled knew what was going on in India. There seems to have been an anomalous blip in 1942. From a British public relations point of view, the failed outcome of the mission was very satisfactory. The *New York Times* said that by rejecting 'this gift of freedom' the Indian leaders would lose the American comradeship that had been theirs for the asking.

The Cripps Mission had done the trick. It had carried the government through one of its lowest points in the war. It had put a stop to criticism from the United States. Churchill had been able to kick the Indian problem away for the foreseeable future. He was delighted. He made a wholly insincere reference to Cripps's having 'rendered a very important service to the common cause and the foundations have been laid for the future progress of the peoples of India'.[31] In his memoirs, written after the war and indeed after Indian independence, he still allowed himself to gloat about hearing the news of the failure of the mission: 'I was able to bear this news, which I had thought probable from the beginning, with philosophy.'[32]

23

War: Quit India

Cripps Mission or no Cripps Mission, the loss of Burma had revitalized the independence campaign, and Gandhi had launched his Quit India programme, a campaign of civil disobedience. The subcontinent was gripped by violent demonstrations. Rail and telegraph communications were struck. In Madras, Bihar and the United Provinces, British servicemen were attacked and murdered. Savage repression followed as the Government of India responded with enormous force. Aircraft were used to strafe saboteurs as they tore up railway lines. In Bombay, demonstrators were beaten with rattan canes. Agitators within the Congress Party were arrested, and many were imprisoned until the end of the war. Fifty-seven infantry battalions, British and Indian, were used to disperse the rioting. Live rounds were fired, killing and wounding about 3000 demonstrators. In terms of numbers, this was much more serious than anything that had happened at Jallianwala Bagh.

Not everyone responded to Gandhi's call. Churchill was particularly pleased that the 'martial races' had been loyal. Army recruitment rose to 9,00,000 during 1942. The Muslim League and Sikhs stood apart from the demonstrations, and overall, the effect of Quit India was less marked than it might have been. The United States, disappointed by the failure of Hindus to respond to the Cripps Mission, had lost patience and interest.

In the short term, however, the effect of Quit India was threatening, particularly in the context of Japanese success, and 60,000 people had been arrested by the end of 1942. Linlithgow told Churchill in the course of the summer that he was 'engaged here in meeting by far the most serious rebellion since that of 1857, the gravity and extent of which we have so far concealed from the world for reasons of military security. Mob violence remains rampant over large tracts of the countryside'.[1]

In an attempt at conciliation, two Indians, Maharajah Jam Sahib of Nawanagar and Sir Ramaswami Mudaliar, were allowed to attend the War Cabinet in London (although not to see uncensored Cabinet papers). Churchill met the two men in the garden of 10 Downing Street and asked them,

> What have we to be ashamed of in our government of India? Why should we be apologetic or say that we are prepared to go out at the instance of some jackanapes? . . . Look at the condition even now. An Indian maid with bangles on can travel from Travancore to Punjab all alone without fear of molestations. That is more than can be said in this country today, where our Wrens and Waafs cannot go two miles with the same feeling of security . . . I am not going to be a party to a policy of scuttle.[2]

Gandhi was arrested, and he and his household were taken by special train to the Aga Khan's palace in Poona. The regime was very comfortable, and when his staff, concerned about his diet, discussed with the head jailer the fact that Gandhi was not eating much and might need goat's milk, they were told that a team of loyal goats was already on standby.

Rejecting any help from the goats, Gandhi began a hunger strike. He looked as if he was going into a coma. Churchill wasn't too concerned. He sent a secret telegram to Linlithgow, saying that he understood that Gandhi usually had glucose in his water 'when doing his various fasting antics' and asked whether he was up to his antics again. Linlithgow said that this was not the case. The Surgeon General and others thought that he *was* being fed glucose, possibly without being aware of it. At any rate, between 24 February and 2 March 1942, the last day of his fast, Gandhi's weight increased by a pound. Churchill was far from sympathetic, calling Gandhi an 'old humbug' and a 'rascal'. He told Field Marshal Smuts that he thought Gandhi had 'been eating better meals than I have for the last week!' Improbable: few people in any of the warring nations would have eaten better than Churchill.

For Churchill, quite simply, Gandhi was 'a thoroughly evil force, hostile to us in every fibre'.[3] Two less similar personalities can scarcely be imagined than Churchill, the sturdy man of action, and Gandhi, elusive, spiritual and ultimately almost impossible to pin down.

Although the United States was now rather fed up with the Indian politicians, Roosevelt and Chiang Kai–shek continued to comment, protest and criticize over Quit India disturbances. Churchill greatly resented the interference. He told Roosevelt that Britain was perfectly capable of maintaining order and securing India's contribution to the war effort. He did so despite the fact that Linlithgow was expressing considerable doubts about whether the Indian Government could weather the storm. Churchill sanitized the record in his war memoirs. What had been feared, a rebellion akin to the 'Sepoy Mutiny of 1857 . . . fizzled out in a few months with hardly any loss of life'.[4]

*

As 1942 went on, a degree of order was restored, and Linlithgow concluded that the government had to give some indication of its policy post-Cripps. Amery drafted a statement that included a reference to attaining complete self-government after the war. Churchill tried to qualify this by adding the words 'within the British Commonwealth of Nations'. Amery managed to eliminate that, and Churchill sank into a mood of pessimism. He told the King that Parliament was now prepared 'to give up India to the Indians after the war. He felt they had already been talked into giving up India'.[5] The King recorded Churchill's gloomy prognostication and said that his Prime Minister thought that too much had happened to make continued rule in India possible.

Even in this mood, which proved to be transient, nothing like a total scuttle was envisaged. During the Cripps Mission, Amery told Linlithgow to make quite sure that whatever happened, a considerable area surrounding Delhi was to be retained as federal territory and was not to pass into the hands of any dominion that might temporarily emerge. In January 1942, Linlithgow, his master's voice, said that nothing would be done to make it impossible for Britain to regain after the war any ground that she had given away in the course of the struggle for victory and survival. Rab Butler, with a powerful interest in India throughout his life, wrote to Amery complaining that the draft declaration, which was never promulgated, did not make clear what he understood to be implicit: that Britain would continue to have a role to play in India after her control of the component parts had come to an end.

As so often, Churchill soon rallied. In September 1942, he declared that:

> [F]or the last twenty-five years the Conservative Party has gone on the wrong tracks, it has lost confidence in itself, and it has given way perpetually until the present state of affairs has come

about. It is all wrong, thoroughly wrong. If we have ever to quit India, we shall quit it in a blaze of glory, and the chapter that shall be ended then will be the most glorious chapter of that country, not merely in relation to the past but equally in relation to the future, however distant that may be . . . no apology, no quitting, no idea of weakening or scuttling.[6]

In this spirit, he drew a line under Roosevelt's interference. On 10 November 1942, when he made the speech at the Mansion House with the reference to not presiding over the liquidation of the British Empire, he had survived his wobble.

24

War: The Bengal Famine

'Churchill was a racist' would not have been scrawled on his statue but for the argument that Churchill was to blame for the dreadful famine that hit Bengal in 1942–1943. The Bengal famine was also at the heart of the Cambridge Conference. When I have given talks on British policy in India, I have received more questions— always from Indians or British Asians—about the famine than about anything else. A judgement on Churchill and the Famine is at the crux of our debate.

In 1943–1944, Bengal suffered a massive catastrophe, a famine on a colossal scale. Between 1.5 and 4.5 million people died following a cyclone in April 1942 that flooded Bengal and Orissa and destroyed the harvest. On top of the failure of the crop, the loss of Burma had meant that 2 million tonnes of rice, or 15 per cent of the 13 million tonnes that were consumed each year in Eastern India, had been lost. The famine was partly due to these practical factors, partly to a lack of organized administration at the local level, and partly to private greed. The argument is that

[I]t is reasonable to argue that the real reason for which India was fighting—the defence of India and its people—was shamefully neglected by the Indian government, here meaning the London government. Bengal in 1943 may be understandable as an event, but it was also unconscionable, irreparably damaging Britain's right to govern, and a leitmotif, together with the repression of political dissent in 1942, for [the] criticism of colonialism ever since.[1]

Organizational skills and administration were available—they were being used to conduct a military war. They were not used to prevent the famine. Efforts were made both in London and in Delhi to divert grain to India, but not with sufficient grip and drive.

But in truth, not only does some of the blame lie on the Indian Government in Delhi and Bengal, but individual Indians were also at fault. The famine was not entirely due to a failure in the harvest. Although the crop yield was the worst for the century, it was only a little less than it had been in 1942. The natural disaster was compounded by human greed and the actions of merchants who hoarded stock to inflate prices. Even Wavell, who succeeded Linlithgow as viceroy and was generally on the side of India here and against London, described this as 'graft and knavery'. Local practices that excluded people from food relief on the basis of their caste or religion exacerbated the problem. Between 1 and 3.5 million Indians who died in the famine were low-caste or from religious minorities.[2]

*

The debate about Churchill's attitude towards Bengal was stimulated by a review in 2014 of Boris Johnson's biography of Churchill.[3] The review prompted a refreshed study of Churchill and the famine.[4] The evidence that emerged tended to endorse Sir

Martin Gilbert's judgement, suggesting that Churchill had done everything he could to mitigate the fate of the starving people of Bengal in the context of a war in which others were also suffering. It approved Churchill's own conclusion about the allegation against him: 'I should think it was hardly possible to state the opposite of the truth with more precision.'[5] It's fair to say that this conclusion is not widely shared.

*

At the outset of the famine, Churchill's primary objective was to do nothing to destabilize India as the base for the war against Japan. To this end, he pressed Wavell to deal with shortages even at the cost of diverting war shipping. When Canada offered aid, Churchill was conscious that Canadian wheat would take two months to reach India as opposed to wheat from Australia, which could be available in three or four weeks. He obtained 3,50,000 tonnes of wheat from Australia in addition to that from Canada.

The famine continued into 1944. Churchill was aware that India needed more than she was receiving, but he was concerned about the operational risks that would result from diverting shipping from other vital purposes.[6] That concern did not result in a denial of help. When he was annotating copies of the *Annual Register* in his days with the Fourth Hussars, he read that the viceroy in 1873–1874, Lord Northbrook, had refused to stop exporting Indian grain. Churchill's annotations approved of Northbrook's action, saying that the Government should not interfere in private trade.[7] But there was none of that laissez-faire attitude now. He continued to interest himself in the matter, asking the Secretary of State for War for an urgent estimate of how much food was really needed. One week after the reference to the operational risks involved, the Cabinet recommended diverting food from the Middle East to India.

The effective resistance in the Cabinet came not from Churchill but from the Minister for War Transport, Lord Leathers, who had responsibility for keeping available foodstuffs on the move. In the immediately following months, Leathers concluded that there was by now a surplus of food grains in India. He and Amery were of the view that the fear of famine meant that peasants were holding back their supplies of grain in case of further shortages. As far as Churchill was concerned, despite concluding that India had underestimated its rice crop, he approved the supply of a further 4500 tonnes of wheat.

But problems continued: unseasonable weather and a major explosion in the Bombay docks. This, in turn, prompted more hoarding. Churchill had been reluctant to involve the United States, but in the face of all this, he now made a heartfelt request to Roosevelt:

> I am seriously concerned about the food situation in India . . .By cutting down military shipments and other means, I have been able to arrange for 350,000 tons of wheat to be shipped to India from Australia . . .
>
> I have had much hesitation in asking you to add to the great assistance you are giving us with shipping but a satisfactory situation in India is of such vital importance to the success of our joint plans against the Japanese that I am impelled to ask you to consider a special allocation of ships to carry wheat to India from Australia . . . I have resisted for some time the viceroy's request that I should ask you for your help. But . . . I am no longer justified in not asking for your help.[8]

Roosevelt replied, saying that he was full of sympathy but that he was unable, on military grounds, to consent to the request. Churchill is blamed for exacerbating the famine, and Roosevelt enjoyed a reputation as India's champion.

*

The charge against Churchill is essentially that he deliberately and personally discouraged the implementation of famine relief and that he did so because he attached little value to Indian lives.[9] The argument is that he halted shipments of food that might have relieved the suffering but insisted that food exports from India to Britain continued while the famine killed 2000 people a month in Calcutta alone. An example of this argument is a sensationalist book by Madhusree Mukerjee, *Churchill's Secret War: The British Empire and the Ravaging of India during World War II*.

Ms Mukerjee's book was attacked by the Nobel prize-winning economist and an expert on famine in India, Amartya Sen, and has been substantially discredited. Professor Sen concludes that food availability in 1943 was significantly higher than in 1941.[10]

> There was indeed a substantial shortfall compared with demand, hugely enhanced in a war economy . . . but that is quite different from a shortfall of supply compared with supply in previous years . . . Mukerjee seems to miss this crucial distinction, and in her single-minded minded . . . attempt to nail down Churchill, she ends up absolving British imperialist policy of confusion and callousness.[11]

Even Amery, who recorded many negative responses to the famine on Churchill's part, said at the Quebec Conference that the case against diverting vital war shipping to India was 'unassailable'. Similarly, he told Wavell that Churchill was 'not unsympathetic' to the situation but that his hands were tied. Later, after D-Day, Amery returned to the subject again, telling Wavell that 'Winston . . . will naturally run any risk rather than one which immediately affects the great military stakes'. Gandhi would have understood. He paid very little attention to the famine, telling Wavell that the goal of independence was much more important than the lives lost in the famine.[12] Like Churchill, he felt he had to take an overview.

*

The balancing exercise was crude but essential. As always in war, priorities had to be weighed. By 1943, the conflicting pressures of defending India against Japan and feeding her people had become intense. This balancing act applied not just to the need for food but also to logistical implications. Britain and America were now fighting in Italy and preparing to launch a second front in northern France; until that front was created, it was also essential to supply Russia, which was fighting the war almost single-handed. All of this meant that cargo space was limited. The case for supplying the population of Bengal did not go to default. It was repeatedly put before the War Cabinet. It was argued forcefully by Amery, supported initially by the viceroy, Linlithgow, and then Wavell. Wavell argued for relief not simply on humanitarian grounds but because the famine would affect military operations in Burma.

When Wavell had taken over from Linlithgow, he was shocked by the famine and by the extent to which it was the outcome of mismanagement and profiteering on the part of the Bengal Government. He told Amery that the death rate from the famine was a thousand or possibly two thousand deaths a week. He repeatedly requested an increase in shipping.

Before he went out to India—indeed, on the day that he was sworn in to the Privy Council and lunched with the King and Queen—Wavell attended a Cabinet meeting where Churchill was crudely dismissive about the famine, said that it was 'more important to save the Greeks and liberated countries from starvation than the Indians', and thought that while something might have to be done for those Indians directly involved in war work, there was no need to do anything in the rural districts.[13]

Churchill's words chill and appal. But at a practical level, the effective resistance in the Cabinet to Wavell's pleas came not from Churchill but from Leathers. Leathers and others thought that the viceroy exaggerated the disaster to turn attention away from the Indian Government's mismanagement and failure to deal with corruption.

At a Cabinet meeting on 4 August 1942, for example, Churchill himself had been sympathetic and had approved the sending of barley from Iraq and wheat from Australia to Bengal. In the following month, Amery was able to obtain another 50,000 tonnes of grain. Leathers, on the other hand, was the man who argued against unduly upsetting the established supply pattern. He thought that the Indian Government was exaggerating the crisis.

Leathers was supported by Churchill's friend, tame boffin and interpreter of statistics, Lord Cherwell, who was written off by Wavell as 'that old menace and fraud'. Amery had to fight not only Leathers and Cherwell but other members of the Food Grain Committee too. The Secretary of State for War, Grigg, was with them in wishing to penalize the Indian profiteers rather than take steps to reduce the famine. They advocated hanging a number of profiteers.

The fact that Leathers argued against diverting supplies to Bengal does not necessarily mean that he was wrong in doing so, however hard-hearted that may sound. Leathers was a self-made man of enormous ability, by virtue of which he had become a pre-eminent force in British shipping long before the war. Churchill had been a director of two subsidiaries of Leathers's firm, William Cory and Sons Limited, a major player in freight shipping. He formed a very favourable view of Leathers, who had already advised the Ministry of Shipping on port problems during the First World War. In May 1941, he appointed him Minister of War Transport. Leathers thus had enormous logistical responsibility at a time when freight and personnel were moved much more on the water than by air. In crisis conditions, difficult choices have to be made. Some needs have to take priority over other needs, even when the latter are very real. When freight was being destroyed at an alarming rate, the needs of the different theatres in terms of men and material interlocked with feeding requirements. On top of all this, Leathers had to coordinate his activities with those of the United States. It was well understood at the time that the United States had more ships than seamen, and Britain had more seamen than ships. The freight movements of the two nations were thus intricately interlocked. Only someone with immense judgement or none could look at the responsibilities with which Leathers was charged and say with certainty that he acted wrongly. He had more opportunity to lose the Second World War for Britain than most generals.

Essentially, therefore, overall war needs argued for giving priority to the offensive theatres rather than relieving the famine; Leathers, Amery and others, rather than Churchill, formulated policy here; and Roosevelt was indifferent to Churchill's pleas.

*

Why did the famine take place at all? There has been much modern analysis of the famine and exploration of why it happened and what its different elements were.[14] After the fall of Burma in the previous year, huge numbers of soldiers were stationed on the border between Bengal and Burma. But Bengal was a rich and efficient agricultural region and should have been able to cope with the demand. Amartya Sen has demonstrated that famines are more likely to occur as a result of human agency than bad weather. The agricultural model in Bengal was a free-market one and not a command economy. Administration in the province, carried out by elected representatives, was riven by conflict and rivalry. Among them, the most important figure was the Minister of Civil Supplies, Hussain Suhrawardy, who was convinced that there was no shortage of grain and that traders were manipulating the market. This theory was accepted by Linlithgow and Leo Amery. It was hardly surprising then that the War Cabinet did not give priority to diverting ships from other essential war purposes, accepting, as it did, what it was being told: that there was not a true shortage.

In a famine, it's always easy to blame merchants for hoarding. This was particularly the case when the merchants were largely Hindu and the Bengal government was largely Muslim. Warehouses were raided, but there was little evidence of excess stocks of rice. Other provinces were reluctant to divert supplies to Bengal. Some of them, too, had been experiencing shortages. Restrictions on cross-border trade, some of them entirely informal, were not lifted. Professor Tirthankar Roy identifies three possible causes of the famine—nature, administration and London, and the markets—but is unable to place culpability on any one of them. For the purposes of this book, which is about Churchill's personal role, what is important is that Roy exonerates the Prime Minister:

> There is little evidence that Churchill's personal views about Indians influenced the policies of the War Cabinet. With Japan's entry into the war and the fall of Singapore in February 1942, the Empire's resources were a critical asset for Britain to fight a war that stretched from Europe to North Africa to Asia. Any prime minister would be reluctant to fight a war and negotiate with nationalists at the same time. Besides, Churchill's reactionary views on the Empire notwithstanding, the context for almost everything that he said about Indians and the Empire was related to the Indian nationalist movement. Negotiating with it during the War could be pointless and dangerous, because moderate nationalists were demoralised by dissentions and the extreme nationalist, Subhas Bose, wanted the allied powers to lose the War (at least on the Eastern Front) and was trying to achieve that result. You do not negotiate with those who want you destroyed.

What has any of that to do with the famine? The War Cabinet did not divert enough ships from the theatres of war to Bengal, or order India to divert army rations to feed people. Was it culpable? The Cabinet believed what Calcutta and Delhi told it: that there was no shortage of food in Bengal. The Cabinet took decisions in the knowledge that the Axis powers were sinking one ship every day and had sunk around a million tons of shipping in 1942. The regions where rice might be available were the most dangerous waters to enter. Army rations were already reduced; any further cuts could risk a mutiny.[15]

*

And so there is no evidence that Churchill *did* anything that resulted in a reduction in famine relief. There is also no evidence that he *said* anything that had that effect. But he did say a lot of things that make his role look very bad to modern readers and that reveal his archaic prejudices. Some of Churchill's most offensive racist comments date from this episode. He talked about the 'starvation of anyhow underfed Bengalis' being 'less serious than that of sturdy Greeks', and about Indians 'breeding like rabbits' and getting paid £1 million a day for 'doing nothing about the war'.

These comments were disgraceful in their own time and even more offensive in today's judgement. I have referred to Churchill's childish use of extreme language to shock others' sensibilities. I have suggested that his behaviour owed something to the culture of the times in which he had been born, seventy years before the Famine, although that may not seem to be sufficient excuse. He expressed himself in this way at a point in the war when he was physically exhausted, when victory was far from assured, and when he was pulled in different ways by his American and Russian

allies who pressed for a second front in Europe before the time
was right in his judgement. He carried an unimaginably heavy
burden of responsibility.

This was no longer the lithe, exuberant young soldier
on the North–West Frontier. Equally, he was not the solid,
adamantine figure of the Karsh photograph. The Graham
Sutherland portrait, which he so disliked,* painted for his
eightieth birthday and showing him looking stubborn, porcine
and stupid, may have been a cruel caricature, but at this stage
of the war he was frequently described as utterly exhausted,
worn-out and (though he rallied marvellously again and again)
irreparably aged.

And, as I have suggested, ill-judged language of this sort
was not inconsistent with Churchill's enormous humanity. His
hatred for the Kaiser's Germany during the First World War
had not stopped him from advocating that fat grain ship for
Hamburg the moment victory was won. His remarks about
starving Bengalis don't seem to have had any practical effect,
although they led Amery to tell him that his views were like
those of Hitler.

It is difficult to ask those informed by the culture of the
twenty-first century to ignore the argot of the nineteenth century
and look at actions rather than what was said in the heat of debate
that preceded those actions, but in my view, when the evidence
is weighed, Bengal is not the most serious of the charges that
Churchill faces over India.

The episode is full of nuance, and a final judgement on it
will be subjective, depending on the weight attached to different
issues. Eclipsing all, it has to be remembered that in a world war,
there is bound to be collateral suffering. There is no question

---

* 'It makes me look like a down-and-out drunk who has been picked
out of the gutter in the Strand.'

that there was a grave humanitarian crisis and that an appalling number of lives were lost. It was not within the government's power to make the consequences of a natural disaster disappear. The culpability of Churchill and his government depends on whether or not more could have been done to divert food and transport from other essential wartime destinations. Ultimately, the lot of people in India would have been infinitely worse if a half-hearted prosecution of the war resulted in victory by the Germans and Japanese.

There is no doubt that Leathers was unsympathetic, but at a point in the war where shipping was limited, starvation was not confined to India, and humanitarian and strategic conditions had to be balanced, there could be no formula that would have satisfied all parties. The case for famine relief was made well in the Cabinet by Amery, supported by first Linlithgow and then Wavell, and by Auchinleck as Commander in Chief.[16] And later in the year, Wavell allowed himself to judge that the famine had been dealt with well by the Indian Government.

Those on the spot, whose responsibilities did not extend to the threats to stability on account of food shortages in the liberated parts of southern Italy and Greece, saw a partial picture, and Wavell, for instance, may have thought of resignation in the face of what he saw as inactivity. During the Dutch 'hungerwinter' of 1944–1945 the RAF dropped substantial quantities of food into the Netherlands. Wavell, still remembering Bengal, said that there was a very different attitude 'towards feeding a starving population when the starvation is in Europe'.[17] He overlooked the strategic significance of the low countries in the wake of D-Day. And we have seen that Churchill relayed Wavell's concerns to Roosevelt and asked for help in shipping supplies that were stockpiled in Australia for use by South–East Asia Command in the war in the east. Roosevelt, with his own logistical commitments to distant theatres, was unable to help.

It was not the United States but Britain and Churchill, who by the end of 1944, had delivered over 1 million tonne of grain and brought the famine to an end.[18]

*

The positive argument against Churchill may not be strong; he may not have done anything active to make the famine worse, but the negative argument is more difficult to answer. The famine occurred on his watch, and he did not do anything to alleviate it and acquiesced in decisions that others had made—though that raises the unanswerable question of whether the greater war effort should have been sacrificed for the sake of humanity.

There is almost no mention of the Bengal famine in Churchill's memoirs. He refers to food shortages at the overall imperial level and not specifically to India's problem. His concerns involved bringing oranges and lemons from the Mediterranean to Britain and providing for the domestic poultry keeper. Why was he silent about Bengal? Was he concerned about American sensibilities? Did he feel that he had something to be ashamed of? Or did he just think it wasn't particularly important in the larger picture? I suspect the last of these explanations is the true one. If that is the case, he does not endear himself to the modern reader.

25

War: The Indian Army Triumphant

While Churchill and his government had been very concerned about the risk of defeat in the East in 1942, very little was said about the victorious outcome there in 1944. It is suggested that the reason was that India and the imperial dimension were no-go areas in relations with America. 'The growth of "the forgotten army" was thus not only caused by the fact that Burma was seen as a strategic backwater but was also a deliberate act of censorship by the British.'[1]

That wasn't good enough. The remarkable scene, when on the battlefield of Imphal, Slim, together with his three corps commanders, Christison, Stopford and Scoones, were knighted by the viceroy is an extraordinary cameo celebrating the repulse of an invasion of India and the greatest defeat ever imposed on the Japanese. In contrast to other events, such as Montgomery taking the German surrender on Lüneburg Heath, it is forgotten, like the forgotten army itself. The significance of the war in the Far East was not downplayed just by Churchill in his war memoirs but indeed by most historians, who saw it as peripheral to the war in Europe, North Africa and on the seas.

Churchill's interest in the Japanese War was inevitably very much subordinate to the war for survival, the war with Germany. He said that there was a veil over his mind about the Japanese War. All proportions were hidden in mist.[2] The significance of the war with Japan for him was that it brought the United States in on Britain's side. In his war memoirs, he recorded no sense that the war was the outcome of a shift in Japan's relationship with the West, including Britain, portraying it very much as an opportunistic attack on Pearl Harbor. From a literary point of view and from the point of view of the narrative that he wished to construct, a narrative in which Britain—but particularly Churchill—was at the centre of a battle for national survival and the survival of freedom, the importance of the Japanese attack on Pearl Harbor was that 'Hitler's fate was sealed. Mussolini's fate was sealed. As for the Japanese, they would be ground to powder.'[3] The Japanese incursion into the Second World War was not to be incorporated into a narrative of pre-war events in which Britain played an important part. 'No American will think it wrong of me if I proclaim that to have the United States at our side was to me the greatest joy.'[4] That was what mattered about Japan's entry into the war.

In Churchill's war memoirs, the chapter in which he describes the reconquest of Burma is a brief one. He devoted less than two pages to the Battles of Kohima and Imphal. His purpose was principally to play down dissension between him and America at this point in the war. Roosevelt had wanted to employ Chinese troops in a way that Churchill thought would undermine Britain's imperial presence after the war. What Churchill wanted to do when he wrote his memoirs was flatter the American ally whom he was again courting in the post-war world. These were important preoccupations, much more important than giving the Indian Army its due for its remarkable reconquest of Burma. To recognize the achievement of Slim's forgotten army would mean, says Cat Wilson, that 'Churchill would have had to revise his opinion of Indian troops, something he was never prepared to do'.[5] Churchill had little interest in dealing with the reconquest of Burma. The Fourteenth Army, who achieved their outstanding feat, called themselves 'the forgotten army', and Churchill was as forgetful as anyone. He told the 'syndicate', the team who put the war memoirs together and wrote the bulk of them, that he could not 'spare more than 3,000 words . . . on the struggles in Burma'.[6] This was to be his treatment of the largest volunteer force ever to exist.[7] He did say that 'the famous Fourteenth Army, under the masterly command of General Slim, fought valiantly, overcame all obstacles, and achieved the seemingly impossible'. But he went out of his way in the brief two paragraphs that he devoted to the victory to stress the role of elements other than the Indian Army in achieving victory, 'those other Services without whose aid the struggles of the Army would have availed little': the Royal Navy, the Allied Air Forces, the Engineers 'both British and American'.[8]

26

The Beginning of the End

Churchill's mood on India continued upbeat from now until the end of his first government in 1945. He turned his back on the idea of expedient concessions that could be withdrawn when the war was over. Increasingly, it became clear that Britain would survive the war, and he was determined to push the jewel firmly back into the crown.

By August 1944, he was telling Amery about his plans for renewing and strengthening the Raj. There would be a purge of British officials who had lost the will to govern and had become 'more Indian than the Indians'. The powers of the money-lenders and the landlords would be reduced. There would be land reform to benefit the peasants and the Dalits. Britain would form a bond not with the educated elite of Congress, whom he disliked so much, but with the masses. He even talked about rural collectivisation on 'Russian lines'. Amery told Churchill that he didn't see much difference between his outlook and Hitler's.[1] Stalin might have been a better comparison. Churchill returned to proposals of this sort in March 1945. He had always regarded the landlords and the moneylenders as not typical of the real India, and he was determined to deprive Congress of their support.[2]

He referred repeatedly to the cost to Britain of defending India. By June 1945, the cost of that defence had risen to £1.292 million. In his war memoirs, he said that 'no greater portion of the world's population was so effectively protected from the horrors and perils of the World War as were the peoples of Hindustan. They were carried through the struggle on the shoulders of our very small island'.[3]

He remained convinced, against the evidence, that the Indian Army was disloyal. He had been born just seventeen years after what he would have called the Mutiny of 1857. He told the Cabinet that Britain was creating a monster by putting modern weapons in the hands of the sepoys, who would shoot her in the back.

*

Churchill had found Linlithgow a congenial viceroy with a shared taste for stasis and a shared belief that the mass of Indians had no interest in politics. As has been seen, just as Churchill dreamed that Britain might stay forever on top of a tripos, Linlithgow thought that Britain could for at least another generation.

But all good things must come to an end and Linlithgow's term in office could not be extended indefinitely. The circumstances surrounding the appointment of his successor, General Archibald Wavell, have already been examined as have Churchill's reasons for appointing a man of whom he thought so poorly that he believed he could have been the chairman of a golf club. He didn't want a dynamic viceroy. He wanted a dull administrator, and he quite wrongly thought that Wavell was that kind of man. Wavell understood perfectly well that he was expected simply to keep India quiet until the end of the war. He surprised everyone by demonstrating the motivation, initiative and ability that were needed to address great political issues.

Before he went to India as viceroy, Wavell and Churchill sailed together to New York on the *Queen Mary*. Wavell wasn't impressed by Churchill's views on India. On the voyage, Churchill complained again about the folly of putting modern weapons into the hands of 'Sepoys'. 'I've tried to reassure him, both verbally and by written note, but he has a curious complex about India and was always loathe to hear good of it and apt to believe the worst. He has still at heart his cavalry subaltern's idea of India, just as his military tactics are inclined to date from the Boer War'.[4] Churchill's paranoid fear about the loyalty of the Indian Army had no basis in fact, in the intelligence reports about morale in the Army, or in its effectiveness and courage in battle.

Hoare also saw the anachronistic source of Churchill's idea of India:

> The splendid memories gathered round the Indian Empire blinded him to the changes that had come about since the days of Clive, Wellington, Lawrence and Kipling. The India that he had served in the Fourth Lancers was the India of polo and pig-sticking, of dashing frontier expeditions, of paternal government freely accepted, and the Great White Empress revered as a mysterious goddess. 'Settle the country, make the people happy and take care there are no rows', the words of Henry Lawrence to his band of brothers, still seemed to him sufficient for maintaining the British Raj.[5]

Attlee's diagnosis was similar:

> Churchill's views on India were very much conditioned by his first-hand experience of that country. When he was a young man in India, the Empire was at its most self-conscious,

and, being at the height of its strength, was liberal (though paternal), not reactionary and repressive. For Winston, the British Empire, free trade, the expansion of opportunity, world order, the progress of man, and war on cruelty and injustice, all went together, with his vision of England, so to speak, crowning everything. He never really grew up to the view that, for instance, Indians did not see things like this, and that by the time he had got to middle age the facts of life had changed, that the role of Britain in the Empire had been altered altogether.[6]

Attlee here is enunciating a very measured appraisal of Churchill on India, and his words deserve to be weighed carefully. He had never been an outspoken critic of Churchill. He understood his complexities. Before he wrote these words, he had, of course, worked closely with Churchill as his deputy throughout the war. He differed significantly from Churchill on Indian policy, and here he records the essence of their differences. His criticism is, however, carefully nuanced.

*

The Cabinet gave a dinner for Wavell on the eve of his departure for India. When Churchill spoke at the dinner, he 'made a pure die-hard speech, glorifying our past record in India' but saying nothing about the future except that his opposition to self-government was unchanged and that he expected to be proved right on this as he had been about Germany.[7] Amery commiserated with the new viceroy: 'You are wafted to India on a wave of hot air.'[8] Wavell was unsurprised by Churchill but was surprised that the Cabinet collectively was 'spineless, uninterested and dishonest'.

*

As early as 10 September 1943, Wavell proposed to Amery that there should be a new attempt to secure a provisional central government—explicitly on the Cripps basis. The proposal arrived when Churchill was in North Africa and was considered by the India Committee with Attlee in the Chair. The Committee wasn't too impressed. Wavell said there were three possibilities: the continuation of 'the present policy of inaction', an executive composed of individuals chosen for their personal ability, or the revival of the Cripps idea of a national government with a representative council working as a quasi-Cabinet. Attlee thought it was impossible to negotiate with the political parties when one of them was trying to block the war effort, and he preferred an informal widening of the executive. The India Committee, by a majority, told Wavell to be less ambitious than he wished and simply talk to the political leaders.

By this stage, Churchill was back from North America and had put a stop to even that insipid response. There was to be no immediate initiative, no negotiation with Gandhi. Churchill told Wavell that negotiations with Gandhi would take place only over his dead body. He said that political initiatives were to be avoided 'lest the achievement of victory . . . should be retarded by undue concentration on political matters while the enemy is at the gate'. Congress had to abandon its present policy of non-cooperation.

At the end of 1943, Wavell reflected on his appointment:

> I accepted the viceroyalty in the spirit of a military appointment—one goes where one is told in time of war without making conditions or asking questions. I think I ought to have treated it in a political spirit and found out what the policy to India really was to be, and I think I could have made my own conditions, for I think Winston was really hard put to it to find someone. However, here I am and I must do my best,

although I am frankly appalled at the prospect of five years—
hard to the mind and soft to the body.[9]

Most of a year later, in October 1944, Wavell wrote in his diary,

I have been viceroy a year today. The hardest year's work I
have done. In some ways I have done reasonably well, the
food problem and getting some sort of a move on post-war
development. I have found HMG's attitude to India negligent,
hostile and contemptuous to a degree I had not anticipated, or
I think I might have done more. Still the more one sees of the
political problems and of the Indians, the more one realises that
there are very dark days ahead for India, unless more wisdom
and good will are shown, and I think they will have to begin
from the top, from Whitehall.[10]

For HMG and Whitehall, read Churchill. Although Attlee put
the prosecution of the war ahead of purely Indian considerations,
the Labour Party had committed itself in 1943 to granting
independence immediately if it won the next General Election.
Amery was in favour of movement towards independence, albeit
at a measured rate. Churchill's views had plenty of support among
the die-hards of his party, but they were on the back benches. It
was he who kept the government's foot on the brake.

Wavell was aware of that. Just four days after the diary entry
that has just been quoted, he wrote to Churchill himself, giving
him a résumé of his first year. He didn't pull his punches: 'I
propose to write entirely freely and frankly, as I know you would
wish. I have served you now for over five years and we should
know one another reasonably well. I know you have always found
me a difficult and troublesome subordinate. I've not always
found you an easy master to serve.' So far as his responsibilities
for appeasing communal differences and making proposals for

political advance were concerned, he conceded that he had made no progress whatsoever. He considered that it had probably been a mistake, twenty or thirty years earlier, to commit Britain to the political reform of India with a view to independence. It would have been better to have prescribed economic development first. But the Cripps visit had put early independence beyond doubt. India couldn't be held by force—not because Britain didn't have the means, but because ruthless force and coercion would be needed, and these were not acceptable.

He then made a critical point. 'India was the first major British possession to be a candidate for independence.' What standard of organizational efficiency was a prerequisite for independence? What had Macaulay meant when he talked about that 'proudest day in English history' when Indians, 'in some future age, demand European institutions?' Other territories that had been propelled into some sort of independence—Egypt or the mandated Middle East—had never been integral parts of the Empire. India had been. Was independence to be delayed until India would be as peaceable, predictable and boring as an English suburb? As late as 1946, Enoch Powell, who served in military intelligence in India from 1943 to 1946, said that India would require at least another half century of direct British rule.[11]

The failure to address this question lies at the heart of much of the confused debate. Wavell, practical and pragmatic, did address it: 'India will never, within any time that we can foresee, be an efficient country, organized and governed on Western lines. In her development to self-government we have got to be prepared to accept a degree of inefficiency comparable to that in China, Iraq or Egypt . . . [W]e cannot continue to resist reform *because it will make the administration less efficient*. [The emphasis is the author's.] His conclusion was that a speedy move had to be made if India were to be kept within the Commonwealth—certainly before the end of the Japanese War.[12]

Remember that he was writing directly to Churchill. He was addressing this searing indictment to the man who *was*, in effect, HMG. He was expressing himself in terms that were not normally addressed to Churchill by a subordinate at any time, let alone in 1944 at the summit of his success. Wavell was a brave man. He continued:

> I am bound to say that after a year's experience in my present office I feel that the vital problems of India are being treated by HMG with neglect, even sometimes with hostility and contempt . . . there remains a deep sense of frustration and discontent amongst practically all educated Indians, which renders the present arrangements for government insecure and impermanent . . . the present government of India cannot continue indefinitely, or even for long . . . if our aim is to retain India as a willing member of the British Commonwealth, we must make some imaginative constructive move without delay.[13]

Wavell proposed a provisional governmental institution based on Cripps, together with a conference of political leaders. Churchill did not reply at all for a month, and then dismissed the matter casually: 'These very large problems require to be considered at leisure and best of all in victorious peace.'

Wavell didn't accept the rebuff. He appealed to Attlee and the India Committee. Cripps was, of course, positive and wanted Wavell to come home and talk to the Committee. The other members were entirely negative. All they conceded was that there should be a review of what was to be done about India and that Wavell should be involved in that review. This was agreed on 18 December 1944, but Wavell was told not to hurry over. Indeed, Attlee did his best to discourage him from coming at all. Attlee had lost sympathy with his old Congress friends, whom he thought were trying to dominate Indian politics in a thoroughly undemocratic way. On 27 March 1944, he told the India Committee that 'he was frankly horrified at the thought of the substitution for the present government of a brown oligarchy subject to no control either from parliament or electorate'.[14]

So Wavell didn't find himself welcomed back to London until March 1945, and when he arrived, he was met by a wall of opposition and negativity. He remained at home for more than two months. By now, Labour had withdrawn from the coalition, and Churchill led a Conservative caretaker government in the run-up to the General Election. Attlee and Cripps were no longer members of the India Committee. Sir John Simon, Rab Butler and Churchill remained hostile to any Wavell initiative.

Wavell was very disillusioned. He was not a self-important man, but he did find it extraordinary that the India Committee, with the viceroy at home and available, was attempting a technical and detailed formulation of Indian policy without taking advantage of his advice. When he was invited to a meeting of the Committee on 14 May, it was his first official contact with or communication from the committee for exactly three weeks. On 24 May, he wrote a personal letter to Churchill, detailing how long he had been home before he heard anything from the India Committee and pointing out that he had not heard from the Prime Minister for seven weeks.

A few days later, he and his family queued to get into a News Theatre: '[T]he feeling was quite familiar after all these weeks of waiting on ministers. But we did get into the theatre in the end; while I'm still in the queue for a decision on India.'[15]

Churchill told the Cabinet that Wavell had betrayed his country's interests in order to curry favour with the Indians. Amery was so outraged that he told the Prime Minister to stop 'talking damned nonsense'. Finally, Churchill was persuaded that something had to be done. Churchill acquiesced with great reluctance, writing an emotional letter to his wife while he was on the way to the Yalta Conference: 'Meanwhile we are holding on to this vast Empire, from which we get nothing, amid the increasing criticism and abuse of the world, and our own people, and increasing hatred of the Indian population.'[16]

What finally was agreed upon was a conference in Simla, where political leaders would discuss the idea of forming a new executive council more representative of organized political opinion and including an equal number of Hindus and Muslims. That arithmetic guaranteed it would not succeed. The fact that only the commander in chief and the viceroy would not be Indians and that all the portfolios other than defence would be held by Indians sounded promising but meant nothing given the communal divide.

Poor Wavell! He must have wondered why he made these visits back to London. No one wanted to see him, and when they did, awkward and inarticulate as he was, he cut a poor spectacle and had to put up with people being rude to him. On this occasion, the receptionist who was provided for him in his room at the India Office did not even know how to spell his name. Churchill told him that, as the country was still at war, constitutional progress could be kept on ice. Wavell had to be supported by Amery. Churchill didn't even want to stick with the offer that Cripps had made. He took the view that it was an offer that had been made when Britain was in dire straits. It hadn't been accepted and had, therefore, lapsed and could be disavowed.

The fact that while Wavell was hanging around, kept out of important meetings and denied access to documents, Germany had surrendered, the opposition parties had withdrawn from the Government and Churchill had formed his Caretaker Government strengthened Wavell's position: if he were not allowed to go back to India with some sort of proposal, India would become a live issue in the election campaign. It was for this reason that he was allowed to go back and call the Simla Conference, which was intended to establish a truly Indian viceroy's Council with significant powers.

The Simla Conference opened on 25 June 1945, before the General Election, and was bitter and inconclusive. Churchill's last gesture to India before Independence was to approve in the Conservative Manifesto a very vague reference to 'granting India a fuller opportunity to achieve Dominion Status'. The Labour Manifesto didn't go any further. The Liberals did talk of 'complete self-government for India' but the Liberals were unlikely to be in a position to implement the contents of their Manifesto.

Churchill left office on 26 July. The Simla Conference had foundered long before the election result was announced. Churchill had ensured that Wavell's powers were so circumscribed that failure was inevitable. Before the attitude of Congress was really clear, the leader of the Muslim League, Jinnah, had objected to the proposal that Congress would have the power to nominate some of the Muslim members.

Wavell was magnificently magnanimous. In his final address to the Conference, he said, 'I wish to make it clear that the responsibility for the failure is mine. The main idea underlying the conference was mine. If it had succeeded, its success would have been attributed to me, and I cannot place the blame for its failure on any of the parties.' It was a pity that he had no support in London and that his political masters could not rise to the heights of which he was capable.

27

Independence and Afterwards

For much of the inter-war years, as has been seen, Clement Attlee was the principal Labour spokesman on India, the party's Indian expert. He had been one of the Labour representatives on the Simon Commission in 1927, returning to the subcontinent several times after that introductory visit.

He wasn't an enthusiastic member of the Commission, fearing that the time he would spend on it could imperil his chances of getting government office. Ramsay Macdonald assured him that that would not be the case, and Attlee discharged his responsibilities on the Commission, as he did everywhere, with thoroughness and a sense of responsibility. To the knowledge of India that he gained while visiting India with the Commission and afterwards, when he took a major part in writing the Report, he added further research and discussion over the following years. During the war, he continued to take a special interest in India, chairing the India Committee in Churchill's absence and seeking to temper Churchill's views with more moderate sentiments. He was, however, like his Labour colleague, Ernest Bevin, a strong supporter of the Empire. He was no firebrand; his approach to India was progressive but moderate.

Like most Labour politicians, he knew the Congress leaders much better than the Muslims. He and his friends were beguiled by the arguable and defensible case that the westernized Congress leaders put forward. They all seemed to share a liberal mindset that was essentially reasonable. As a result, he failed to recognize the steely determination with which Congress politicians would press their point when discussion really began. He also failed to understand the strength of Muslim nationalism and *its* determination not to budge. In the short period between taking office as Prime Minister in 1945 and Independence in 1947, Attlee had to face up to the irreconcilable desire of Congress for a single India and the Muslim League's increasing insistence on two Indias. He learned, too, that it was not easy for either Congress or the League to accept that Britain would walk away, leaving India divided if need be. Attlee repeatedly said in later life that Indian independence might have occurred earlier if these realities had been understood in 1945.[1]

*

By now, it was clear to Wavell that it was too late for the sort of orderly transfer of power that would be done over a generation. That would have been possible in the 1930s but it was out of the question in 1945. He wanted public commitment to an early exit followed by withdrawal in a phased military operation. Attlee was very much against Wavell's plan for retreat—rather strangely, given that he instructed Wavell's successor, Mountbatten, to commit to independence in 1948 precisely in this way. He said of Wavell's plan for withdrawal, codenamed BREAKDOWN: 'I thought that it was what Winston would certainly quite properly describe as an ignoble and sordid scuttle and I wouldn't look at it. I came to the conclusion that Wavell had shot his bolt.'[2]

In fact, Churchill had pretty well given up on India. When Wavell paid a courtesy call on him after the Conservatives lost the 1945 election, the former prime minister was staying temporarily at Claridge's. He had now really given up on India. He told Wavell that without 'the anchor' [Churchill] India was now on 'a lee shore with rash pilots'. At the end of their meeting, Churchill walked Wavell to the lift. As the door closed, he said to him, 'Keep a bit of India.'[3] Much later, he told his cousin Clare Sheridan that his life and work had 'all been for nothing . . . The empire I believed in has gone'.[4]

Churchill's views hadn't changed, but he recognized that it was too late to do anything. 'India must go,' he said. 'It is lost. We have consistently been defeatist. We have lost sight of our purpose in India.'[5] That was what he said in private; in public, he kept his distance from government policy. He wrote to Attlee on 14 May 1946: 'I consider myself committed up to the Cripps Mission in 1942, though you know what a grief this was to me.' But if there were not an agreement between 'the great forces composing Indian life . . . I must resume my full freedom to point out the dangers and evils of the abandonment by Great Britain of her mission in India'.[6]

Attlee, as was always his policy after the 1945 General Election, kept Churchill fully informed on what was happening, partly as a matter of courtesy to his wartime chief and partly to avoid eruptions in the House of Commons. He told Churchill that Wavell was to be replaced by Mountbatten. He might have expected no great difficulty, as Churchill had criticized and undermined Wavell throughout his own time and, on the other hand, was known to be a huge admirer of the dashing naval officer with his royal connections. He even explained to Churchill that Wavell was to go specifically because the Government rejected his evacuation plan—where again, Churchill might be expected to agree. Attlee hadn't wanted Churchill to cause any difficulties in the Commons and was accordingly surprised and disappointed by the fact that he did just that. Attlee could not reveal to the House as he had privately to Churchill that Wavell had advised scuttle.

> This put me in perhaps the most embarrassing situation of my whole career since I could not divulge in detail all the facts of the matter and therefore could not give the lie to Winston. I find it very hard to forgive him for this. The extraordinary thing is that I *can* forgive him. Winston could get away with this. In any other man it would have been damnable and utterly unpardonable.[7]

Churchill did nothing to help Attlee—unfair. All Attlee could say in reply was something that so many said of Churchill in relation to India: 'I think his practical acquaintance of India ended some fifty years ago. He formed strong opinions—I might say prejudices—then. They have remained with him ever since.'[8]

*

On 18 May 1947, the new and last viceroy, Mountbatten, returned to London to get approval for a change to a plan that the Cabinet had already endorsed. They were taken aback to learn that the earlier plan, which Mountbatten had told them would be acceptable to all parties, needed to be replaced. Now, he recommended partition and an accelerated departure date. His plan included dominion status for India together with—an important new element—membership of the Commonwealth.

While he was in London, he visited Churchill, who had always admired his dash and elan. Mountbatten had been just the sort of flamboyant maverick that Churchill loved. He persuaded Churchill to support his policy. Churchill accepted that Indian unity could not be preserved and urged the Muslim leader, Jinnah, to accept the partition deal. Jinnah required very little urging.

Churchill, not yet out of bed for the day, was mollified by the idea that independence would be moderated by membership in the Commonwealth. Mountbatten regarded that as one of his great achievements. The Conservative Party did not oppose the Government's Indian legislation. It would be wrong, however, to think that by now Churchill was happy with Indian developments, either out of regard for Mountbatten (whom Attlee may well have appointed to spike Churchill's guns) or because he thought the cause was lost. He did not abandon his anachronistic and rebarbative views. He was distressed that the Attlee government was abandoning a continued British role in India. In speeches right up until Independence, he continued to rumble darkly about what was happening. Even after Independence, on a social occasion when Mountbatten approached Churchill full of bonhomie, he was rebuffed bitterly: 'Dickie, stop. What you did in India is as though you had struck me across the face with a riding whip.'

*

Churchill's reaction to the approaching independence was a sad acquiescence. He knew that India was going to go. He told one acquaintance that Britain had lost sight of its purpose in India. 'India breaks my heart,' he told Amery. When Mountbatten announced that Britain would withdraw on 30 June 1948 (in fact, the withdrawal came a year before that), Churchill made a speech in the Commons in which he suggested entrusting the problem to the United Nations, as in fact, the Labour Government would do with Palestine. He ended with one of his magnificent perorations:

> It is with deep grief I watch the clattering down of the British Empire, with all its glories and all the services it has rendered to

mankind . . . we must face the evils that are coming upon us, and that we are powerless to avert . . . but, at least, let us not add—by shameful flight, by a premature, hurried scuttle—at least, let us not add, to the pangs of sorrows so many of us feel, the taint and smear of shame.

After Independence, when Partition and its attendant slaughter were underway, Churchill blamed the Government for the 'hideous massacres, the like of which have never stained the British Empire in all its history'. When the Constituent Assembly described India as a 'sovereign, independent republic' Churchill was half-minded to argue that it should not be allowed to stay in the Commonwealth. Later, Attlee privately told Churchill that this would be unwise. 'Mr Churchill in response at once went off the deep end with his usual attitude on Indian matters, and suggested that India should now be a foreign power.'[9] He pulled back, of course, and accepted the deal: India was now an independent republic associated with the Commonwealth, recognizing the British monarch as its head.

For all his gut-felt opposition to Independence, at a human level, he did not want Indians excluded from the Commonwealth. Churchill wrote to his old friend, Jan Christian Smuts, and told him, 'My heart gave the answer, "I want them in." Nehru has certainly shown magnanimity after sixteen years imprisonment.'[10] There's an echo in these words of Churchill's own magnanimity, typical and redeeming.

As Prime Minister again in 1951, Churchill found he could indeed work with Nehru. Even before then, while still Leader of the Opposition, he had begun to build bridges. Now he backed the Indian leader and saw him as a crucial figure in the defence of South Asia from communism. After all the years of unreasoning opposition to India and vituperation of the Indian political classes, he was doing as he always did, accepting a change in circumstances, whether a defeat or a victory, in a practical, amicable and constructive way. He had done this with South Africa after the South African War—Smuts remembered that. He adjusted very speedily to the changed relationship with Ireland. In 1918 and 1945, he moved at once from enmity with Germany. Now, he embraced independent India. That was the mark of the man.

28

The Heart of the Paradox

Born when he was and into the circle he occupied, it was inevitable that Churchill's views on India and Empire started from the Whiggish premise that Britain had been in the vanguard of a movement that had transferred and, to an extent, was still transferring the world from uncomfortable barbarism to what he described as being 'at or around the summit of the civilised world'. He wanted the advantages of 'civilisation'—health, education, adequate food, medicine—and he wanted them for everyone. He wanted them for, amongst others, races that had not yet achieved 'civilisation' and were not yet fit for democracy. It seemed to him incontestable that a delegation of Kenyan Indians who came to see him in 1921 were 'a vulgar class of coolies, and that they could not yet be allowed the same political rights as white men'.[1] He agreed with Cecil Rhodes that there should be 'equal rights for civilised men'; he did not believe for a moment that all inhabitants, or even the majority of inhabitants of the Empire, were civilized. That's a view that may sound appalling and untenable today, but he was far from alone in holding it in his time.

And yet, in 1907, at the Colonial Office, Churchill reacted in horror to news of the massacre of Kisi tribesmen and was equally shocked by hearing reports of 'disgusting butchery' of Africans in Natal. These reactions, humane as they were, did not indicate that he regarded 'the African Aboriginal, for whom civilisation has no charms' as being entitled to or capable of holding the status of a European.

This belief in a distinction between 'civilised' and 'uncivilised' peoples must be distinguished from his cruel but thoughtless disparagement of other races, whether Germans (Huns), Italians (Organ-grinders), Negroes (N*****s), Chinese (Chinks and pigtails), Bedouins (Cut-throats who lived on camel dung), Arabs (worthless) and Indians (Baboos). This vocabulary, I have tried to suggest, though I aware how few readers of today will accept the argument, was offensive and ill-advised but of less consequence than it would appear to be. His ranking of the 'civilised' and educated (usually white) above the 'uncivilised' and uneducated (usually, but not always, not white) was also a product of its times, but less offensive: in its day, defensible on what his contemporaries would have regarded as objective observation. He must, as we all must, be judged by the values and attitudes of his time. Scarcely anyone in his days would have maintained that all societies were equally 'civilised'. In his practical concern for the underdogs of all colours, he was ahead of many of his time.

When we consider the immoderate language he used, we should also remember the immoderate nature of his debating stance. Churchill worked by dialectic. He took the most extreme position he could in opposition to an argument that he did not accept. He held that the outcome of extreme debate would be an acceptable compromise. He had worked like this all his life. Those who were not familiar with the approach could find it disconcerting and offensive. Poor Alan Brooke, as Chief of the Imperial General Staff for most of the war, found Churchill's

debates with the service chiefs enormously wearing and wasteful
of time. His diaries overflow with his frustration at something
that was the opposite of calm, rational discussion.

This habit of enunciating extreme positions that Churchill
would not, in calm reflection, have adhered to for a moment—
indeed, would not have wished to have seen recorded—is reflected
in many of the outrageous things that he said about India in the
1930s and, much more memorably, in the Second World War.
A good example was given when Rab Butler, then Minister of
Education, visited Churchill at Chequers in March 1943. Churchill
'launched into a most terrible attack on the "Baboos", saying that
they were gross, dirty, and corrupt, and that he was quite happy
to see Pakistan hived off from the rest of India'. Butler, for whom
India was one of the three crucial elements of his life,* said that the
whole purpose of the Raj had been to stand for unity, Churchill
replied, 'Well if our poor troops have to be kept in a sweltering,
syphilitic climate for the sake of your precious unity, I'd rather see
them have a good civil war.' Clemmie, who was present and well
aware of Winston's ways, told him that, of course, he didn't mean
what he was saying. Churchill admitted that this was the case
but—and this is the crux of the matter—added, 'but when I see
my opponents glaring at me, I always have to draw them out by
exaggerated statements'.[2] If Churchill is to be judged fairly, that
trait of challenging his opponents with outrageous exaggeration
has to be kept in mind.

In his very moving tribute in the House of Lords that he
made the day after Churchill's death, Lord Attlee brought

---

* The others were 'academic groves' and politics. His father was
Settlement Officer of Campbellpur District of the Central Provinces
when Rab was born in the rest house attached to the fort at Attock,
which had been built by the Mughal Emperor Akbar. He never forgot
travelling across India with his parents followed by a camel train.

out important truths about his great colleague, opponent and friend:

> Not everybody always recognised how tender-hearted he was. I can recall him with the tears rolling down his cheeks, talking of the horrible things perpetrated by the Nazis in Germany. I can recall, too, during the war his emotion on seeing a simple little English home wrecked by a bomb. Yes, my Lords, sympathy— and more than that: he went back, and immediately devised the War Damage Act. How characteristic: sympathy did not stop with emotion; it turned into action . . . he had sympathy, an incredibly wide sympathy, for ordinary people all over the world . . . he saw himself . . . as an instrument. As an instrument for what? For freedom, for human life against tyranny.

His overall view is that Churchill was *not* reactionary but rather in favour of social reform and liberal administration and concerned for the welfare of the masses and the unity of the country.

Churchill attacked the 'Hindoo Priesthood' on the basis of books like Catherine Mayo's *Mother India*,* a popular publication mentioned earlier that contained propaganda material about bigotry and prejudice in the subcontinent. Catherine Mayo's book was published in 1927. It was sensational and popular, but manipulative; she was assisted by the Indian Civil Service. It focused on the Dalits, whose welfare was ostensibly such a concern for Churchill. In the *Daily Mail* article of 16 November 1929, which is mentioned above, he wrote that 'Dominion Status

---

* The book was published in 1927 as propaganda for the anti-independence case. It was a simplistic attack on Indian politicians and obvious targets like the treatment of women and the Dalits. It was well received by those who wanted to read its arguments and provoked rebuttals from those who did not.

can certainly not be attained by a community that brands and treats 60 million of its members, fellow human beings, toiling at their side, as "Untouchables", whose approach is an affront and whose very presence is pollution.' *Mother India* also dealt with child marriage, the position of women, the lack of sanitation and other social ills. It was anti-Hindu and reinforced Churchill's own bias towards Muslims. Of course, Churchill undoubtedly paraded concern for the subordinated masses as part of his divide and rule tactics, but it would be simplistic to imagine that this essentially humane and emotional man was devoid of sympathy for those who so manifestly deserved it.

As a young minister at the Colonial Office, Churchill was regarded by the right as an opponent of the Empire, 'a Little Englander' in the sense in which that phrase was used at that time. His conservative opponents described him as a danger to the Empire, opposed to imperial expansion and grand visions of the country. In 1920, from the left—indeed, the very left—the Independent Labour Party's James Maxton said that the Empire was approaching complete disintegration and that 'it was not going too far to say that Mr Churchill had played a primary part in bringing about that state of affairs'. At that time, he was not only working to get rid of the Middle Eastern mandates as fast as possible; he was also negotiating with the Irish Nationalist leader, Michael Collins, to split off Southern Ireland, even though he was aware that doing so might end his political career.

While Churchill wanted to maintain the Empire, that did not mean that he was against the devolution of power from the Centre to the periphery. Speaking in Canada in August 1929, he said, 'I have put through Parliament two of the most daring experiments in self-government ever attempted in connection with the Transvaal and the Irish Free State.' He had been in favour of radical reform in Egypt to protect the well-being of the *fellahin* at the cost of the landowners.

Churchill's views on India were not simply those of an unreconstructed die-hard. They were the outcome of how he read events since 1914 and their implication for him of national decline. This is brought out well in the exchange between him and Linlithgow in 1933, when Churchill argued that he did not see the future as a mere extension of the past.

*

These are, of course, ambiguities and contradictions. Some are the result of a crabbed age encroaching on a more liberal youth. In January 1914, Churchill was remarkably frank about Britain's imperial activities: 'We have got all we want in territory, and our claim to be left in the unmolested enjoyment of vast and splendid possessions, mainly acquired by violence, largely maintained by force, often seems less reasonable to others than to us.' When he quoted these words many years later, he omitted 'mainly acquired by violence, largely maintained by force'. By then, his stance was much less liberal, and his concerns about 'colonial immigration' were so great that, in one year at the end of his time as Prime Minister, there were thirteen separate cabinet discussions on the matter.

In 1953, the Conservative Lord Winterton wrote to Leo Amery, congratulating him on the first volume of his memoirs: 'I am particularly pleased that you have, whilst paying a tribute to Winston's great patriotism, stated, which is indubitably the case, that he has never been an imperialist in the sense that you and I are.' Leo Amery had said, in the context of the Bengal famine, that on the subject of India, 'Winston is not quite sane.' And yet, he agreed with Winterton's view that Churchill was not an imperialist. For Amery, Milner and the others, the imperial mission was a matter of the future—of extending the Empire, vitalizing it with democratic structures and promoting it as a permanent and substantial force in the world. Such a policy involved a diminution of Britain's stature to being *part* of such a commonwealth rather than its possessor. Churchill's views were much less complex. As a Victorian liberal, a doctrine of peace, retrenchment and reform discouraged a commitment to imperial expansion. At the same time, as an old-fashioned patriot, he had no wish to see Britain diminished, either as a mere part of the Commonwealth or by surrendering the jewel that distinguished his country from ordinary democracies.

*

This diminution in Britain's status is at the heart of Churchill and India and of the paradox that a man who could be sensitive, sympathetic and liberal to other imperial possessions could also be so shamefully and pettily hostile to India's legitimate aspirations. I have argued that his language can be explained and possibly forgotten. But his consistent policy towards India from 1930 onwards cannot be excused or justified. It was dishonest, mendacious and immoral and neither typical nor worthy of a man who, in no other aspect of his public life, could attract such adjectives.

The reason for the Indian anomaly was simply that with India, Britain remained, on the surface at least, that great empire into which he had been born, the most magnificent empire that world history records. Without India, Britain was a small offshore island, indistinguishable from innumerable European democracies. By the time the Second World War was coming to an end, thanks more than anything else to his own exertions and leadership, Britain was, on one argument, at the most heroic moment of her history—her finest hour. Another view was that the country was exhausted, bankrupt and forever reduced—no longer a great power.

In terms of sheer quantum, losing India was quite different from paring off peripheral fragments of Empire. At the midnight hour, when, as Nehru put it, India had her tryst with destiny, no less than three-quarters of its subjects departed from the British Empire. Things would never be the same again.

'The loss of India,' Churchill had said in 1934, 'would mark and consummate the downfall of the British Empire. That great organism would pass at a stroke out of life into history. From such a catastrophe there could be no recovery.'[3] When Lord Randolph Churchill returned from India, his message was that if we wanted to secure the future of British India, then Britain had to exert its right to rule; the alternative would be the loss of India and the rest of the Empire.[4] This critical quality of India as the mother of Britain's greatness was one of the visions passed from father to son.

In 1930, Churchill could not have foreseen how Britain would stand in 1945, financially bankrupt, largely irrelevant to a world dominated by two superpowers, morally and physically exhausted by the exertions by which she had saved herself and the free world. He could, however, see Britain already weakened by the First World War, losing, as he saw it, the will to maintain her position in the world. Even in that 1930 vision, Britain was, in his view, at a critical point in what he liked to call her long history. One choice would be to continue in a dominating role, moulding the destiny of the world. The other was to subside into mediocrity, the pomp of yesterday one with Nineveh and Tyre, without a role or a purpose. With India, the former was possible. Without it, the latter was inevitable. For a man such as Churchill, the choice was inevitable, and what he did to India to achieve his objective is explained but can never be excused.

Notes

Chapter 1

1. Taylor, A.J.P., *English History, 1914–1945* (Oxford: Oxford University Press, 1965), p. 4, fn.
2. Roberts, A., and Gebreyohanes, Z., 'Cambridge "The Racial Consequences of Mr Churchill," a Review', in The Hillsdale Churchill Project, 14 March 2021 (https:\\winstonchurchill.hillsdale.edu\cambridge-racial-consequences\.

Chapter 2

1. Churchill, R.S., *Winston S. Churchill, Vol. I, Youth, 1874–1900* (London: Heinemann, 1966), p. 197.
2. Churchill, *Winston S. Churchill, Vol. I*, p. 286.
3. WSC to Lady Randolph Churchill, 4 August 1896, quoted in Churchill, *Winston S. Churchill, Vol. I*, p. 288.
4. WSC to Lady Randolph Churchill, 4 October 1896, quoted in Churchill, *Winston S. Churchill, Vol. I*, p. 297.
5. WSC to Lady Randolph Churchill, 12 November 1896, quoted in Churchill, *Winston S. Churchill, Vol. I*, p. 297.
6. Churchill, R.S., *Winston S. Churchill, Companion Vol. I, Part II* (London: Heinemann, 1969), p. 696.

7. Churchill, *Winston S. Churchill, Companion Vol. I, Part II*, p. 697.

8. WSC to Lady Randolph Churchill, 14 April 1897, quoted in Churchill, *Winston S. Churchill, Vol. I*, pp. 298–99.

9. WSC to Lady Randolph Churchill, 31 March 1897, quoted in Churchill, *Winston S. Churchill, Vol. I*, pp. 333–34.

10. WSC to Lady Randolph Churchill, 25 February 1897, quoted in Churchill, *Winston S. Churchill, Vol. I*, p. 315.

Chapter 3

1. Churchill, W.S., *My Early Life* (London: Thornton Butterworth Limited, 1930), Reprint Society Edition, pp. 114–15.

2. Cornwallis-West, G., *Edwardian Hey Days* (London: Putnam, 1930), p. 119.

3. Churchill, R.S., *Winston S. Churchill, Companion Vol. I* (London: Heinemann, 1969), p. 869.

4. Pelling, H., *Winston Churchill* (London: Palgrave Macmillan, 1989), pbk. edn., pp. 42–44.

5. Lady Randolph Churchill to WSC, 26 February 1897, quoted in Churchill, R.S., *Winston S. Churchill, Vol. I, Youth, 1874–1900* (London: Heinemann, 1966), p. 329.

6. WSC to Lady Randolph Churchill, 21 April 1897, quoted in Churchill, *Winston S. Churchill, Vol. I*, p. 341.

7. Churchill, *My Early Life*.

8. Personal communication from Colvin's family.

9. Personal communication from Colvin's family.

10. Churchill, *Companion Vol. I*, p. 792–93.

11. Pelling, *Winston Churchill*, pbk. edn., pp. 51–52.

12. See Toye, R., *Churchill's Empire: The World That Made Him and the World He Made* (London: Macmillan, 2010), pbk. edn., p. 41; also, Piers Brendon, P., *The Decline and Fall of the British Empire, 1781–1997* (London: Jonathan Cape, 2007), p. 205.

13. Churchill, W.S., *The Story of the Malakand Field Force, An Episode of Frontier War* (London: Longman's Green & Co., 1898), p. 5.

14. Churchill, R.S., *Churchill, Companion Vol. I, Part II* (London: Heinemann, 1969), p. 821.

15. See Toye, *Churchill's Empire*, pbk. edn., p. 45.
16. Churchill, W.S., *The Second World War*, Vol. 1, *The Gathering Storm* (London: Cassell, 1964), p. 5.
17. Pottle, M., (ed.), *Champion Redoubtable: The Diaries and Letters of Violet Bonham–Carter, 1914–1945* (London: Weidenfeld & Nicolson, 1998), p. 252.
18. Churchill, *Winston S. Churchill, Companion Vol. I*, p. 777.
19. See James, L., *Churchill and Empire: Portrait of an Imperialist* (London: Weidenfeld and Nicolson, 2013), p. 125.
20. Churchill to Lady Jennie Churchill, 18 November 1896, quoted in Churchill and Gilbert, *Winston S. Churchill, Companion Vol. I*, p. 703.
21. WSC to Lady Randolph Churchill, 7 March 1898, quoted in Churchill, *Winston S. Churchill, Vol. I*, p. 374.

Chapter 4

1. Churchill, R.S., *Winston S. Churchill, Companion Vol. I, Part II* (London: Heinemann, 1969), p. 676.

Chapter 5

1. Churchill, R.S., *Winston S. Churchill, Companion Vol. I* (London: Heinemann, 1969), p. 698.
2. Pelling, *Winston Churchill*, pbk. edn., pp. 74–75.
3. Quoted in Sheldon, M., *Young Titan: The Making of Winston Churchill* (New York: Simon & Schuster, 2013).
4. Churchill, W.S., *My Early Life* (London: Thornton Butterworth Limited, 1930), p. 387.
5. Quoted in Bright, J., and Thorold Rogers, J.E., (eds.) *Speeches and Questions of Public Policy* by Richard Cobden, Vol. 1, p. 40.
6. Quoted in *Better Times: Speeches by the Right Hon D. Lloyd George MP Chancellor of the Exchequer*, (London: Hodder and Stoughton Ltd., London First Edition, 1910), p. 43.
7. Churchill, R.S., *Winston S. Churchill, Companion Vol. II, Part I* (London: Heinemann, 1969), pp. 183–84.
8. Churchill, *Winston S. Churchill, Companion Vol. II, Part I* (London: Heinemann, 1969), p. 219.

9. Churchill, R.S., *Winston S. Churchill, Vol. II, Young Statesman 1901–1914* (London: Heinemann, 1967), p. 96.

Chapter 6

1. Churchill, R.S., *Winston S. Churchill, Vol. II, Young Statesman 1901–1914* (London: Heinemann, 1967), p. 101.
2. Churchill, *R.S., Winston S. Churchill, Companion Vol. II* (London: Heinemann, 1969), p. 95.
3. WSC to Nathan Laski, 30 May 1904, quoted in Churchill, *Winston S. Churchill Vol. II*, p. 82.

Chapter 8

1. James, L., *Churchill and Empire: Portrait of an Imperialist* (London: Weidenfeld and Nicolson, 2013), p. 139.
2. Quoted in Judd D., *Empire: The British Imperial Experience from 1765 to the Present* (London: HarperCollins, 1996), p. 259.
3. Diver, M., *Far to Seek: A Romance of England and India* (Massachusetts: Houghton Mifflin, 1921).
4. James, L., *The Rise and Fall of the British Empire*, pbk. edn (London: Little Brown, 2002), p. 419.
5. Quoted in James, *Churchill and Empire: Portrait of an Imperialist*, p. 143.
6. Gilbert, M., *Winston S. Churchill Vol. IV, World in Torment, 1916–1922* (London: Heinemann, 1975), p. 401.
7. Gilbert, *Winston S. Churchill, Vol. IV*, p. 405.
8. Gilbert, *Winston S. Churchill, Vol. IV*, p. 407.
9. Hansard, quoted in Gilbert, *Winston S. Churchill, Vol. IV*, p. 408.

Chapter 9

1. Minute, 9 February 1922, quoted in Gilbert, M., *Winston S. Churchill, Companion, Vol. IV* (London: Heinemann, 1975), p. 1763.
2. Quoted in Callahan, R.A., *Churchill: Retreat from Empire* (Delaware: Scholarly Resources Inc.,1984 and Tunbridge Wells: Costello, D.J. Ltd., 1984), p. 28.

3. Soames, M., (ed.) *Speaking for Themselves: The Personal Letters of Winston and Clementine Churchill,* (London: Black Swan, 1999), p. 226.

4. Toye, R., *Churchill's Empire: The World That Made Him and the World He Made* (London: Macmillan, 2010), pbk. edn., p. 143.

5. Gilbert, *Winston S. Churchill, Companion Vol. VI,* p. 1349.

6. Reynolds, D., *Island Stories: An Unconventional History of Britain* (London: William Collins, 2019), pbk. edn, p. 43.

7. Quoted in Reynolds, *Island Stories,* p. 43.

8. Gilbert, *Winston S. Churchill, Vol. IV,* p. 801.

9. Gilbert, *Winston S. Churchill, Vol. IV,* p. 809.

10. Gilbert, M., *Winston S. Churchill, Vol. III, The Challenge of War, 1914–1916* (London: Heinemann, 1972), p. 774.

11. Gilbert, *Winston S. Churchill, Vol. III,* pp. 794–95.

12. Quoted in Gilmour, D., *Curzon: Imperial Statesman* (London: Penguin, 1952), p. 526.

13. Gilbert, *Winston S. Churchill, Vol. III,* p. 602.

14. Gilbert, *Winston S. Churchill, Vol. III,* pp. 329–30.

Chapter 10

1. Churchill, W.S., *My Early Life* (London: Reprint Society Edition, 1944), p. 5.

2. Norwich, J.J., *The Duff Cooper Diaries: 1915–1951* (London: Weidenfeld & Nicolson, 2006).

3. Gilbert, M., *Winston S. Churchill, Vol. VIII, Never Despair, 1945–1965* (London: Heinemann, 1988).

4. Gilbert, *Winston S. Churchill, Vol. VIII.*

5. Gilbert, M., *Winston S. Churchill, Vol. V, 1922–1939* (London: Heinemann, 1976), p. 59.

6. Gilbert, *Winston S. Churchill, Vol. V,* p. 163.

7. Jenkins, R., *Churchill* (London: Macmillan, 2001), p. 394.

8. Jenkins, R., *The Chancellors* (London: Macmillan, 1998), pbk. edn., p. 309.

9. Gilbert, *Winston S. Churchill, Vol. V,* p. 314.

10. Gilbert, *Winston S. Churchill, Vol. V,* p. 314.

11. Gilbert, *Winston S. Churchill, Vol. V,* p. 321.

12. Gilbert, *Winston S. Churchill, Vol. V*, p. 322.
13. Gilbert, M., *Winston S. Churchill, Companion, Vol. V* (London: Heinemann, 1979), p. 1431.
14. Gilbert, *Winston S. Churchill, Vol. V*, p. 326.

Chapter 11

1. CO537/5698, Number 69,'The Colonial Empire: Summary of Our Main Problems and Policies': CO International Relations Department Paper Annex: 'Some Facts Illustrating Progress to Date'.
2. Kaye, J.W., *A History of the Sepoy War in India, 1857–1858*, Vol. III (England: Longmans, Green & Co., 1896), p. 649.
3. Judd, D., *Empire: The British Imperial Experience, From 1765 to the Present* (London: HarperCollins, 1996),p. 239.

Chapter 12

1. Birkenhead to Reading, 10 December 1925, Quoted in Birkenhead, F., *Halifax: The Life of Lord Halifax* (London: Hamish Hamilton, 1965), p. 222.
2. Roberts, A., *'The Holy Fox': A Biography of Lord Halifax* (London: Weidenfeld & Nicolson, 1991), p. 19.
3. Birkenhead, F., *The Life of F.E. Smith 1st Earl of Birkenhead* (London: Eyre & Spottiswoode, 1959), p. 209.
4. Churchill, W.S., *My Early Life* (London: Thornton Butterworth Limited, 1930), pbk. edn., p. 35.
5. Walker, P.G., *The Commonwealth* (London: Martin Seeker & Warburg Limited, 1962), pp. 86–87.
6. Quoted in Mansergh, N., *The Commonwealth Experience* (London: Palgrave Macmillan, 1982), p. 266.
7. Quoted in Walker, P.G., *The Commonwealth* (London: Secker & Warburg, 1962), p. 47.

Chapter 13

1. Quoted in Lowe, D.A., *Lion Rampant: Essays on the Study of British Imperialism* (London: Routledge, 2016), p. 161.

2. Birkenhead, F., *Halifax: The Life of Lord Halifax* (London: Hamish Hamilton, 1965), p. 247.
3. Birkenhead, *Halifax*, p. 307.

Chapter 14

1. Gilbert, M., *Winston S. Churchill, Vol. V, The Prophet of Truth 1922–1939* (London: Heinemann, 1976), pp. 358–59.
2. Gilbert, *Winston S. Churchill, Vol. V*, p. 386.
3. Callahan, R.A., *Churchill: Retreat from Empire* (Delaware: Scholarly Resources Inc., 1984 and Tunbridge Wells: Costello, D.J. Ltd., 1984), p. 34.
4. Churchill, *Daily Mail*, 16 November 1929.
5. Chartwell Papers 2/169/62, Quoted in St John, I., 'Writing to the Defence of Empire', in Chandrika Kaul (ed.) *Media and the British Empire* (London: Palgrave, 2006), pp. 105–06.
6. Jenkins, R., *Churchill: A Biography* (Plume; Reprint edition, 2002).
7. Gilbert, *Winston S. Churchill, Vol. V*, p. 379.
8. Gilbert, *Winston S. Churchill, Vol. V*, p. 403.
9. Rhodes–James, R., *Memoirs of a Conservative* (London: Weidenfeld & Nicolson, 1969), p. 385.
10. Self, R., (ed.) *The Austen Chamberlain Diary Letters* (Cambridge: Cambridge University Press, 1995).
11. C.R. Attlee to T. Attlee, 3 April 1933, quoted in McKinstry, L., *Attlee and Churchill: Allies in War, Adversaries in Peace* (London: Atlantic Books Ltd., 2019), pbk. edn., p. 115.
12. James, *Memoirs of a Conservative*.
13. Young, K., *Churchill and Beaverbrook* (London: Eyre & Spottiswoode, 1966).
14. Gilbert, *Winston S. Churchill, Vol. V*, p. 480.
15. Gilbert, *Winston S. Churchill, Vol. V*, p. 476.

Chapter 15

1. Reynolds, D., *Island Stories: An Unconventional History of Britain* (London: William Collins, 2019), pbk. edn., pp. 28–29.

2. First Viscount Templewood, *Nine Troubled Years* (London: Collins, 1954), p. 98.
3. Hoare to George Stanley quoted in Gilbert, M., *Winston S. Churchill, Vol. V, The Prophet of Truth 1922–1939* (London: Heinemann, 1976), p. 582.
4. Gilbert, *Winston S. Churchill, Vol. V*, p. 597.
5. Hoare to Willingdon, quoted in Gilbert, *Winston S. Churchill, Vol. V*, p. 605.
6. Gilbert, *Winston S. Churchill, Vol. V*, p. 606.
7. Gilbert, *Winston S. Churchill, Vol. V*, p. 611.
8. Gilbert, *Winston S. Churchill, Vol. V*, pp. 612–13.
9. Gilbert, *Winston S. Churchill, Vol. V*, p. 617.
10. First Viscount Templewood, *Nine Troubled Years*, p. 48.

Chapter 16

1. Norwich, J.J, *The Duff Cooper Diaries: 1915–1951* (London: Weidenfeld & Nicolson, 2006).
2. Churchill, R.S., *Winston S. Churchill, Companion Vol. I, Part II* (London: Heinemann, 1969), p. 1216.
3. Masani, Z., 'Artillery Row', in *The Critic*, December 2021–January 2022, Issue 23.
4. PRO, CAB 23/39, Minutes of a conference of ministers held at 10 Downing Street, 5 February 1922, Quoted in Addison, P., The Political Beliefs of Winston Churchill, *Transactions of the Royal Historical Society, 5th Series, Vol XXX* (1980), pp. 41–42.
5. French, P., *Liberty or Death: India's Journey to Independence and Dominion* (London: HarperCollins, 1997), pbk. edn., p. 92.
6. Lough, D., *No More Champagne: Churchill and His Money* (London: Head of Zeus, 2015).
7. Roberts, A., *Eminent Churchillians* (London: Weidenfeld & Nicolson, 1994).
8. Catterall, P., (ed.), *The MacMillan Diaries* (London: Macmillan, 2003).
9. Rose, N., 'Churchill and Zionism', in Blake, R., and Louis, W.R., *Churchill A Major New Assessment* (New York: W.W. Norton & Company, 1993).

10. Lord Moran, *Winston Churchill: The Struggle for Survival 1940–1965* (Boston: Houghton Mifflin Company, 1966), p. 370.
11. Lord Moran, *Winston Churchill*, p. 131.
12. Quoted Dockter, A.W., *Men of a Martial Nature: Winston Churchill and British Indian Muslims*, www.academia.edu.

Chapter 17

1. James Grant Duff, of the Company. See Bayly, S., *The New Cambridge History of India* IV.3 *Caste, Society and Politics in India from the Eighteenth Century to the Modern Age* (Cambridge: Cambridge University Press, 1999), pbk. edn., p. 89.
2. Bayly, *The New Cambridge History of India*, p. 103.
3. Bayly, *The New Cambridge History of India*, p. 129.

Chapter 18

1. Evans, R.J., 'Breaking up is Hard to Do: Joining the European Union—and the Messy Business of Leaving it.' In the *Times Literary Supplement* Number 6139, 27 November 2020, p. 4.
2. Sanghera, S., *Empireland: How Imperialism has Shaped Modern Britain* (London: Viking, 2021), p. 6.
3. Toye, R., *Churchill's Empire: The World that Made Him and the World He Made* (London: Macmillan, 2010), p. xiv.
4. Dalrymple, W., *The Anarchy* (London: Bloomsbury, 2019).
5. Bolts, W., *Considerations on India Affairs* (London: Brotherton & Sewell, 1772).
6. Macaulay, T.B., Minute of 2 February 1835 on Indian Education.
7. *Financial Times* quoted by Sanghera, S., *Empireland: How Imperialism Has Shaped Modern Britain* (London: Penguin Viking, 2021), p. xi.
8. Sanghera, *Empireland*, p. 123.
9. Quoted in Sanghera, *Empireland*, p. 123.
10. Tharoor, S., *Inglorious Empire* (London: C. Hurst & Co., 2017).
11. Furber, H., Quoted in Sanghera, *Empireland*, p. 129.
12. Churchill, R.S., and Gilbert, M., *Winston S. Churchill, Vol. II, Young Statesman 1901–1914* (London: Heinemann, 1967), p. 100.

13. *Hansard*, 3, 292, 1885, Col. 1540.

14. Quoted in Toye, *Churchill's Empire*, p. 10.

15. Quoted in Addison, P., *Churchill on the Home Front* (London: Faber & Faber, 2013), p. 125.

16. Foot, M., *Loyalists and Loners* (London: Faber & Faber, 2011), pp. 305–08.

17. Churchill, 1920, quoted in Satia, P., *Spies in Arabia* (Oxford: Oxford University Press, 2009), p. 225.

18. Gilbert, M., *Winston S. Churchill, Vol. IV, World in Torment 1916–1922* (London: Heinemann, 1975), p. 912.

19. Gilbert, M., *Winston S. Churchill, Vol. IV*, pp. 913–14.

Chapter 19

1. Clarke, P., *The Cripps Version: The Life of Sir Stafford Cripps 1889–1952* (London: Penguin, 2003), pbk. edn., pp. xiv–xv.

2. Roosevelt, E., *As He Saw It* (New York: Duell, Sloan and Pearce, 1946), pp. 36–38.

3. Gilbert, M., *Winston S. Churchill, Vol. VI, Finest Hour 1939–1941* (London: Heinemann, 1983), p. 1163.

4. Stafford, D., *Roosevelt and Churchill, Men of Secrets*, pbk. edn. (Independently Published, 2022), p. 221.

5. Telegram of 31 July 1940, Quoted in Gilbert, *Winston S. Churchill, Vol. VI*, p. 689.

6. Amery, L., *Political Life*, Vol. I (London: Hutchinson, 1953), p. 253.

7. Rizvi, G., *Linlithgow and India: A Study of British Policy and the Political Impasse in India, 1936–1943*, (London, Royal Historical Society, 1970), p. 3.

8. Butler, R.A., *The Art of the Possible* (London: Hamish Hamilton, 1971), p. 111.

9. Linlithgow to Lumley, 25 November 1942, *Transfer of Power in India (TOPI)*, Vol. III (Cambridge: Cambridge University Press, 1973), p. 218.

10. Barnes, J., and Nicholson, D., (eds), *The Empire at Bay: The Leo Amery Diaries 1929–1945* (London: Hutchinson, 1988), p. 676.

11. French, P., *Liberty or Death: India's Journey to Independence and Division* (London: HarperCollins, 1997), pbk. edn., p. 178.
12. Morris. J., *Farewell the Trumpets* (London: Faber & Faber, 1978), p. 481.
13. French, *Liberty or Death*, p. 174.

Chapter 20

1. Quoted in Toye, R., *Churchill's Empire: The World that Made Him and the World He Made* (London: Macmillan, 2010), pbk. edn., pp. 197–98.
2. Satia, P., *Time's Monster: History, Conscience and Britain's Empire* (London: Allen Lane, 2020), p. 195.
3. Colville, J., *The Fringes of Power: Downing Street Diaries, 1939–1955* (London, W.W. Norton & Co., 1986), p. 103.
4. Barnes, J., and Nicholson, D., (eds), *The Empire at Bay. The Leo Amery Diaries 1929–1945* (London: Hutchinson, 1988), p. 367.
5. Glendevon, J., *The Viceroy at Bay: Lord Linlithgow in India 1936–1943* (London: HarperCollins, 1971), pp. 180–81.
6. Glendevon, *The Viceroy at Bay*, p. 182.
7. Churchill to Amery, 31 May 1941, Quoted in Moore, R.J., *Churchill, Cripps and India 1939–45* (Oxford: Clarendon Press, 1979), p. 41.
8. Callahan, R.A., *Churchill: Retreat from Empire* (Delaware: Scholarly Resources Inc and Tunbridge Wells: Costello, D.J. Ltd, 1984), p. 185.

Chapter 21

1. Gilbert, M., *Winston S. Churchill, Vol. V, 1922–1939* (London: Heinemann, 1976), p. 495.
2. Quoted in Lewin, *The Chief: Field Marshal Lord Wavell, Commander-in-Chief and Viceroy 1939–1947* ((London: Hutchinson, 1980), p. 211.
3. Gilbert, M., (ed.) *The Churchill Documents,* Vol. 17 (London: Hillsdale College Press, 2014), p. 69.

4. For an account of the war in the east, see Lyman, R., *A War of Empires: Japan, India, and Britain, 1941–1945* (London: Osprey, 2021).

5. Churchill, W.S., *The Second World War, Vol. II: Their Finest Hour*, WC to Anthony Eden, 6 June 1940 (London: Orion, 1950), p. 146.

6. Churchill, W.S., *The Second World War, Vol. III: The Grand Alliance*, WC to Chief of Staff Committee, 17 February 1941, in Appendix C (London: Orion, 1950), p. 653.

7. Wilson, C., *Churchill on the Far East in the Second World War: Hiding the History of the 'Special Relationship'* (London: Palgrave Macmillan, 2014), pp. 120–21.

8. Wilson, *Churchill on the Far East in the Second World War*, p. 121.

9. Churchill, W.S., *The Second World War, Vol. IV: The Hinge of Fate* (London: Orion, 1950), p. 146.

10. See Callahan, R., 'Did Winston Matter?' In Roy, K., (ed.) *War and Society in Colonial India* (New Delhi: OUP India, 2006).

11. Lyman, *A War of Empires*.

12. Churchill to Ismay 24 July 1943, National Archives PREM 3 143/8.

13. Lyman, *A War of Empires*.

Chapter 22

1. Quoted in Moore, R.J., *Escape from Empire: The Attlee Government and the Indian Problem* (Oxford: Oxford University Press, 1983), p. 8.

2. Clarke, P., *The Cripps Version: The Life of Sir Stafford Cripps, 1889–1952* (London: Penguin, 2003), pbk. edn., p. 138.

3. Clarke, *The Cripps Version*, p. 139.

4. Linlithgow to Zetland, 21 December 1939, Quoted in Clarke, *The Cripps Version*, p. 141.

5. *Hansard* V Series 383, pp. 302–05.

6. Wilson, C., *Churchill on the Far East in the Second World War: Hiding the History of the 'Special Relationship'* (London: Palgrave Macmillan, 2014), p. 92.

7. Barnes, J., and Nicholson, D., (eds), *The Empire at Bay: The Leo Amery Diaries, 1929–1945* (London: Hutchinson, 1988), p. 786.

8. Moore, R.J., *Churchill, Cripps, and India, 1939–1945* (Oxford: Clarendon Press, 1979), p. vi.

9. Barnes and Nicholson (eds), *The Empire at Bay*, p. 783.

10. *Transfer of Power in India (TOPI)*, Vol. I, Document No. 66.

11. Barnes and Nicholson (eds), *The Empire at Bay*, 26 February 1942.

12. French, P., *Liberty or Death: India's Journey to Independence and Division* (London: HarperCollins, 1997), pbk. edn., p. 188.

13. Toye, R., *Churchill's Empire* (London: Macmillan, 2010).

14. Bryant, C., *Stafford Cripps: The First Modern Chancellor* (London: Hodder and Stoughton Ltd, 1997).

15. French, *Liberty or Death*.

16. Brookshire, J., *Clement Attlee* (Manchester: Manchester University Press, 1995).

17. Linlithgow to Amery, 21 January 1942, *TOPI*, Vol. I, p. 23.

18. Attlee to Amery, 24 January 1942, *TOPI*, Vol. I, p. 35.

19. Moore, *Churchill, Cripps, and India*, p. 70.

20. See Downing, T., *1942: Britain at the Brink* (London: Little, Brown, 2022).

21. Churchill to Linlithgow, 10 March 1942, Quoted in Moore, *Churchill, Cripps, and India*, p. 74.

22. Quoted in Glendevon, J., *The Viceroy at Bay: Lord Linlithgow in India, 1936–1943* (London: HarperCollins, 1971), p. 225.

23. Churchill to Cripps, 2 April 1942, Quoted in Moore, *Churchill, Cripps, and India*, p. 96.

24. Barnes and Nicholson (eds), *The Empire at Bay*, 10 April 1942.

25. Churchill to Cripps, 10 April 1942, Quoted in Moore, *Churchill, Cripps, and India*, p. 122.

26. Barnes and Nicholson (eds), *The Empire at Bay*, 10 April 1942.

27. *TOPI*, Vol. I, pp. 73–81.

28. Amery, L., *My Political Life*, Vol. III (London: Hutchinson, 1955), p. 205.

29. Barnes and Nicholson (eds), *The Empire at Bay*, p. 795.

30. French, *Liberty or Death*, p. 146.
31. Gilbert, M., *Winston S. Churchill, Vol. VII, Road to Victory 1941–1945* (London: Heinemann, 1986), pp. 87–88.
32. Churchill, W.S., *The Hinge of Fate: The Second World War*, Vol. IV (London: Orion, 1950), p. 192.

Chapter 23

1. *Transfer of Power in India (TOPI)*, Vol. II, p. 853.
2. *TOPI*, Vol. III, p. 3.
3. Gilbert, M., *Winston S. Churchill, Vol. VII, Road to Victory, 1941–1945* (London: Heinemann, 1986), pp. 350–51.
4. Churchill, W.S., *The Hinge of Fate: The Second World War*, Vol. IV (London: Orion, 1950), p. 457.
5. Wheeler–Bennett, J., *King George VI: His Life and Reign* (London: Macmillan, 1958), p. 703.
6. *TOPI*, Vol. III, p. 2.

Chapter 24

1. Lyman R., *A War of Empires: Japan, India, and Britain, 1941–1945* (London: Osprey, 2021).
2. Sarkar, A., https:\\winstonchurchill.hillsdale.edu\bengal-famine-sarkar and Herman, A., Absent Churchill, Bengal's Famine Would Have Been Worse', https:\\winstonchurchill.hillsdale.edu\churcills-secret-war-bengal-famine-1943 [*sic*] 3 October 2017
3. Hensher, P., 'Does Boris Johnson Really Expect Us to Think He's Churchill?', In *The Spectator*, 25 February 2014.
4. The Hillsdale Churchill Project (https:\\winstonchurchill.hillsdale.edu\did-churchill-cause-the-bengal-famine\
5. Churchill in the Commons, 8 December 1944.
6. War Cabinet Papers, 14 February 1944, 65/41.
7. Wilson, C., *Churchill on the Far East in the Second World War: Hiding the History of the 'Special Relationship'* (London: Palgrave Macmillan, 2014), p. 110.
8. Churchill to Roosevelt, 29 April 1944 (Churchill Papers 20/163).

9. See, for instance, Mukerjee, *M.*, *Churchill's Secret War: The British Empire and the Ravaging of India during World War II* (Basic Books; Reprint edition, 2011).

10. Mukerjee, M., https:\\winstonchurchill.hillsdale.edu\churcills-secret-war-bengal-famine-1943 (*sic*)

11. Sen, A., In *New York Times,* Quoted in *Critic*, December 2021–January 2022, Issue 23.

12. Herman, A., 'Absent Churchill: Bengal's Famine Would Have Been Worse', https:\\winstonchurchill.hillsdale.edu\churcills-secret-war-bengal-famine-1943 [*sic*].

13. Moon, P., (ed.), *Wavell: The Viceroy's Journal*, p. 19 *et seq.*.

14. See particularly Roy, T., 'The Bengal Famine of 1943', In *History Today*, Vol. 69, Issue 7, July 2019.

15. Roy, 'The Bengal Famine of 1943'.

16. James, L., *Churchill and Empire: Portrait of an Imperialist* (London: Weidenfeld and Nicolson, 2013), pp. 304–05.

17. Quoted in Hastings, M., *All Hell Let Loose* (London: Harper Press, 2011).

18. James, *Churchill and Empire,* p. 306.

Chapter 25

1. Lyman, R., *A War of Empires: Japan, India, and Britain, 1941–1945* (London: Osprey, 2021).

2. Kelly, D., quoting Churchill to Martin Gilbert, 11 October 1988 quoted in Wilson, C., *Churchill on the Far East in the Second World War: Hiding the History of the 'Special Relationship'* (London: Palgrave Macmillan, 2014), p. 44.

3. Churchill, W.S., *The Second World War, Vol. III: The Grand Alliance* (London: Cassell & Co., 1950), p. 539.

4. Churchill, *The Second World War, Vol. III*, p. 539.

5. Wilson, *Churchill on the Far East in the Second World War*, p. 130.

6. Churchill College Archive Centre, 7 November 1950.

7. Wilson, *Churchill on the Far East in the Second World War*, p. 116.

8. Churchill, W.S., *The Second World War, Vol. VI* (Boston: Houghton Mifflin, 1953), p. 538.

Chapter 26

1. Barnes, J., and Nicholson, D., (eds), *The Empire at Bay: The Leo Amery Diaries, 1929–1945* (London: Hutchinson, 1988), p. 872.
2. Amery, L., *The Empire at Bay*, pp. 1032–33.
3. Churchill, W.S., *The Second World War, Vol. IV: The Hinge of Fate* (London: Orion, 1950), pp. 304–05.
4. Moon, P., (ed.), *Wavell: The Viceroy's Journal* (Oxford: Oxford University Press, 1973), pp. 4–5.
5. First Viscount Templewood, *Nine Troubled Years* (London: Collins, 1954), p. 99.
6. In 1965 Memorial Collection: *Churchill: By His Contemporaries*, published by the *Observer*, available in https://winstonchurchill.hillsdale.edu/clement-attlee-part-2/.
7. Barnes and Nicholson (eds), *The Empire at Bay*, p. 945.
8. Moon, P., (ed), *Wavell: The Viceroy's Journal*, 8 October 1943, p.23.
9. Moon (ed.), *Wavell*, p. 45.
10. Moon (ed.), *Wavell*, p. 93.
11. Wilson, J., *The Chaos of Empire: The British Raj and the Conquest of India* (New York: PublicAffairs, 2016), pp. 496–97.
12. Moon (ed.), *Wavell*, pp. 94–99.
13. *Transfer of Power in India (TOPI)*, Vol. V, p. 64, also quoted in Moore, R.J., *Churchill, Cripps, and India, 1939–1945* (Oxford: Clarendon Press, 1979), p. 141.
14. *TOPI*, Vol. V, p. 345.
15. Moon (ed.), *Wavell*, pp. 129–33.
16. Churchill to Clementine Churchill, Soames, M., (ed.) *Speaking for Themselves: The Personal Letters of Winston and Clementine Churchill* (London: Black Swan, 1999), p. 512.

Chapter 27

1. See Harris, K., *Attlee* (London: Weidenfeld and Nicolson, 1982), p. 362.

2. Attlee, C., and Williams, F., *A Prime Minister Remembers* (London: Heinemann, 1961).

3. Moon, P., (ed.), *Wavell: The Viceroy's Journal* (Oxford: Oxford University Press, 1973).

4. Leslie, A., *Cousin Clare: Biography of Clare Sheridan* (London, Hutchinson, 1976), pp. 304–05.

5. Gilbert, M., *Winston S. Churchill, Vol. VIII, Never Despair* (London: Heinemann, 1988).

6. Churchill to Attlee, 14 May 1946, Churchill College Archives.

7. *Observer*, 31 January 1965.

8. *Hansard*, 6 March 1945.

9. Hyam, R., (ed.), *British Documents*, p. 177.

10. WSC to JC Smuts in *Selections from the Smuts Papers*, Vol. VII, August 1945–October 1950, p. 298.

Chapter 28

1. Hyam, R., *Understanding the British Empire* (Cambridge: Cambridge University Press, 2010), pp. 237–39.

2. Butler, R.A., *The Art of the Possible* (London: Penguin, 1973), p. 111.

3. Churchill, 'Shall we give up India? Fair play for Lancashire!', in *Answers*, 21 July 1934, p. 3.

4. *Hansard*, 4 May 1885.

Index